ESSAYS IN MUSICAL ANALYSIS

ESSAYS IN MUSICAL ANALYSIS

By
DONALD FRANCIS TOVEY

Volume III
CONCERTOS

London
OXFORD UNIVERSITY PRESS
New York   Toronto

Oxford University Press, Ely House, London W. 1

GLASGOW NEW YORK TORONTO MELBOURNE WELLINGTON
CAPE TOWN SALISBURY IBADAN NAIROBI LUSAKA ADDIS ABABA
BOMBAY CALCUTTA MADRAS KARACHI LAHORE DACCA
KUALA LUMPUR SINGAPORE HONG KONG TOKYO

FIRST EDITION 1936
ELEVENTH IMPRESSION 1969

PRINTED IN GREAT BRITAIN

CONTENTS

CONTENTS vii

DOHNANYI

CONTENTS

ADDENDUM

SINCE my analysis of the work known as Haydn's Violoncello Concerto, op. 101, was written, a miniature score has been published giving the work in its original form, with a preface explaining that Dr. Hans Volkmann has proved that this concerto is not by Haydn but by Haydn's pupil, Anton Kraft (1752–1820). The demonstration is admittedly not complete, but I find no difficulty in giving Kraft the credit for a very pretty piece of work in a form in which Haydn never put forward his full powers, and which, if genuine, would have belonged to a period at which his style and forms were imitable enough to tempt many publishers to secure a market for other composers by ascribing their works to a master whose early popularity was so remarkable. My analysis will not, I think, be found to contain anything committing me to uphold this charming concerto as a great work. The average quality of Haydn's output at Esterhaz is such that the greatest scholars have been compelled, when selecting the unquestionably authentic symphonies, to make a longer list of doubtful than of spurious works. A stroke of genius will settle the question, and so will any high power of composition: that is why I see red when musical philologists cast doubts on Bach's tremendous D minor Concerto. But the absence of these qualities will not settle the question with early works ascribable to Haydn. The only thing that puzzled me in the present instance was the prominence of a definitely Mozartean cliché in the opening themes of the first movement and slow movement. The slow movement begins with two bars of pure Mozart followed by two of pure Haydn. In an analytical programme it was no part of my business to disturb the listener by questions which are vexing as long as they raise doubts. Now that I have no doubt, I shall in future give Anton Kraft the credit of his very pretty work; and I shall expect my audience not to be snobbish about it.

LXXXIV. INTRODUCTION TO VOLUME III

THIS volume deals mainly with the classical concerto as described in the first essay: secondly, it deals with a few *concertante* works in variation form. These ought by rights to have included Beethoven's Choral Fantasia, but it is so obviously an unconscious study for the finale of the Ninth Symphony that the temptation to put it after that work was irresistible. The rest of the volume is devoted to concertos and *Conzertstücke* that are not based on the classical notion of the ritornello.

The origin and character of the earlier polyphonic type of concerto is fully discussed in the first essay (LXXXV); but works of that kind (including some modern examples) have already been dealt with in Vol. II as arising from the general problem of applying polyphonic forms to orchestral music.

Although this volume thus presents a greater coherence of subject than the other volumes of these essays, it is by no means better calculated for continuous reading. On the contrary, the difficult and complex theory of concerto form, though elaborated systematically in the first essay, is repeatedly summarized in several others; and the reader will be well advised to treat this volume, like the others, in the way in which all my essays were treated by readers who saw them in their original form of programme-notes. They are separate accounts of individual works of art. Two individual works of art do not quote one another when they use the same forms; and the same illustration may serve for more than one analysis if it is the best illustration for more than one case.

LXXXV. THE CLASSICAL CONCERTO
(1903)

INTRODUCTION

Without a sound appreciation of those peculiarities of form which distinguish the classical concerto from the classical symphony the concerto can only be very imperfectly understood, whether by performers or by listeners; for the rational enthusiasm for great classics is the outcome not only of natural taste, but also of long familiarity with all that is purest in art; and so far as the opportunity for such familiarity is wanting, so far will current ideas and current criticism be vague, Philistine, and untrue. Now the number of great works in the true concerto form is surprisingly small; far smaller than the number of true symphonies. And of this small collection a good two-thirds has been contributed by Mozart, whose work has for the last fifty years been treated with neglect and lack of intelligent observation, for which we at the present time are paying dearly with a notable loss both of ear for fine detail and of grasp of musical works as definite wholes.[1] On the other hand, every virtuoso whose imagination is fired with the splendid spectacular effect of a full orchestra as a background for a display of instrumental technique has written concertos that express little else than that effect. Thus the name of concerto is assumed by literally hundreds of works that have not even an academic connexion with the classical idea of concerto form and style; while of the very small collection of true concertos the majority, those of Mozart, are ignored, and the remainder not nearly so well understood as any classical symphony. No composer attempts a symphony without a strong sense of responsibility, and some appreciation of the greatness of the classics of symphonic art, and so neither the number of spurious symphonies nor their tendency is such as to set an entirely false standard of criticism for the art. But that current criteria of the concerto are false, no one who seriously studies that form can doubt. The idea that the professed purpose of the form is technical display has been actually maintained by musicians who yield to none in their reverence and love for the great concertos of Beethoven and Mozart. Yet that idea is in flat violation of almost every fact in the early history of the form; and those who hold it seem to let it

[1] I do not know how many people in 1903 foresaw the vindication of Mozart, of which on the Continent the main impulse was given by Richard Strauss, and which dates in England from the memorable performance of the *Zauberflöte* at Cambridge some eight years after this essay appeared. That performance marked the first stages of Professor E. J. Dent's work upon Mozart's operas.

remain comfortably in their minds side by side with the opposite, and scarcely less untrue notion, that in the works of Bach and his contemporaries the solo part of a concerto is no more than *primus inter pares*. The first idea springs from the assumption (difficult to avoid, where bad works so overcrowd good ones) that art-forms are invented by bad artists to be disgustedly improved off the face of the earth by the great men; and the second springs from the difficulty of recognizing in ancient art anything that does not happen to take much the same shape in modern art.

The only way to avoid these pitfalls is to seek out the typical artistic idea that is to be found in the concertos of the greatest composers. To avoid repeating what I have written elsewhere, I propose to follow out this train of thought in an historical, or at all events chronological, sketch, instead of applying it merely to any particular concerto. Opinions differ so much as to the way in which musical history should be written that I hesitate to call this sketch historical. Its object is to trace the successive forms in which what I shall call the concerto-idea has been realized. Those forms in which it has been falsified by vanity, or obscured by imperfect skill or vague thought, will not come under discussion at all, though to many historians that which is transitional and immature is often more interesting, and always more easy to discuss than that which is permanent and self-consistent.

To avoid a frequent source of misunderstanding, I must point out that neither here nor in any other of my analytical essays is the basis of analysis technical. It is frequently urged as an objection to all musical analysis that to investigate 'how it is done' distracts the mind from the poetic enjoyment of a work of art. So it does; you cannot, for instance, enjoy the first movement of Beethoven's Eroica Symphony if you insist on thinking the while of Beethoven's seven or eight different sketches of its exposition. They are among the most wonderful documents recording the profound workings of a creative mind; but the only way in which they can help you to enjoy the symphony is by directing your attention to what it is. Follow up the sketches, then, as they approach the final version from something now more monotonous, now more violent, now smaller, now dangerously large, always changing with the surprising purpose and power of a creator who ruthlessly rejects all that will not remain as an inspiring force for all time, when what common admirers of genius call 'the inspiration of the moment' has gone the way of dreams and moods. Follow this up until it leads you to the ideal, the realized Eroica Symphony; and you will no longer think that there is anything prosaic in investigating 'how it was done'. But you will see this only if, as you listen to the symphony, you forget the sketches utterly, as Beethoven himself forgot them. They have helped you, not because they showed you 'how it was done', but because they drew your attention to *what* was done; and on that, and that alone, your attention must remain fixed, or the whole object of all that loving and laborious sketching is lost.

Musical analysis then is concerned with *what* is done. Unless the composer has left sketches, any attempt to speak of '*how* it is done' is downright charlatanry, a pretence of solving a problem that is beyond the human intellect. Beethoven himself must have found his old sketch-books a series of perpetual surprises if he ever looked at them a year or two after finishing a work.

An analysis that gives a faithful account of what is done in a work of art cannot but be a help, so long as it is not one-sided and is used in a practical way. Hence in my early essays I have aimed at quoting or at least mentioning every theme in the works analysed, so that the material may lie conveniently before the eye. On the other hand, I have from the outset abandoned any attempt to confine the letterpress to what can be read in the concert-room. Quotations in musical type can be seen while they are heard; but the kind of prose explanation that can be read while the music is going on is as useless in the concert-room as it is at home.

Lastly, as this is an essay on a musical subject I have tried to treat it from a musical point of view. This again is not a limitation to technical matters; music is music, and does not become technical as soon as it is not discussed as if it were a nondescript mixture of intellect and emotion and poetry. As a plain musician I believe music to be music; poetry, a form of literature; painting, one of the plastic arts; and *all* to be poetry. But when I discuss music I shall speak of things musical, as beautiful harmony, breadth, firmness and depth of modulation, nobility of form, variety and contrast of tone, clear and well-motived contrast and harmonious fullness in those simultaneous combinations of melodies which we call counterpoint, for it is these things and others equally musical that make a concerto or a symphony what it is. And if it is objected that these things, as they occur in classical music, are non-poetical, or mere technical means of expressing some poetic idea that lies behind them, I can only reply that, so long as music remains music, this poetic idea will only be attainable through these musical phenomena. Certainly a criticism or an admiration that scorns the musical phenomena does not thereby become poetical; on the contrary, the man who expects music to give him poetical ideas while he refuses to listen to it as music, will infallibly, if he looks at other things as he looks at music, value poetry for the information it conveys when paraphrased in prose, architecture for the problems it solves in engineering, science for its practical use, and in short, everything for its lower and more accidental qualities, and this is the very type and essence of the prosaic mind.

To sum up: I believe the classical concerto to be a highly dramatic and poetic art-form, having nothing in common with the popular and pseudo-academic idea of the form except a few misleading superficial resemblances. I therefore propose to illustrate the poetic and dramatic expression of this form by an analysis that has nothing to do with technique, though it will use any good technical term that may substitute a word for a paragraph; nor anything to do with *a priori* theories of absolute music which will apply equally well to absolute nonsense, though it declines to talk of poetry when its business is to describe musical facts. I merely attempt to describe what may be *observed* by any one really fond of music, who takes pains to study the works of great composers in a spirit that endeavours to understand the ways of minds other than one's own.

THE CONCERTO PRINCIPLE

The primary fact that distinguishes all works that have in them the character of the concerto style, is that their form is adapted to make the best effect expressible by opposed and unequal masses of instruments or voices. Whenever in classical or indeed in any really artistic music, you find that an art-form is to be expressed by a mass of instruments (under which head we may for present purposes include voices), and that this mass inevitably divides itself into two parts that cannot without some embarrassing limitation or *tour de force* be made to balance each other: then you will assuredly find that the form has been modified so as not merely to fit these conditions but to make them a special means of expression.

Hence arises at least half of the prejudice which many fairly experienced lovers of music, and nearly all inexperienced students of composition, feel against the concerto forms. When our experience is no more than enough to give us a keen pleasure in following the normal outlines of an art-form, and in seeing how they give reality and inevitableness to the contrasts and crises of the music, then we are prone to resent any influence that modifies the form, and we do not stop to see whether the new form may not be as grand as the old.

That the conditions of concerto form are in themselves unnatural or inartistic can certainly not be maintained in face of the facts. Nothing in human life and history is much more thrilling or of more ancient and universal experience than the antithesis of the individual and the crowd; an antithesis which is familiar in every degree, from flat opposition to harmonious reconciliation, and with every contrast and blending of emotion, and which has been of no less universal prominence in works of art than in life. Now the concerto forms express this antithesis with all possible force and delicacy. If there are devotees of 'absolute music' who believe that this is the very reason why these forms are objectionable, as appealing to something outside music, we may first answer that, if this were so, then neither Brahms, Beethoven, Bach, Mozart, Haydn, nor any person of so much calibre as Clementi, ever was an 'absolute musician', or had anything to do with such a mysterious abstraction. And secondly we may reply that this dramatic or human element is *not* outside the music, but most obviously inherent in the instruments that play the concerto; and that, so far as such a feebly metaphysical term as 'absolute music' has a meaning, it can only mean 'music that owes its form, contrasts, and details solely to its own musical resources'. As long as musical instruments or voices exist, there will always be the obvious possibility of setting one instrument or voice against many; and the fact that this opposition exists also in human affairs is no reason why music should cease to be 'absolute' or self-supporting —unless we are likewise to reason that man ceases to be human in so far as his five senses are shared by lower animals.

We must now see how the classical composers, to whom music was music no matter how profoundly it reflected humanity, adapted their art-forms to this condition of the antithesis between one and many, or between greater and less. I hope to show that the distinctive mark of the classical work is that it delights in this opposition and makes it expressive, while the pseudo-classics and the easy-going, thoughtless innovators, though they continually try to use it, miss the point with a curious uniformity amid diversity of error, and find every special condition of a concerto embarrassing and uninteresting.

Let us take these conditions in their earliest and, in some ways, simplest form. It is no use going farther back than the aria of Alessandro Scarlatti, or, to keep to familiar examples, Handel, in whom the conditions are not appreciably more developed. The Handelian aria is a clear and mature, yet an early and simple art-form. It owes almost its whole vitality to the opposition and relation between the voice and the accompaniment. When Handel was at work it was already dying of conventionality. And on this point I must beg leave to digress.

Conventionality is generally understood to mean something vaguely to the following effect: that a device may occur a very large number of times, say five hundred, in as many different works of art, and yet be in every instance the right thing in the right place, and therefore good and not conventional; but that the moment it occurs a five-hundred-and-first time, it becomes conventional and bad for all future occasions; so that we are entirely at the mercy of custom and history in the matter, and must know whether we are listening to No. 500 or to No. 501 before we can tell if either is beautiful or conventional. Now, though this is the real basis of more than half the current uses of the term, no one will believe it to be true when it is put before them in this form. The real meaning of 'conventionality' is either an almost technical, quite blameless, and profoundly interesting aesthetic fact, more often met with where art aspires beyond the bounds of human expression than elsewhere; or else the meaning is that a device has been used unintelligently and without definite purpose. And it makes not an atom of difference whether this use is early or late: thus the device of the canon is, more often than not, vilely conventional in the late fifteenth and early sixteenth centuries, and extremely beautiful wherever it occurs in Schumann and Brahms. So long as a thing remains the right thing in the right place, custom has simply nothing to do with it. Custom may help us to understand what might otherwise be distressing in its remoteness from our humdrum ideas; and custom frequently is an unmitigated nuisance, making us feel towards classical works as an overgrown choir-boy whose voice is cracking must sometimes feel towards the forms of worship which have become too familiar to impress him—but custom never makes good criticism or in any way ministers to the enjoyment of art, so long as it is allowed to dictate to us.

This digression was necessary here, because all the concerto forms show an unusual number of constantly recurring features, and it is of great importance that we should never be misled into estimating these features as conventional merely because they are frequent. Indeed, the really conventional composer abolished them long ago. After using them in a hopelessly unintelligent way for some centuries, he naturally concluded that what he could not understand was of no use to any one, and so he avoided them in the very same conventional spirit in which he had at first used them. The original composer is nowhere more triumphantly unconventional than when he chooses an old device because he knows its meaning, and applies it rightly, in the teeth of all popular criticism and current notions as to originality and genius. Let us see how far Handel and Bach bear this out.

The arias of Scarlatti and Handel (and, of course, all opera and oratorio writers between archaic periods and Gluck) obviously depend on the antithesis between a voice and an instrumental accompaniment. This accompaniment is generally conceived as orchestral; and accordingly (though the orchestra is not often very formidable except in warlike scenes where trumpets and drums are treated vigorously), there is almost always the contrast between the single voice and the chorus of instruments. In fact, wherever Handel is not either employing some special instrumental effect, itself of a solo character, or else writing merely for voice and figured bass, his usual direction for the top part of the accompaniment is 'tutti unisoni'. But in any case the relation between voices and instruments is such that, as Gevaert teaches in his works on instrumentation, as soon as the living utterance of the voice strikes upon the ear, the orchestra falls into the background. This natural phenomenon is too powerful to be obscured by any perversions of modern taste. The callous and stupid use of it ought to have no influence on us. It has no influence on great artists, though they often shock contemporary critics, who have no better criterion of vulgarity than that it is what vulgar people do. As long as we know too much of what vulgar people do, we shall be worried and misled by the fact that, among other things, they ape their betters. Let us study their betters.

In great music, then, we may expect that such a contrast as that between a voice and an orchestra will always have its original value, and will be more, instead of less, impressive as the range of the art increases. Now it so happens that there is in a lesser degree just that kind of contrast between the quality of tone (not merely the volume) of a solo instrument and that of an orchestra. The solo player stands out from the orchestra as a living personality no less clearly, though somewhat less impressively, than the singer. Hence there was, in the period from Alessandro Scarlatti to Handel, the closest affinity, amounting in some cases to identity, between certain vocal and concerto forms. If we could understand a beautiful Handel aria so as to have some idea, however incomplete, of that wherein it differs from his hack-work, then we may hope to understand a Beethoven concerto.

When a voice or instrument is accompanied by something which it either thrusts into the background as soon as it is heard, or else fails to penetrate at all, a moment's reflection will convince us that the easiest way to give both elements their best effect is to let the accompaniment begin with a statement of the material, and then to bring in the voice or solo with a counter-statement. This arrangement brings out the force of the solo in thrusting the orchestra into the background, while at the same time the orchestra has had its say and need not seem unnaturally repressed as it probably would seem (supposing it to be at all powerful) if it were employed only to support the solo. Again, this ritornello of the orchestra will, as its name implies, return effectively at the end of the piece when the solo has reached its climax. The solo is probably more active, as well as more personal and eloquent, than the orchestra, and can therefore make a brilliant climax if it chooses; but it cannot make its climax very powerful in sound as compared with what the orchestra can obviously do with ease; and so this one missing element may be supplied, and the design rounded off, by bringing in the ritornello forte on the last note of the solo, thus ending the piece. Here we have the beginning and end of an enormous number of typical concerto forms. A single unbroken melody might be arranged in this way as a complete piece for a voice and orchestra, with no further elaboration and no other appearances of the orchestra except the opening ritornello and its recapitulation at the close; but generally the voice or solo goes farther afield and attains more than one climax in foreign keys, so that the orchestra introduces parts of its ritornello perhaps three or four times in such a movement.

Obviously much depends on the skill and sensibility of the composer in choosing different parts of this ritornello, bringing the solo into fresh relationship with it at each entry. Very early in the history of the operatic aria an important device was discovered, which is usually associated with the name of Alessandro Scarlatti. Its essential point is that the voice does not complete its first strain at once but allows the orchestra to finish it instead, and then begins again from the beginning, this time to continue. The device obviously has great value in establishing a more subtle relation between voice and accompaniment than is possible when they persist in alternating only in large and complete sections. It soon became 'conventional', that is to say a mere formula in the hands of composers who knew and cared nothing about the contrast and harmony of voice and accompaniment; and Mr. Fuller-Maitland, who describes it fully and accurately in the fourth volume of the *Oxford History of Music*, gives many instances of it in various stages of true feeling and decadence from Bach, in whose hands no device is more conventional than the very laws of nature, to Greene, who, in one of his anthems, shows its last trace in a futile piece of mechanism lazily indicated by a da capo sign.

And yet the device has never died, aesthetically speaking, though we may not be conscious of its ancestry. Wherever a solo depends for its effect on entering after an orchestral ritornello, there we shall find the trace of Alessandro Scarlatti's principle—that the solo should first be inclined to enter into dialogue with the orchestra—the speaker should conciliate the crowd before he breaks into monologue.

I do not propose here to trace how Bach was influenced by his predecessors in this matter. Bach is an original composer, and no conventional ideas about originality will prevent him from using the most hackneyed device in its fullest and oldest meaning. His

chief concerto form is in every particular derived from the typical
vocal aria form, at least as regards the first movement.

A little consideration of the new conditions involved will help
us to arrange the facts clearly. The opposition of solo and orchestra
began early to take a greater variety of forms than was possible
in the vocal music of the same periods. The main type of early
concerto was the *concerto grosso*, in which the opposition was
between such a number of solo players as could produce quite
a complete mass of harmony to oppose against the orchestra
proper. This opposition of the concertino against the orchestra or
concerto grosso (from which the form takes its name) could even
be reduced to a state of things in which all played together and
split into whatever groups they pleased; as in Bach's magnificent
Third Brandenburg Concerto, which is for a string orchestra which
plays in three parts in the ritornello, and divides itself into nine by
way of representing solo passages—no further indication of a distinction between solo and tutti being given. Still, apart from the
likelihood that Bach was writing for only nine players, and that
in performance by a larger band the nine-part passages should be
played by the leaders alone, this dividing of the orchestra at once
produces a fairly strong impression of that entry of individual tone
which we know to be the most expressive feature of the concerto
style; and this first movement of the only concerto throughout
which Bach does not write for a detached solo-group or single
solo, differs in no other way from the rest of his concertos.

We need only think of an aria enormously enlarged, with
its square-cut melody turned into a concentrated group of pregnant, sequential figures, such as befit a serious and monumental
movement that will not for a moment be confined within the
limits of lyric melody. We shall find all the other features of the
aria here: the ritornello, of course, states the main figures of
the movement in their most forcible shape; then the quasi-solo
of the orchestra divided into nine parts begins its version of the
theme, but, just as in Scarlatti's arias, bursts into a tutti before
the phrase is finished, though the greater scale of the movement
(and a higher organization in every respect) is indicated by the
fact that this interruption is in a new key. Another interruption
occurs before the resumed nine-part passages can deliver a longer
sentence; and we have to go some way into the movement before
these quasi-solos have any long uninterrupted discourse. Throughout the work the principles of alternation between quasi-solo and
tutti are most subtle and delicate in their adaptation to the peculiar
conditions of this band. Sometimes the three basses coalesce into
tutti while the six upper parts remain individual; in one most
impressive place, the basses do this in order to bring out a difficult

passage, thus retaining their value as solo parts. Sometimes basses
and violins will each coalesce while the three viola parts flourish
separately. In short, the combinations are endless, and are all
in the highest degree expressive of the peculiar concerto opposition of forces. This is what Bach does under conditions in
which the possibilities of concerto style are least obvious.

The Second Brandenburg Concerto is for four solo instruments
and orchestra. Here the principles of the form are far more obvious.
Yet they cannot be so strongly marked in a concerto for four
instruments as in a concerto for one; and if Bach's extant concertos
be studied as glorified arias, the vital aesthetic principles will
reveal themselves in endless variety. (Incidentally these principles
will help us to restore by conjecture the original forms of works
extant only in arrangement.) Bach, far more than Handel, likes to
organize both his larger arias and his concertos by making the solo
enter with a different theme from that of the ritornello, so that when
the orchestra breaks in on the first solo with Scarlatti's interruption
(or something to that effect) the bit of ritornello so introduced has
a new meaning. Sometimes he translates into these larger instrumental forms the things that happen in an aria where a solo
instrument as well as a voice is opposed to the orchestra. Further
details must be left to other analyses of Bach's vocal and instrumental works. Here we can only add that Bach, like the masters
of later concerto forms, makes the relation of solo and tutti more
intimate and less contrasted in middle and final than in first
movements.

In short, Bach's concerto forms are completely identical with
his vocal forms, except those that are dramatic, like some of
Handel's, and those that employ the orchestra merely as a support,
such as fugues and the severer forms of figured choral.

In the case of festive choruses, where form and brilliance are
more important than fugue and solemnity, this identity is such that
actual concerto movements have been arranged by Bach as choruses.
And the arrangements are so amazingly successful that there is
nothing but external evidence to prove that the chorus is not the
original. The best illustration of this is the first chorus of a delightful cantata, *Vereinigte Zwietracht der wechselnde Saiten*, written to
celebrate the election of one Dr. Kortte to a professorship. The
very title of the cantata throws light on the concerto idea; for
Vereinigte Zwietracht is a singularly accurate and forcible rendering
of the root meaning of *concertare*; and Bach generally calls the solo
part (*Cembalo, Violino*, or whatever the case may be) *certato*.[1]

[1] The true interpretation of this significant point is among my earliest
recollections of that great musical scholar, A. J. Hipkins, whose kindness
to me began in my childhood.

When we compare Bach's rendering of this 'united contest of turn-about strings' with the third movement of the First Branden-burg Concerto, we find that the framework, themes, and counter-point are bar for bar the same, with the exception of an occasional expansion (two bars inserted here, half a bar there), to make the approaches to climaxes longer and more suitable to the grander massiveness of choral writing. But what will strike us most forcibly is that the chorus parts are derived, not from the horns and other wind-parts of the original, but entirely from the single solo part, a struggling violino piccolo (Quart-Geige, or kit), that has more difficulty in getting the upper hand of the orchestra than any other solo in the whole classical repertoire. The transformation of this thinnest of solo threads into massive and stirring four-part choral writing is one of Bach's most astonishing feats of easy and unerring mastery. Any ordinary man would have reasoned as follows: 'This movement is the only one in the concerto with a true solo, all the rest of the work being on the lines of the concerto grosso, and depending on the opposition of masses of strings, wood-winds, and horns. And this solo part is not very brilliant, nor does it give me any material I cannot get more easily from the winds. There-fore I will either neglect it, or absorb it into the arrangement I pro-pose to make of the wind-parts, which shall become the chorus. And now that I look at the structure of the movement, I see that there is much repetition caused by this tiresome little solo part, the motive of which will vanish when my chorus carries all before it. So I will cut out all these conventional repetitions, and make the form of my chorus free and terse.' And so our *a priori* theorist achieves a breathless chorus in a jerry-built form. Thus the easy-going innovator (for all conventional minds are bursting with innovation) has arrived at the forms of many popular concertos of modern times. Bach's ways have nothing to do with *a priori* theorizing. In the true sense of the word he is the greatest of theorists, for he *sees*, he *understands*, and his vision is perfected in action.

Bach, or rather his chorus, seems to reply to our reasoner: 'You complain that the violin part is overshadowed, and you point out that the rest of the work is a concerto grosso. But this first movement is not; and your complaint only proves that the violin arrested your attention from the moment it appeared, and made you wish that the orchestra allowed you to hear it better. The violin spoke to you like a voice, and you found it too weak; it shall become a chorus, and you shall learn that the whole orchestra always was its loyal bodyguard. The repetitions you think conven-tional shall continue to mean here exactly what they always meant —the transformation of a formal statement into the living and

moving utterances of a personality; with this new splendour that
the personality is that of a happy multitude inspired by one joy.
The form of such a movement as this need no more change with
a reversal of its balance of tone than the forms of the mountains
change as the light falls at morning and evening. Let the horns
become trumpets, let us hear the thunder-clap and roll of drums
where the chorus sings of "der rollende Pauken durchdringender
Knall"; let the voices have more room here and there; but do not
dream of losing the vital beauty that not only gives the movement
its form, but is its very cause, the opposition of a *personality* to the
impersonal orchestra. It is no matter whether that personality be
an instrument, personal because isolated, or a chorus, personal
because having human speech. The moment it appears it rivets
our attention, and the orchestra itself becomes an eager listener
expressing its sympathy in harmonious assent.'

As if to demonstrate that the affinity between choral and concerto forms is no accident of an insensitive age, Handel once
adapted some non-ritornello choruses (such as 'Lift up your heads')
into a huge concerto. The results are absurd enough to make the
difference between right and wrong in this matter self-evident.

THE SONATA-FORM CONCERTO

We have seen how the early aria form was adapted to the conditions of a concerto; though we did not enter into many particulars about the aria itself. We must be more careful with the forms
that underlie the concertos that are now to be discussed. The
best way to avoid a tiresome abstract of ordinary sonata form will
be for us to base our analysis on the difference between the sonata
forms and those of Bach. The cardinal difference between sonata-
style movements and those of the time of Bach is that the sonata
movement changes on dramatic principles as it unfolds itself, whereas the older forms grow from one central idea and change only in
becoming more effective as they proceed. Bach's grandest movements will show this no less than his smallest. You cannot, indeed,
displace a bar without upsetting the whole; but the most experienced critic could not tell from looking at a portion out of its context whether it came from the beginning, middle, or end of the
work. Yet almost any sufficiently long extract from the first movement of a sonata by Mozart or Beethoven would give a competent
musician abundant indications of its place in the scheme.

It would be convenient if we could say that the polyphonic idea
of form is the development of a single theme, while the sonata idea
is the development and contrast of several; but it would not be
at all true. The first movement of Bach's B minor Sonata for

cembalo and flute has fifteen distinct figures—which is more than can be found in the extremely rich first movement of Brahms's G major Violin Sonata—and yet it is a perfect example of the true spirit of polyphonic form; while Haydn often gives us quite mature sonata movements in which it is impossible to find more than one theme. Still, the great thing to bear in mind is that the themes of the old polyphonic movement, if there are more than one, flow one into the other. The movement grows without ever show-ing impressive preparation for the advent of something new; and its surprises, many though they may be to a sympathetic listener, are never much connected with new themes or indeed with any-thing we do not seem to have known from the first. But a Haydn movement sets out in search of adventures; and if there is only one theme, that theme will somehow contrive to enter in another place disguised as its own twin brother. There will always be a vivid impression of *opposition* of ideas, and of change as well as develop-ment. And Haydn's frequent use of one theme where orthodoxy expects two is a result of amazing invention working on a decep-tively small scale and seizing every conceivable means of making the dimensions of his work seem spacious, and its outlines free.

Hence the early instrumental forms were such that a short pregnant ritornello could sum up the principal material of a move-ment in a single line, while the solo was under no need to intro-duce more fresh matter than suited its disposition. But the material of sonata forms cannot be so briefly summed up; the ritornello, if it is used at all, must be larger and must contain more than one paragraph.

The great masters of sonata form were not to be persuaded to abandon the ritornello. The larger range of sonata movements, the treatment of the orchestra on lines as dramatic as those of the new forms, and the rise of a corresponding style of solo playing—all these facts conspire to make the ritornello more instead of less necessary than before. Bach's concerto orchestra was almost always merely a string band; when he adds wind instruments to it, these show a strong tendency to detach themselves as subordinate solo parts; and so completely does he falsify the current idea about the parity of his orchestral and solo parts, that his great Double Concerto in C major for two cembalos reduces the string-band to a mere support, necessary and effective, but in no way opposed to the cembalos, who wrestle only with each other. Under these conditions Bach even abandons the ritornello. Not so the masters of sonata form: their orchestra uses wind instruments in every possible combination with the strings, sometimes opposed in groups, as in the old concerto grosso, sometimes in solos, and constantly in perfect blending of tone with the strings as part of the compact chorus. Such an orchestra cannot be allowed to remain permanently in the background. On the other hand, the solo will need to be more brilliant than ever before, if it is to stand out against this orchestra which has already so much contrast of its own. The modern concerto form must rest more than ever on the old and natural concerto idea, the entry of a personal voice instantly arresting attention, and by mere force of its individuality thrusting even the most elaborate orchestra into the background. And the more rich the orchestra, and the greater the number and range of themes, the longer and more effectively may the appearance of this individual voice be delayed by an orchestral ritornello, if only this remains truly a ritornello and does not merge into pure symphonic writing. Here we have the key to the true method of conveying sonata form in terms of a concerto. The ordinary account of the matter, as given in standard treatises, is that the orchestra gives out the first and second subject with most of their accessories, more or less as in a symphony, but all in one key, instead of the first being in the tonic and the second in the dominant; that the solo then appears and restates these subjects somewhat more at leisure and in their proper complementary keys; after which there is a shorter recapitulation of part of the tutti in the new key, whereupon the solo again enters and works out an ordinary sonata development and recapitulation more or less in combination with the orchestra; after which the movement ends with a final tutti, interrupted by an extempore cadenza from the solo player. Now this scheme is, no doubt, rather like a concerto as it sounds to us when we are not listening; but it is falsified in all its most important particulars by nearly every concerto in the classical repertoire except Beethoven's in C minor; and the whole subsequent history of Beethoven's treatment of the form indicates that he learnt to regard the structure of the first tutti of his C minor concerto as a mistake.

Let us try to discover the true concerto form by analysing a great work of Mozart, the Pianoforte Concerto in C major (Köchel 503), referring to parallel cases wherever they may help us.

Mozart begins with a majestic assertion of his key, C major, by the whole orchestra, with mysterious soft shadows, that give a solemn depth to the tone (Ex. 1).

Ex. 1.

Allegro maestoso.

The second of these sombre changes passes into C minor with extraordinary grandeur and breadth, and a new rhythmic figure (Ex. 2) rises quietly in the violins.

Ex. 2.
C minor.

(a)

This new figure bursts out forte in the bass[1] with a counterpoint on the violins (Ex. 3), in the major again, and with the full orchestra.

Ex. 3.

Bass 8ve. *lower.*   (a) *inverted.*

It modulates broadly and firmly to the dominant, which key it explores triumphantly, and finally annexes by trumpeting the rhythmic figure three times on G. Now this is not quite in the manner of a symphony. True, many of Mozart's earlier symphonic first themes consist, like Ex. 1, of little more than a vigorous assertion of the tonic and dominant chords; but they continue in a style that only slowly becomes more epigrammatic and melodious, and hardly rises to any surprising harmonic effect throughout the whole movement; whereas this concerto opening is mysterious and profound in its very first line. It shows at once a boldness and richness of style which is only to be found in Mozart's most advanced work. A symphony in this style would certainly begin with something more like an articulated regular theme, however openly it might be designed to emphasize the tonic and dominant of the key. (Compare the opening of the Jupiter Symphony. The Jupiter Symphony is the *locus classicus* for an architectural opening, but it takes no such risks as the opening of this concerto.) These solemn procedures have much the effect of an *introduction*. That impression is somewhat modified as the music carries us out with its tide, and we realize that we have indeed begun a grand voyage of discovery. This cannot be an introduction that leads to something with a beginning of its own, but

[1] In the only printed parts accessible (published, to its lasting disgrace, in connexion with the complete critical edition), all this is blurred by a stupid crescendo. The parts are simply plastered all over with additional marks of expression that show a total deafness to fine orchestration, dignity, and vividness of style, and only one faint gleam of intelligence, that the editor does not give his name. The only way to avoid hours of labour in clearing up this mess is to play from manuscripts faithfully copied from the score.

it must be a preparation for some advent; and we can best realize
how grand it is if we try to imagine the effect with which a chorus
might enter at this close on the dominant (end of the passage
beginning at Ex. 3). The entry of a chorus, singing the psalm
Dixit Dominus, would be almost perfectly appropriate; indeed
Mozart's church music, which is mostly of an earlier period,
rarely attains to such power and solemnity as this opening. If we
turn to Brahms's *Triumphlied*, we shall find that the orchestral
introduction, though not nearly so long as these first fifty bars,
is not unlike them in the way in which it covers its ground and
seems to be leading up to something. But of course a chorus
thrusts the orchestra far more into the background than a solo
instrument can. Our opening tutti must develop further, for the
orchestra will not sound relevant if repressed by the feeble tone of a
single instrument before it has stated several contrasted themes.

We have, then, paused on the dominant. Observe again that
the modulation to the dominant is not like the normal early modulations of symphonies. Though, if taken out of its context, the
close of this passage would seem to be clearly in G, yet it here
sounds only like very strong emphasis on the dominant of C. True,
in symphonies of an earlier period Mozart would have followed
his close by a second subject in G; but the effect of doing so is
always a little epigrammatic—the taking advantage of a natural
emphasis on the dominant so as to turn it into a new tonic; and
I believe that Mozart differs, even in his earliest works, from
ordinary composers in seeing that the device *is* epigrammatic,
whereas they only saw that it was convenient and obvious. But
it certainly would not tell in a work in the advanced style of this
concerto. The only way to prepare the mind for G major after this
grand opening would be to go to *its* dominant and pause on that.
But the present close in G (in spite of the F sharp and all the
firmness and emphasis) has not taken our minds out of C at all. We
feel that we are *on* the dominant, not *in* it. Again, if this were
a symphony and Mozart wished to begin his second subject, or
preparations for it, at this point he would be almost certain to plunge
into a remote and quiet key, most probably E flat, rather than use
the old colourless device described above. And it is interesting to
note that this is exactly what Beethoven did in the same circumstances in his C major concerto, when he had not yet realized the
difference between symphonic form and the form of the concerto-
ritornello. (Another reason for making particular note of this
possibility of E flat will appear later.)

What does Mozart do? He remains in C; and this fixity of key
stamps the introductory ritornello character of the music more
and more firmly the longer it continues. Out of that Beethovenish

rhythmic figure ♩.♫|♩ arises a quiet march in C minor, half
solemn, half gay, and wonderfully orchestrated (Ex. 4).

Ex. 4.

(a)

&c.

This is repeated by the wind, with soft trumpets and drums, in
the major. 'Here', explains the believer in standard accounts of
concerto form, 'we evidently have the second subject, which the
solo will eventually restate in the dominant.' Wait and see.

After this counter-statement there is a delightful kind of
Hallelujah Chorus (Ex. 5), which settles with majestic grace into
a quiet cadence-figure (Ex. 6);

Ex. 5.

&c.

p

Ex. 6.

&c.

&c.

Light semiquaver accompaniment.

and the grand pageant of themes closes in triumph. Then the strings
seem to *listen*, for one moment of happy anticipation. As they
listen the pianoforte enters, at first with scattered phrases (Ex. 7).

Ex. 7.
Strings.   Pfte.

These quickly settle into a stream of florid melody, which
grows to a brilliant climax in accordance with the artistic necessity that the solo should hold its own by doing that which most

distinguishes it from the orchestra, and should therefore be florid just in proportion to the amount of orchestral impressiveness.[1]

On the top of this climax the full orchestra re-enters with Ex. 1, on the same principle as the bursting in of the ritornello upon the first utterances of the voice or solo in the polyphonic arias and concertos. The impressive soft shadows of this theme are now beautifully illuminated by running passages in the pianoforte, which continues the theme in close dialogue with the wind-band. Ex. 2 follows, yet more impressive, thrilled with the rise and fall of pianoforte scales. Instead of leading to a triumphant outburst in the major, it is continued in the minor with very dark colouring and great breadth of rhythm, and culminates on the dominant of C minor, which the full orchestra sternly emphasizes with the rhythmic figure (a) ♩ ♫ ♩. . Here, then, we have another pause on the dominant, not unlike that which we had shortly after Ex. 3. What does the pianoforte do now? It quietly modulates to E flat, exactly as we saw that Beethoven was tempted to do in the opening tutti of his first concerto. And that modulation, which is a mistake in a ritornello[2] because of its symphonic character, is for the same reason beautiful when the solo has entered and established its relation to the orchestra. Here Mozart gives the pianoforte a new theme (Ex. 8) pervaded by that omnipresent rhythmic figure (a).

Ex. 8.

Transition Theme.

(a)   &c.

[1] Hence the source of all our delusions as to the relation between the concerto and the bravura styles. A modern concerto *must* be technically difficult, because all the easy ways in which a solo can stand out against an orchestra are harmonically and technically obvious, being the elementary things for which the instrument must be constructed if it is to be practicable at all; and as the orchestra becomes more varied and powerful, the soloist must dive deeper into the resources of his instrument. Hence the concertos of Mozart are in general far more difficult than any earlier ones; those of Beethoven the most difficult of all except those of Brahms; while the concertos of the virtuoso-composers, which exist mainly for technique, are easier than any others, since whatever types of passage they employ are written on progressions schematic at best, so that they can in time be mastered once for all like the knack of spinning a peg-top; whereas the great composer's passages never take your hand where it expects to go, and can be mastered by the muscle only in obedience to the continual dictation of the mind. Mozart's passages are in this respect among the most treacherous in existence.

[2] I continue to apply this term to the whole opening tutti of the largest concertos. The longest opening tutti does not, if rightly designed, lose the unity that characterizes the true ritornello, even if it contains many important changes of key.

This modulates to the dominant of G in a broadly symphonic style, thoroughly expressive of the intention to establish the new key with firmness. Contrast what we felt about the passage following Ex. 3. After dwelling on this new dominant with sufficient breadth, the pianoforte settles down into the second subject. This will come as a surprise to orthodox believers in text-books, for it has nothing whatever to do with Ex. 4, which seemed so like a possible second subject. Indeed the only part of it that has anything to do with the ritornello is a variation of Ex. 3, which obviously belonged originally to the first subject, though we may remember that the pianoforte had avoided it when it fell due after the solo statement of Ex. 2.

I need not describe the second subject in detail. Its new and main theme (Ex. 9) is first stated by the pianoforte—

Ex. 9.

and then counterstated and expanded by the wind instruments. The derivative of Ex. 3 follows (see Ex. 10) and leads brilliantly to a climax,

Ex. 10.
(*cf.* 3.)

(*a*) *inverted.*

with all that variety of colour and rhythm and continual increase of breadth which is one of the most unapproachable powers of the true classics, distinguishing them no less from the classicists, who do not know that they lack it, than from the romantic composers, the greatest of whom contrive to make their work depend on renouncing it in favour of epigram and antithesis.

On the top of this climax the orchestra, long pent-up, bursts in with Ex. 3 of the ritornello. And here Mozart contrives one of his most subtle and brilliant strokes. We saw that Ex. 3 originally led to G and closed emphatically in that key, but yet under circumstances that made us feel that we were all the time only on the dominant of C. But now, of course, it begins in G, and Mozart so contrives that it remains there, instead of going on to the present dominant, D, as it would if transposed exactly; and it ends with the *very same notes* for no less than ten bars, *as in its original occurrence*, but now, of course, with the strongest possible feeling of being *in* G, not merely *on* the dominant. Thus Mozart cannot even do a mere repetition without shedding a new light that could not possibly be given by any variation. There is no describing the peculiar and subtle pleasure this device gives. It depends on a delicate sense of key, but has nothing to do with the technical knowledge which enables us to name it; indeed, it is certain to be keenly enjoyed by any attentive listener whose knowledge of music is the result of relish for classical works, stimulated by frequent opportunities for hearing them under good conditions. On the other hand, it is quite possible that many persons skilled in the mechanics of what passes for counterpoint, and having at least a concert-goer's retrospective view of musical history, simply do not hear these effects at all.

The sense of key-perspective can never be made obsolete by new harmonic developments. In otiose styles, whether early or recent, it is in abeyance; but a genuinely revolutionary style is more likely to stimulate than obliterate it. Strauss's opening of *Also sprach Zarathustra* might almost pass for a paraphrase of the opening of Mozart's C major Concerto.

The orchestra ends, trumpeting the rhythmic figure (*a*) on G as a finally established key. The pianoforte re-enters, repeating the figure on the dominant of E. And now it goes straight on with the march theme (Ex. 4) in E minor, which is to furnish our development section. The concerto has been grand and surprising, leaving us continually mystified as to what is to happen, and now it takes shape.

This theme that so happily pulls the whole design together all the way back from its single previous appearance in the ritornello, now moves calmly through a long series of very straightforward sequences through various keys. But though the sequences are simple in their steps, they are infinitely varied in colouring, and they rapidly increase in complexity until, to the surprise of any one who still believes that Mozart is a childishly simple composer, they move in eight real parts.

These eight parts are in triple, or, if we count added thirds, quadruple canon, two in the strings, four in the wind with the added thirds, and two of light antiphonal scales in the pianoforte. No such polyphony has occurred since in any concerto, except one passage in the middle of the finale of Brahms's D minor.

Then there follows a majestic dominant pedal for the next eight bars, not at all polyphonic; the wind rises in a scale which the pianoforte crosses in descent, and just at the most satisfactory moment the full orchestra enters with the opening theme, Ex. 1; and we find ourselves in the recapitulation. The pianoforte shares the continuation, as in its first solo, and proceeds without alteration through the expanded version of Ex. 2 to the E flat theme, Ex. 8. This takes a new direction of very beautiful harmony and leads to the second subject. From this point the recapitulation bids fair to continue to follow its original exactly; but we find that the counter-statement of Ex. 9 is expanded in a new sequence of modulations in minor harmonies, and suddenly we find ourselves again in the broad daylight of the major key, listening to Ex. 4 as it was given in counter-statement in the ritornello! The pianoforte has a brilliant part of its own in this incident. Then the rest of the recapitulation follows, with Ex. 9 as if nothing had happened. And, of course, at the end the orchestra enters with Ex. 3, and comes to a pause on a 6/4 chord, whereon the pianoforte extemporizes a cadenza. After this the orchestra crowns the work with its final triumph of formal balance by repeating, what we have not heard since the first entry of the solo, the closing themes, Ex. 5 and 6.

It will be seen that this whole wonderful scheme entirely fails to fit the orthodox account of concerto form. Evidently the opening tutti has no connexion with the notion of a sonata exposition in one key; it is a true ritornello, differing from that of an aria only in its gigantic size. If further proof were wanted, Constance's great bravura aria 'Martern aller Arten' in the *Entführung* would furnish it, besides showing the use of auxiliary solos in the ritornello, a device revived by Brahms in the slow movement of his B flat Concerto. Of course there are plenty of cases where the second subject is represented in the ritornello, especially where the work is not on the largest scale; but there is no foreseeing what the solo will select from the ritornello. All that we can be sure of is that nothing will be without its function, and that everything will be unexpected and inevitable. I doubt whether three important concertos of Mozart (at least fifteen are important) could be found that agreed as closely in form as Beethoven's three greatest concertos (G, E flat, and the Violin Concerto). In one point they almost all agree, even down to the smallest works; and that is the splendid device of inserting in the recapitulation of the second subject a theme from the ritornello that was not represented in the original solo statement. In Beethoven's hands the concerto grew so large that this device would no longer be weighty enough to pull the design together, and so it has remained peculiar to Mozart.[1]

---

[1] Further investigation will show that this device is the result of a larger principle which I had not grasped in 1903. The recapitulation in the tonic is a recapitulation of the opening tutti as well as of the first solo. It does not omit the features peculiar to the solo, but it adds to them those features of the ritornello which the solo had not at first adopted. In particular, it is likely to follow the course of the opening much more closely than in the first solo; and the subsequent appearance of a previously neglected theme is the most conspicuous result of this tendency. In Beethoven and Brahms the main principle is quite as clear, though it may not be marked by a special theme.

It is unnecessary to give a full account of the other movements; concertos, as they proceed, naturally use, like all sonata-works, more sectional forms, in which solo and orchestra alternate more simply than in the first movement. This is further necessitated by the fact that it can no longer be effective to lay such tremendous emphasis on the entries of the solo, now that it has so gloriously won its way into friendship with the orchestral crowd. Hence the ritornello idea does not find such full expression in these later movements, though Mozart is very fond of using a simple kind of ritornello at the beginning of his larger slow movements, as in the present work. I give the three main themes of this ritornello in Ex. 11, 12 and 13.

Ex. 11.
(a)
(b)
Ex. 12.
Ex. 13.

The pianoforte turns Ex. 12 into a second subject and adds more themes to it; returning then by a really colossal passage on a dominant pedal to the main theme in the tonic, and a regular recapitulation of both subjects. Ex. 13 is reserved to round off the movement.[1]

Concerto finales are practically certain to be some kind of rondo. Mozart soon found out how to make the rondo form bring out the solo in the most appropriate way. He gives to the main theme (which is usually announced by the solo) a large number of orchestral accessories, which do not recur with the returns of the

[1] In some of Mozart's andantes, notably that of the G major Concerto, the themes of the ritornello are so closely welded together that it is a great surprise to hear what we thought was part of one melody blossom out in a new key as a well-contrasted second subject. (See Essay LXXXVIII.)

theme, until the very end where the solo shares in them as they round off the movement with fine effect.[1]

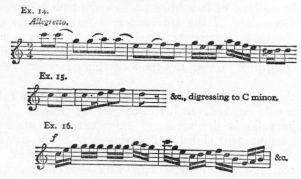

Ex. 14.
Allegretto.

Ex. 15.
&c., digressing to C minor.

Ex. 16.
f
&c.

In the present instance, Mozart announces the main theme by the orchestra, and uses the accessories more extensively, making Ex. 15 modulate to A minor for the middle episode. But Ex. 16 appears only at the end of all, after a very big coda. In this finale the free-rhythmed connecting links between the main sections attain a breadth that was never approached until surpassed by Beethoven. Here are the remaining themes:

Ex. 17.
Entry of Pianoforte.
&c.

Ex. 18. Transition.
&c.

Ex. 19. First Episode.

Ex. 20. Middle Episode (a).
(Allied to No. 17.)

Ex. 21. Middle Episode (b).
Is alluded to by diminution in the Coda.

[1] Mozart found this use of accessory themes in the tonic valuable outside concertos. The finales of the two pianoforte quartets and of the great A major Violin Sonata are excellent examples.

CONCLUSION

Only the analysis of individual works can adequately show the later developments of the true concerto form. These chiefly concern the first movement; for the other movements are not much prevented by the special conditions of concerto form from growing on ordinary lines. But the following generalizations may be useful.

1. Beethoven ceased making the ritornello come to a full stop before the solo entered. In his three greatest concertos the end of the ritornello is dramatic and expectant, so that the solo enters on a dominant chord and ruminates in broad passages of immense dignity and beauty before taking up the themes. These passages correspond to the new theme with which Mozart so often begins the solos of his larger concertos; but, with their entry on the dominant and their non-thematic character, they produce a far more thrilling effect. Mozart's nearest approaches to this are in the concerto just analysed, in the much earlier A major Violin Concerto, where the solo begins with a short, florid adagio, in the brilliant and witty Pianoforte Concerto in B flat (Köchel 450), see Essay LXXXVII, and in another big Concerto in C major (Köchel 467), where the solo enters on the dominant.

2. Beethoven did *not* 'emancipate the orchestra' as is commonly held: he could not possibly have made it more prominent and elaborate than Mozart makes it in such works as that described here. On the contrary, he treated the pianoforte much more constantly in full harmony, and this inspired him with the possibility of accompanying it by very incomplete harmony in the orchestra and so producing numberless wonderful effects that can be heard under no other conditions.

3. Beethoven had the art of inventing themes which pass continually through several keys. This enabled him to give the opening tutti of his G major Concerto great variety of tonality without becoming symphonic or losing its unity as a ritornello.

4. In the same work he secures the novel effect of letting the pianoforte begin, and making the orchestra enter *in a foreign key* with the next phrase, after which the ritornello proceeds on the orchestra alone.

5. In his E flat Concerto he discovered the possibility of a rhapsodical solo introduction before the ritornello.

6. In the same work he found out how to construct a gigantic coda out of a new recapitulation of the later themes of the ritornello, including even the entry of the solo. This removes the one real defect of the classical form, that it entrusts the organization of the coda to the player's extempore powers in the cadenza.

Brahms further developed the concerto form in the following ways.

7. He found a way of modulation that gives the ritornello more than one key, and this, not by a series of transitions (like Beethoven's in the G major Concerto), but by a real contrast of fixed keys, all without loss of the necessary unity and flow.

8. He enlarged the notion of a solo introduction and made it both thematic and rhapsodic, thus saving space in the ensuing ritornello.

9. He did not, as used to be said, score too heavily for the solo; on the contrary he is demonstrably lighter than Mozart; but he uses the modern pianoforte in order to add greatly to the volume of a big tutti.

10. He discovered that if the solo takes most of its material from the orchestra, the orchestra may take some fresh material from the solo; and thus he obtained many new contrasts.

11. He found out how to write a symphonic scherzo for pianoforte and orchestra.

Such innovations do not make a formidable catalogue, but they are the outward signs of spiritual forces that are not concerned in the gyrations of the up-to-date weathercock. In the classical concerto forms the orchestra and solo are so organized that both are at their highest development. The conditions of such a problem do not admit many obviously different solutions; and the concertos that abandon the classical form obtain their unlimited variety by being structures of a much looser and less ambitious order. They stand on their own merits, and can be defined only by individual analysis. Beethoven had no reason, for example, to despise Weber's *Conzertstück*; and later composers, from Mendelssohn onwards, would have seen no reason why it should not have been called a concerto. It is manifestly better than Weber's regular concertos; and composers may as well write the best music they can, without being worried by a terminology that would confine the word 'concerto' to a form which exists in hardly thirty perfect examples.

MOZART

LXXXVI. PIANOFORTE CONCERTO IN A MAJOR (KÖCHEL'S CATALOGUE, NO. 414)

1 *Allegro.* 2 *Andante.* 3 RONDO, *Allegretto.*

This is one of a group of three small pianoforte concertos which Mozart wrote not long before *Figaro*, during the period of the six string quartets which made Haydn acknowledge him as the greatest composer he had ever heard of. These concertos are small as the wild strawberry is small; they are no stunted growths, nor are they school-pieces of 'educational' value; they are highly characteristic and mature masterpieces. The smallest is in F major, and its character is somewhere between that of an Aberdeen terrier and a Dandie Dinmont; it does not happen to show fight, but its quiet sagacity is no sign of weakness. The largest is in C major. To the little old orchestra of strings, two oboes, and two horns, for which all three are written, it adds trumpets and drums, with which it makes dramatic jollifications; the slow movement reacts from these in a style which is the source of Mendelssohn's Songs without Words; and the finale is a fairy-tale in which a melancholy adagio twice introduces the marvellous into the design.

The little A major Concerto is in style midway between these two; and it would be difficult to find another work of Mozart in which practically every single theme is so typical of his style. Even small works of art in these large forms usually assert a composer's style more in their treatment of themes than in any large proportion of the themes themselves. Those of the little F major Concerto are almost all common formulas, and so are more than half of those of the little C major; but here it almost seems as if Mozart had concentrated the most personal features of a dozen compositions on this single work. He appears to have been fond of it himself and to have played it or taught it often to his favourite pupils, for he has left two complete sets of cadenzas for it, by no means as perfunctory as his written cadenzas usually are. As a rule it may be taken that Mozart's written cadenzas do not adequately represent what he would extemporize in the places where they are required; but this concerto gives us the exceptions. They are very short, but full of valuable features in design.

The opening tutti of the first movement gives, as usual, the principal themes of the first subject—

Ex. 1.

followed by a vigorous transition theme which I do not quote; and the second subject, a gallant little march, full of Mozart's Tyrolese raillery.

Ex. 2.

Besides these we have an important feature in Mozart's mature concerto form; a prominent theme which is ignored by the solo instrument when it first gathers up the threads of the opening tutti, but which pulls the whole form together when the recapitulation follows the lines of the tutti more faithfully, and puts this theme in its proper place.

Ex. 3.

Lastly, there is the final cadence-figure which (as in the earlier flute concertos and elsewhere) the solo has a way of neatly turning into a new transition theme. I need not quote it, as this description will suffice to identify it.

There are people who still believe that Mozart's whole idea of pianoforte playing was confined to a pretty tinkle. It may surprise them to hear that Mozart's friends were fond of asking him to 'make the pianoforte sound like an organ', and that he delighted in so obliging them. What they meant thereby is shown by the first theme of the slow movement, which the pianoforte, when its turn comes, gives in very full chords.

Ex. 4.

Another theme, which afterwards constitutes the second subject, is remarkable for its likeness to the first theme of the first movement (see Ex. 1).

Ex. 5.

Such resemblances come too often and too prominently in Mozart's concertos to be accidental. They are sometimes placed where they have exactly the same function in each movement, and are always placed where they must attract attention.

The finale, beginning with a lively little formula-tune—

Ex. 6.

continues with an excellent theme full of sly resource, which brings about most of the action throughout the movement.

Ex. 7.

The pianoforte, which, after stating Ex. 6, gave way to a tutti full of accessory themes, re-enters with a new cantabile transition melody, which I need not quote, though it is the source of some pretty dialogue in the coda. It leads to the first episode (or second subject), in which, among other themes, Ex. 7 is developed. Like nearly all concerto finales this movement is a rondo; and so in due course Ex. 6 returns, and then Ex. 7 leads to the middle episode beginning with a playful tune in D major. Look out for the violas with their mocking imitations.

From this middle episode Mozart returns, not to the first subject, but to the solo cantabile transition theme, and so to the recapitulation of the second subject. Then follows a coda in which Ex. 7, the transition theme, and all the accessories given by the first tutti round off the whole design with delightful freedom. Notice, for example, the whimsical pauses in the transition theme when, after the cadenza, it enters into dialogue with the orchestra.

LXXXVII. PIANOFORTE CONCERTO NO. 15, IN B FLAT MAJOR (KÖCHEL'S CATALOGUE, NO. 450)

1 *Allegro.* 2 *Andante.* 3 *Allegro.*

Ludwig Deppe, the originator of the method of pianoforte playing on which I was trained, used to call Mozart's fifteenth concerto 'the most difficult concerto in the world'; as readers of Amy Fay's *Music Study in Germany* may remember. In the days which that book commemorates it was still possible for a responsible critic to remark (as Beethoven himself would have remarked) that we should regard Mozart's cadenzas and passages as child's-play. Amy Fay already thought that 'such a critic ought to go to school again'. Mozart's own opinion is interesting. He produced this concerto as one of three, together with the great Quintet for pianoforte and wind-instruments, in March 1784; having early in February produced the Sonata for two pianofortes. Of this concerto, with its soldierly brother in D major and two others, he writes to his father on 24 May: 'I cannot come to a decision between those two concertos in B flat and D. I consider them both concertos that make one perspire; but in difficulty the one in B flat beats the one in D. Besides, I am very anxious to know which one of the three concertos, in B flat, D, and G, you and my sister like best; for the one in E flat is not at all in the same class, being a concerto of quite a peculiar kind and written rather for a small orchestra than for a big one.'

The Concerto in G is a large work written in April of the same year.[1] From Mozart's letter we learn that the difference between

[1] *Vide* following analysis.

small and large orchestras is not a matter of trumpets and drums. Our Dresden-china Mozart is a fiction which we may remorselessly hand over to the most panclastic of scullery-maids.

Of a symphony smaller than the Linz Symphony Mozart writes that it went '*magnifique*' with forty violins, ten double-basses, six bassoons, and all the wind doubled. This treatment would not suit even a heroic concerto, but the fact puts an end to miniature views of Mozart's style.

The opening theme of this B flat concerto—

Ex. 1.

shows Mozart in his most *schalkhaft* (or naughty) mood, and the change of accent at * shows that his naughtiness is stimulated by his most dangerous wit.

The raillery is continued even more quizzically. But soon Mozart, though refusing to leave the tonic chord, plunges into the usual forte theme which comes to the usual half-close. Then, thinks the usual theorist, we have the usual second subject.

Ex. 2.

But, as we have seen before, it is impossible to tell which, if any, of the themes of a Mozart tutti is going to belong to the second group.

Another tutti theme, beginning with a conspirator's crescendo, leads to the cadence-figure of the whole ritornello. On the stage this would imply a ribald gesture addressed to deluded husbands. See *Figaro*, Act IV, No. 26 '*gia ognuno lo sa*'.

Ex. 3.

While the orchestra is finishing some final chords, the pianoforte enters with a declamatory running figure, which it turns into an introductory cadenza. It then states the main theme, Ex. 1. Having completed this, it proceeds on entirely new lines, and modulates broadly to the dominant, where it gives out a second subject, consisting, with all its accessories, of themes that have never been suggested by the opening tutti at all.

Ex. 4.

At the end of this the orchestra bursts out with a dovetailing of the
two forte themes of the tutti; ending, of course, with the cornute
gesture of Ex. 3. The latter figure of this theme is turned into a
chromatic run by the pianoforte, which thus begins a short but
adequate development. This becomes dignified in becoming episodic; and the return to the first subject is, as always in Mozart,
delightfully comfortable in the impression it gives of accurate
timing.

With the recapitulation we see the full breadth of Mozart's
concerto form. It is quite as much a recapitulation of the first
tutti as it is of the first solo, and consequently it gathers up threads
which the first solo had left unused. Thus it uses the first tutti
forte before preparing for the second subject, and in the course of
the second subject it inserts Ex. 2. Lastly, it follows the end of the
solo not by a forte but by the original conspirator's crescendo.
Even after the (presumably extemporized) cadenza, the orchestra
turns its last chords to fresh account, no longer overlaid by the
pianoforte.

The slow movement is a set of ornamental variations on one of
Mozart's most beautiful themes.

Ex. 5.

Two double variations (i.e. variations in which the repeats of the
two halves of the theme are themselves varied) suffice with a short
coda to make a movement of great breadth and of almost solemn
tone.

With the finale Mozart becomes *schalkhaft* again. Says the Fool
in *King Lear*—

'This prophecy shall Merlin make, for I live before his time,'

and in the same spirit we may suppose Mozart to have foreseen
that one day Schumann would write a pianoforte quartet with a
slow movement which takes Mozart's naughtiest theme seriously.

Ex. 6.
Mozart.

Schumann.

No concerto-rondo by Mozart can do with less than seven different themes. Of these I must quote, besides Ex. 6, two themes from the tutti—

Ex. 7.

Ex. 8.

and (omitting the cantabile transition theme, with which the pianoforte re-enters, and the theme of the middle episode) the beginning of the first episode (or second subject) with its more than intelligent anticipation of Liszt's dovetail-hand technique.

Ex. 9.

The returns to the main theme (Ex. 6) are particularly witty. For the first return Mozart wrote an extra cadenza (not given in the score); and the second is reached from the extreme distance of A minor by a dialogue between pianoforte and oboe.

At the end of the movement Ex. 7 and Ex. 8 are combined in an amusingly dramatic way.

LXXXVIII. PIANOFORTE CONCERTO IN G MAJOR (KÖCHEL'S CATALOGUE, NO. 453)

1 *Allegro.* 2 *Andante.* 3 *Allegretto, with Presto* FINALE.

The Concerto in G, written in 1784, is one of Mozart's richest and wittiest. The slow movement is full of deep and tender feeling, with a certain gravity in its sweetness and light; but the first movement and finale are in the most intellectual vein of high comedy, culminating in an epilogue of pure *opera buffa* on a more expansive plan than almost any other of Mozart's codas. The scoring, for small orchestra without clarinets, trumpets, or drums, is as consummate as that of the three great symphonies; and the pianoforte part is highly polished, without any of the problems Mozart sometimes presents by leaving it in a sketchy state to be filled out extempore by himself as the pianist. He even wrote two separate sets of cadenzas for the first two movements. Both sets are far from perfunctory, and it is difficult to choose between them.

Of the first movement I quote, first, the opening theme—

Ex. 1.

and (passing over its forte sequel) the wistful cantabile which afterwards becomes the second subject.

Ex. 2.

&c. leading to—

&c.

A dramatic incident in a dark key—

Ex. 3.

will show later on that the development is not quite so episodic as it seems. The ritornello ends with three contrasted themes, of which I quote the first, with its *Don Giovanni* sharpened octave.

Ex. 4.

The pianoforte enters with Ex. 1 and follows the course of the ritornello closely until it sees opportunity for modulating broadly to the dominant. Here, however, it introduces the second subject with a quite new theme—

Ex. 5.

&c.

after which the cantabile (Ex. 2), with its introductory quaver figure, appears. It is followed by a series of running and arpeggio themes, until the orchestra caps the climax by entering with its first (unquoted) forte theme. The development has an air of being episodic throughout; but its first part is suggested by Ex. 3. At the end of the recapitulation, this intervenes dramatically in its original shape.

The slow movement is one of those profound utterances of Mozart in terms which are almost confined to formulas; the language of the *Zauberflöte*, the last (so-called 'Jupiter') Symphony, and the *Requiem*. Few casualties of criticism are more amusing than the collision between such works of art and the plausible dogma that 'every important musical composition must have strongly original themes'. The truth is that nobody knows exactly what a theme is, or how many themes make an idea, or even how many ideas may go to a theme and whereabouts in the theme they may be situated.

Externally and conventionally the main themes of this wonderful andante are, first, a solemn pleading phrase, which breaks off with a pause (Ex. 6) and is followed by an arioso formula for oboe with a long swelling first note. This my quotations omit, and I give in Ex. 7 the dialogue for three instruments which arises from it.

Ex. 6.

Ex. 7.

Who would have thought that this dialogue is going to become the second subject in a highly developed sonata form?

A majestic forte theme joins the procession, and the tutti concludes with the one obviously 'original' theme of the movement, a profoundly expressive blend of minor and major modes.

Ex. 8.

The modulations throughout the movement are in a grand dramatic vein, the dramatic note having been already indicated by the unusual pause after the opening phrase (Ex. 6).

Classical concertos contain few examples of the variation form: there are only four in Mozart (the present finale, that of the C minor Concerto, the slow movement of a concerto in B flat, and a so-called rondo written as a new finale to an early concerto in D). The variations in the G major Concerto are among the most witty and ingenious achievements in this form before Beethoven. The wit begins with the theme, of which Ex. 9 is the first strain.

Ex. 9.

From Mozart's petty-cash book we learn that this tune attracted not only the notice of the general public but also that of the birds, or at least that of the bird-fanciers, for he spent thirty-four kreutzers on a starling which delighted him by producing his tune in the following Cloud-cuckoo-land version:

Ex. 9a.

The variations, most of which are double (i.e. with varied or totally contrasted repeats), attain to great remoteness from the external melody; the fourth, in the minor mode, being a mysterious piece of counterpoint on a quite new idea strictly following the structure of the theme.

The fifth and last variation (a double variation with violent contrasts) expands into a coda which leads to the presto finale or epilogue, a comic wind-up big enough for *Figaro* and unique in Mozart's instrumental works. Most of its themes are new. Two of them I quote.

Ex. 10.
Presto.   Horns.

Ex. 11.

The original theme (Ex. 9; not 9a) romps in among the other conspirators as if it had known them all its life.

LXXXIX. PIANOFORTE CONCERTO IN A MAJOR (KÖCHEL'S CATALOGUE, NO. 488)

1 *Allegro.* 2 *Andante.* 3 *Presto.*

The three months of June, July, and August 1788 are famous
for the creation of Mozart's three greatest symphonies; but they
are not more wonderful than the single month of March 1786,
in which the two pianoforte concertos in A major and C minor
were written. These works are in no way inferior to the symphonies, nor are they less sharply contrasted with each other.
The pathos of the C minor Concerto is even more profound than
that of the G minor Symphony, though the texture is less concentrated. The A major Concerto is, with the additional element
of pathos in its remarkable slow movement, as eminently a study in
euphony as is the E flat Symphony, which it further resembles in
revealing the clarinets as Mozart's favourite wind instruments, and
omitting the oboes. Before the year was out Mozart had produced
another concerto (in C major) which fully equals the Jupiter
Symphony in triumphant majesty, and even in contrapuntal display. (See the analysis in the Essay on the Classical Concerto.)

As there is no rule without an exception to prove it, I readily
admit that the first eight and a half pages of this A major Concerto completely tally with that orthodox account of classical
concerto form which I have taken such pains to refute every
time I have discussed a classical concerto. And if a single
concerto, and that a work which the text-books have not selected
as specially typical, can establish a form as 'normal' in points
wherein all the other classical examples differ from it and from
each other so radically that these points can hardly be identified
at all; then perhaps Mozart did here produce an orthodox first
movement—as far as the middle of the ninth of its twenty-two
pages. But at that point things begin to happen which cannot
be found in any other concerto.

However, it is perfectly true that of the five themes (or more,
according as you take broad phrases or single clauses) which the
orchestra gives in its opening tutti, the pianoforte takes up the first
four quite faithfully in their order, making Ex. 1 the first subject;—

Ex. 1.

continuing the forte orchestral sequel (which I do not quote) as a
regular transition leading to the dominant; transposing to that key
(with the aid of only two extra bars) the exquisitely graceful and

gallant theme which the orchestra had already in the first instance
marked off by a formal preparatory half-close—

Ex. 2.

and following it with the next theme. This is a somewhat more
dramatic paragraph, in which three bars, with rustling inner movement tinged with minor harmony, are answered by a spirited major
close, which in its turn gives way to a plaintively quizzical question
and answer in the 'relative minor' (F sharp in the tutti, C sharp
when we have it in the solo statement). The continuation of this
is the only part of the first tutti which the pianoforte expands
into a longer and more brilliant passage so as to prepare for a
big re-entry of the orchestra, instead of passing on to the formal
little orchestral cadence theme with which the first tutti had
closed.

But quickly upon this big re-entry of the orchestra there comes
the inevitable shock to orthodoxy. The need for such a shock is
more pressing than any matter of terms or technicalities. The
objection to the 'orthodox' accounts is that they inculcate spurious
forms, and so induce composers to revolt from the study of classical
music because it is identified in their minds with what they instinctively feel to be bad. Now in the present instance, if Mozart
had not at this point some stroke of genius in preparation—if his
only intention were to write a development on the preceding themes
and return to a regular recapitulation—his form would be orthodox,
but stiff; at all events no better than Spohr's concerto form, and
considerably less good than the best of so modest a master as Viotti,
who (as Joachim and Brahms agreed) was quite capable of intelligent experiments. By what possible means can Mozart, as far as
we have followed him here, manifest the principle governing
the recapitulation of all his other concertos, that the solo recapitulates, not its own version of the first and second subject, but
a fusion of its version with that of the original tutti? Here the
two are as nearly as possible identical. Well, let us see what
happens.

The orchestra has hardly got beyond the beginning of its resumption of the first forte of the opening tutti when it breaks off,
and after a half-bar's silence softly gives out a quite new theme
which brings a deeper and graver mood to add to the grace of the
whole work.

Ex. 3.

The pianoforte takes this up in a florid variation, and with the aid of another new episodic theme in semiquaver movement, works out a broad development in dialogue with the orchestra. Thus, when the recapitulation is reached, the old themes return with complete freshness. And, what is perhaps more remarkable though less obvious, the development had none of the looseness of effect that in ordinary sonatas is apt to result from basing it mainly or entirely on 'episodes'. The episode was here a thing of absolute dramatic necessity. And after the now inevitably and rightly regular recapitulation, Mozart paradoxically vindicates his principle of making the solo refer more closely to the orchestra than to its own exposition of the themes. For when he comes to the last climax of pianoforte passages, it is the pianoforte that breaks off and, after a half-bar's silence, gives out Ex. 3 in its original simplicity and gravity. Afterwards the orchestra too has its say. And the poor pianoforte player has the appalling task of making a cadenza that shall not set the Mozart-lover's teeth on edge. (Mozart has written a cadenza for this concerto, but a more than usually perfunctory and inadequate one. It is doubtful whether he would have regarded any of his written cadenzas to first movements as adequately representing his way of extemporizing, and it is quite certain that he could not wish to be represented by this one; though, like all his cadenzas, it conveys at least one useful hint.) Finally the orchestra rounds off the movement with its little cadence theme which has not been heard since the end of the first tutti.

The slow movement (Mozart's only composition in the key of F sharp minor) is of the most touching melancholy. Its first theme—

Ex. 4.

is stated by the pianoforte alone, and shows in its second bar a feature of late eighteenth-century style which we accept as familiar, without curiosity as to its meaning. One of the most superb vocal gestures of the eighteenth-century singer was the display of an unerring aim in skips from one extreme of the voice to the other, especially when the notes were selected as being opposed to each other in harmony, and so specially difficult to judge accurately. It was, as it ought still to be, the highest boast of the player of an instrument that 'he made his instrument sing'; and Mozart had an unrivalled reputation for that quality in his pianoforte playing. There is not the slightest difficulty in playing the low E sharp in Ex. 3 with the left hand and the next B with the right; and even with one hand the risk of the skip in this slow tempo would be quite unnoticeable; but the whole point of the phrase is that the skip is conceived as an enormous change of vocal register. The pianoforte is a supernatural singer with a compass of five octaves—not more, in Mozart's time; but five octaves is more compatible with a vocal style than seven and a half.

The orchestra introduces another theme—

Ex. 5.

which the pianoforte takes up in a chromatic variation. This leads to A major, in which key we have a lighter and perhaps happier episode. I say 'perhaps', because the childlike new themes are full of prophecy of poor Donna Elvira when her affectionate simplicity is bringing her back into the power of Don Juan. Here, however, there is no sardonic or comic background. The main themes soon return, the pianoforte part being written in a skeletonic way which Mozart certainly must have filled out with ornamentation. I claim to be an absolute purist in *not* confining myself to the written text. With Beethoven the case is already different; yet even Beethoven absent-mindedly sent the score of his C minor Concerto to the publisher after it had been performed, and the publisher returned it rather angrily, pointing out that the pianoforte part had never been written at all. This is the extreme case which decisively shows that the autograph score of a Mozart concerto is not always the best place to look for the pianoforte part as he would have it played.

The most difficult point comes near the end, where the mood is almost that of Wordsworth's—

> Roll'd round in earth's diurnal course
> With rocks, and stones, and trees.

Here there is no doubt that Mozart intends to use the effect of a singer's display of the extreme compass of his voice; and whatever ornamentation one attempts must show this instead of disguising it.

In concertos Mozart's rondo form contains features which he uses elsewhere; and the finale of the present concerto is remarkably like the finales of the great A major Violin Sonata, the two pianoforte quartets, and that most wonderful neglected masterpiece, the Sonata in F for four hands. The essential feature in the concerto-finale is that the solo player states the theme, and the orchestra gives a counterstatement, to which it appends a long string of other themes, none of which is destined to reappear until the last stages of the work, where they all troop in and make a triumphant end. Mozart was delighted with the effect, in other works than concertos, of this string of themes in the tonic and the resulting delay before any new key is established. He then establishes his new key rather abruptly, and enjoys another luxurious string of themes in it. Richard Strauss, one of the greatest Mozart-lovers of modern times, has produced some of the essence of this effect in the structure of *Till Eulenspiegel*. I cannot quote more than three of the themes of the present finale; but there are no less than ten perfectly definite and important ones, not counting various running passages that could easily be distinguished from each other. The end of the tutti distinctly recalls the quizzical F sharp minor incident at the corresponding point in the first movement.

Here is the first of the four themes in the first subject:

Ex. 6.

I do not quote the two transition themes which the pianoforte gives out after the orchestra has had its say. From the second subject I quote its first theme—

Ex. 7.

which in the recapitulation is given in the major, and its irrepressible third theme which figures largely in the coda.

Ex. 8.

The middle episode contains at least two more themes, one in F sharp minor, the other in D major; and when the time comes for returning to the tonic, it is not the main theme but the transition themes that turn up. The main theme is thus all the more welcome when it reappears, and is followed by its train of accessories, divided between the pianoforte and the orchestra. In addition to this, there is a big coda, towards the end of which Ex. 8 sails in with a grandiose subdominant colouring that adds to its glorious effrontery.

XC. PIANOFORTE CONCERTO IN C MINOR (KÖCHEL'S CATALOGUE, NO. 491)

1 Allegro. 2 Larghetto. 3 Allegretto.

I do not propose to repeat here what I have said elsewhere on classical concertos. But besides quoting certain themes I have three general points to make, one special point, and one anecdote.

My first point concerns Mozart's own special treatment of the form of the first movement of a concerto. In no other form does he show so much variety, and I cannot recall any two cases in which his procedure is the same through the whole movement. But there is one interesting general principle. As every concert-goer knows, the first movement begins with a long orchestral ritornello, and the accepted text-book theory (which is very incorrect) asserts that this ritornello contains the first and second subjects all in the main key, and that when the solo instrument enters, it restates and expands these, distributing them into their proper keys and, in co-operation and alternation with the orchestra, building them up into a more or less normal development and recapitulation, the bulk of the coda being, unfortunately, left to the mercy of the solo-player's gift of extemporizing. Now you cannot possibly tell which of the many later themes of the opening tutti is going to belong to the group of first subject, and which to the second. Most people would confidently guess that in the present case the theme which begins in the middle of Ex. 2 belongs to the second subject.

Ex. 1.

Ex. 2.

But the pianoforte seems to know nothing about it, or indeed about any of the orchestral themes except Ex. 1, and even this it only takes up in continuation (from figure (*b*)) when the orchestra violently forces it on the attention. The first pianoforte theme is a long, slowly-moving cantabile which I do not quote. Then the orchestra, as we have seen, intervenes with Ex. 1, which the piano-forte, disregarding the first four bars, develops into a transition passage. This leads with great deliberation to an immense second subject containing any number of new themes, of which Ex. 3—

Ex. 3.

is the second and most important. Besides this there is a rich passage in which the flute gives Ex. 1 in E flat minor, accompanied brilliantly by the pianoforte. There are several other themes and passages, all of them new, thoroughly in the manner of second-subject material, and all utterly subversive of the doctrine that the function of the opening tutti was to predict what the solo had to say. At last the full orchestra enters with what sounds, in retro-spect, like a free version in E flat of the original last phases of the tutti. As a matter of fact this also, except its touching soft close, is really new as well as free.

The development is begun by the pianoforte with its own (un-quoted) opening cantabile. Then the orchestra intervenes with Ex. 1 in F minor, and a broad and simple development ensues, arising mainly from figure (*b²*). The middle stage of this is marked by a passage of fine, severe massiveness, in which the majestic anger of the orchestra is answered by rolling arpeggios from the piano-forte. At last the recapitulation is reached. And now we can see very clearly one of Mozart's peculiar principles of concerto form; a principle far less easily traced in either Beethoven or Brahms, though both these masters use it. With Mozart the principle is definitely this: that the recapitulation recapitulates not so much

the first solo as the opening tutti. Here we have the extreme case,
in which the first solo (and hence everything that has to do with
the second subject) has been entirely new. Hence we are struck
with the full force of the fact that now in the recapitulation the
orchestral and solo materials are for the first time thoroughly combined. Of course the result is quite impossible to fit in with any
ordinary text-book theory of sonata form; the second subject is
ruthlessly compressed, the order of its themes altered, and there
is nothing to correspond with the flute passage founded on Ex. 1.
But Ex. 2 appears in full, and pulls the whole design together as
nothing else could do. This device of holding one of the most
prominent tutti themes in reserve for the recapitulation is peculiar
to Mozart, and is retained by him even where there is no other
evidence of the principle we have just seen illustrated.

My second point illustrates some characteristic differences in the
emotional ranges covered by Haydn, Mozart, and Beethoven.
Neither Haydn nor Mozart produced more than a small proportion
of works in minor keys; and while their ways of characterizing the
minor mode are by no means conventional, nearly all their works
in minor keys have a special character. Tell me that a mature but
unknown large work of Mozart is in a minor key, and I will confidently assert that while it may have humorous passages it will
certainly have both passion and pathos, and that while the pathos
will almost certainly not amount to tragedy, it is very likely that
much of the work will border on the sublime. If a large work
of Haydn is in the minor mode it is almost sure to conceal
pathos beneath a blustering temper in its quick movements. With
Beethoven we reach the world of tragedy. Now the recapitulation of a second subject in a minor movement is likely to make these
distinctions very clear. For, if the second subject was, as usual,
originally in a major key, what is to become of it when it is recapitulated in the tonic? Haydn, in his later works, nearly always
indulges in a 'happy ending' by turning the whole thing into the
tonic major. Mozart (except in the finale of the D minor Concerto,
where he achieves both his own and Haydn's method by adding a
happy epilogue) always makes a pathetic transformation of his
originally happy second subject into the tonic minor. This is
pathetic but not tragic. Beethoven seems, at first sight, to return
to Haydn's practice, but really he has transcended Mozart's; his
major recapitulation has all the power of tragic irony, and the
catastrophe follows in the coda.

Near the end of the first movement of this concerto a curious
detail occurs. The cadenza comes in the usual place, after the recapitulation: there is the usual pause of the orchestra, and blank
space left for the extempore solo; but the usual concluding shake

is not indicated and the orchestra re-enters with a connecting
passage of two bars which is not to be found elsewhere in the
movement. After much thought I have come to the conclusion
that the omission of the shake is not an oversight, and that Mozart
had in view a novel way of ending the cadenza in this case. It is
a pity that this concerto is not one of those for which he wrote
down his own large collection of cadenzas, for these, though perfunctory like all similar attempts to write down what should be
extempore, are priceless evidence as to the style and technique of
this difficult lost art. As it is, I am reduced to guesswork.

The first theme of the child-like slow movement—

Ex. 4.

raises in its fourth bar my last general point, the most difficult of
all the problems that beset the interpreter of Mozart's concertos.
At first sight it seems hard to realize that the naivety of that fourth
bar can be intentional. Yet Mozart must have thoroughly impressed
upon his young pupil Hummel that its whole point was its utter
simplicity; for many years afterwards Hummel, having become the
most brilliant and authoritative pianist-composer in Europe, published an arrangement of eight of Mozart's greatest concertos, in
which he rewrote almost every bar of the pianoforte passages and
brought them up to date. Yet he did not dare to touch this bar,
until at its fifth and last appearance he added one little turn. But
this raises the whole question of extempore ornamentation in
Mozart's concertos. I am far from pretending to settle the problem.
Hummel's ornamentation will certainly not do; but it should be
studied, for he had all the knowledge we have not, though his
temperament was inflated rather than inspired. It is quite certain
that the plain text of Mozart's pianoforte part is often incomplete; for instance, you find a clarinet and a bassoon varying
their repetitions while the pianoforte part at the same moment
has always the old bare outline. Clearly the orchestral players
could not be left to extemporize variations, and the pianist could.
But one is thankful to do as little as possible; for any deviation
from Mozart's style, even a deviation into early Beethoven, sets
one's teeth on edge. I am inclined to think that the problem set by
this slow movement in particular is the reason for the otherwise
inexplicable fact that this C minor Concerto, perhaps the most sublime of all Mozart's instrumental works, is less known at the present
day than the D minor, which happens to look less incomplete.

In Beethoven's young days these things were not difficulties but
opportunities. Players and singers were judged quite as much by

their taste in ornamentation as by their capacity for making the best of what the composer wrote down. According to Dannreuther, even the word *semplice* in the recitatives in Beethoven's D minor Sonata is a special warning to the player not to add ornaments; and we actually find Chopin, in an early posthumous set of variations, inscribing the theme *semplice e senza ornamenti*.

Be this as it may, Mozart's C minor Concerto was in Beethoven's time one of his most famous works, and it made a profound impression on Beethoven. The theme of the finale can only be called sublime.

Ex. 5.

In the first stages of sketching for his C minor Symphony, Beethoven was thinking of making a pathetic finale, and he jotted down a theme in 6/8 time that was little more than a variation of this, a variation that would have passed almost unnoticed among the variations Mozart's finale actually consists of. Some of these variations are pathetic, some childlike (e.g. the cheerful episode in A flat, and the graceful one in C major), and some majestic, as the orchestral fortes and the one in flowing four-part polyphony for the solo. But, as with Greek art, the subtle sublimity is a function of the simplicity and clearness of the surface; until at last the whole pathos of Mozart's work is summed up in the last variation, in 6/8 time.

Ex. 6.

It must have been the haunting second phrase of this (bars 5–8) that made Beethoven exclaim to Ries as they listened to it during a rehearsal: 'Oh, my dear fellow, *we* shall never get any idea like this.' Perhaps this was true enough of Ries. But even of Beethoven himself it is true that he did not strike this particular vain of pathos and romance until his art had gone beyond all possible reach of Mozart's direct influence. Then indeed, in the finale of the Quartet op. 95, Beethoven did produce a heart-rending theme of the same incomparable simplicity.

XCI. FLUTE CONCERTO IN G MAJOR (KÖCHEL'S CATALOGUE 313)

1 Allegro maestoso. 2 Adagio non troppo. 3 RONDO: Tempo di Menuetto.

The two flute concertos of Mozart appear to have been written, together with the Concerto for flute and harp, in 1778. This, in G major, is not less witty and beautiful than the one in D major. In an interesting series of articles in the *Chesterian*, Louis Fleury commented upon the tendency of the flute composers of a hundred years ago to write pretentiously and pompously for this childlike and elfish instrument. The crushing solemnity of the nineteenth-century virtuoso musician certainly did produce depressing developments. Kuhlau wrote magnificent sonatas and duets and concert pieces, which earned him the title of the Beethoven of the flute. We have still to learn that Beethoven was at any time known as the Kuhlau of the orchestra. Mozart had a gentle vein of irony which often goes with a long range of prophetic vision, and we may take it that when he inscribes the first movement of this Concerto in G major *allegro maestoso* he writes the inscription with his tongue in his cheek. He is in fact doing very much what Mendelssohn did in the *Midsummer-Night's Dream* music, when Pease-blossom, Cobweb, and Mustard-seed make their bows to Bottom the Weaver to the accompaniment of a flourish of trumpets on two oboes, while two flutes execute a roll of drums. I quote enough of the first and second subjects of the first movement to show the range of contrast between the majestic attitude of the opening, where you are requested to keep grave—

Ex. 1.

and the second subject, which begins in an unexpected part of the scale and continues in epigrammatic vein.

Ex. 2.

The slow movement is the richest and most beautiful movement in these flute concertos. Here Mozart has boldly substituted two flutes for the oboes which constitute with the horns the usual wind band in his smallest concertos. Thus the solo flute is now standing out against a background largely of the same colour. But the strings are muted; and the horns, in a lower key than in the first and last movements, provide a darker tone. The solemn opening figure, in which the flute has no share, intervenes with dramatic weight at the turning points of the structure.

Ex. 3.

The movement is in the usual arioso sonata form.

The finale is one of those graceful *tempo di menuetto* rondos which Mozart seems to have given up writing in his later works.

Ex. 4.

In spite of its leisurely tempo it gives the flute more scope for its characteristic fantastic agility than the rest of the work. It is broadly designed without any unusual features, and ends quietly, like almost all Mozart's examples in this tempo.

XCII. FLUTE CONCERTO IN D MAJOR (KÖCHEL'S CATALOGUE, NO. 314)

1 *Allegro aperto.* 2 *Andante.* 3 *Rondo. Allegro.*

It is very good for an artist to make the best of a task he dislikes; so long as there is a good best to be discovered for it. It is said that Mozart could not abide either the flute or the harp; yet, as we shall see, when at the command of a Duke in Paris he had to write a double concerto for those instruments, he dissembled his love in a long and charming work, and only on the last page ushered the harp downstairs in an exposed passage which neatly contained the two perfectly simple things which no harpist, ancient or modern, can play.

As for the flute, whatever he may have said about it, he liked it well enough to write two concertos, an andante with orchestra which is conspicuously lovely in tone and feeling, and two quartets for flute and strings which are by no means perfunctory. These five works are all comparatively early, ranging from 1777 to 1778; but Mozart was a mature artist in most art-forms at the age of twelve; and not even an opera can be dismissed as an 'early work' if he was twenty when he wrote it. He took the flute seriously enough in these highly-finished little works: more so than in his supreme masterpiece *The Magic Flute* (which indeed has only two episodes to justify its title).

Of course, he is incapable of such a blunder as to write for a big orchestra with a long and heroic opening tutti, by way of preparing for the entry of his Puck or Ariel. His opening tutti is short, though it summarizes the whole movement from the first subject—

Ex. 1.

to the second, with its warning notes such as usher in a change of key in a Viennese waltz—

Ex. 2.

and its mischievous cadence-theme—

Ex. 3.

the last bar of which (figure (a)) the flute has a characteristic way of detaching for purposes of its own. At the end of the movement this figure tricks the Eminent Critic into giving the performers the exquisite pleasure of being blamed for deficient ensemble when they play the last bars accurately. Throughout the movement the second violins behave with an opera-buffa malice which Mozart particularly cultivated at this period: it makes all his early concerto-tuttis crowded with contrapuntal and operatic life; and it almost conjures up an awful vision of an early Rossini whom one could take seriously, much as, according to Professor Saintsbury, the rhymed headings to the pages of *The Rose and the Ring* evoke the ghost of a Milton with a sense of humour.

As for the flute, Mozart may not have been the earliest to understand its fantastic agility—these questions of priority interest nobody who wants to listen to music—but no one before or since

III   E

has better seen the point of its qualities: the agility that can in the
same breath give and deny local habitation to whatever airy
nothings it is pleased to name; and the innocence which can seem
superhuman rather than cold, so long as the composer does not
give it phrases indicating passions of which it is ignorant. None
of Mozart's flute-music happens to be pathetic, except the slow
movement of the D major Quartet: the exception shows that there
was nothing either in the Flute or in Mozart's idea of it to prevent
his being as pathetic as Gluck in the Elysian scene of *Orfeo*, or
Brahms in the finale of his Fourth Symphony. There is no limit
to the beauty and pathos of childhood, so long as it is true to the
nature of childhood. It so happens, however, that in this concerto
the only serious note is to be found in the serenity with which the
flute answers the quasi-heroic gestures of the first theme of the slow
movement—

and in the second subject in dialogue between flute and orchestra.

As for the finale, two quotations from its numerous collection of
themes will show its lightness of heart, its flexibility of rhythm—

(note in Ex. 6 that the theme, though it foreshadows Blonde's
lively air in the *Seraglio*, has none of that young person's square-
ness of phrasing), and its richness of counterpoint—

in a central episode complicated enough to get the copyist of the
earliest extant band-parts into a thorough muddle.

It is in some ways a pity that music of this order never gets the kind of vulgar valuation that comes to pictures and beautiful pieces of furniture. This Flute Concerto is supremely artistic in every way; its slightness and smallness are functions of its greatness; and we might expect it to fetch a fabulous price if it were an escritoire, or a porcelain dinner-set, or any other form of art which daily usefulness has caused to be produced anonymously in good periods as well as in bad.

XCIII.   ANDANTE FOR FLUTE WITH ORCHESTRA
(KÖCHEL'S CATALOGUE, NO. 315)

The last and perhaps the most beautiful of Mozart's flute works, this Andante may possibly have been intended as a substitute for the andante of the Concerto in G. The very beautiful and elaborate slow movement of that work requires two flutes in the orchestra besides the solo player, and Mozart may have found that this was inconvenient. The other cases in which there is a single movement, slow or quick, for a solo instrument with orchestra are all known to be cases of reviving an old work and substituting the new movement for the corresponding old one. Be this as it may, the new movements are at their best by themselves, and the original works are best in their early form. The production of a concerto at a public concert in Mozart's, and even as late as Chopin's time, was one of those best of all possible events in which every detail was a necessary evil. The first movement was produced in one part of the concert, the slow movement and finale were produced about an hour afterwards when the audience had been gratified by other items which might now find place in a rather primitive variety entertainment. Nothing more clearly proves the genius of the greatest masters of eighteenth-century music than the undoubted fact that their concertos and symphonies have an inviolable unity, which at the time of their composition was appreciable by the composer alone, or to the few who studied the works in private.

More than anything else in the flute works of Mozart, the style and themes of this andante are prophetic of his yet more magic flute of thirteen years later. The position and melodic type of the first theme is very like that of the tune with which Tamino in *Die Zauberflöte* first tries the power of the magic flute, with the effect of bringing on to the stage a complete menagerie of fascinated birds and beasts.

My quotation indicates the picturesque introductory chords for

oboes, horns, and pizzicato strings, which are cunningly developed
later on into a second subject. The movement is worked out in the
typical arioso sonata form, and is one of the ripest examples of
Mozart's style at its comparatively early date of composition, 1778.

XCIV. CLARINET CONCERTO IN A MAJOR
(KÖCHEL'S CATALOGUE, NO. 622)

1 *Allegro.* 2 *Adagio.* 3 RONDO: *Allegro.*

As far as the art of writing for the instrument is concerned, Mozart
may well be considered to have invented or at least discovered the
clarinet. His three compositions in which the clarinet is the leading
wind instrument, namely the Clarinet Concerto, the Trio for pianoforte, viola and clarinet, and the Quintet for clarinet and strings,
belong to the last years of his life and are among his most beautiful
works. The concerto is in the full-sized classical form and by no
means on a small scale. If it were a pianoforte concerto, it would
be among the more important ones, though Mozart has avoided
involving his sharply characterized solo instrument in any polyphonic discussions with the orchestra. Mr. Forsyth in his admirable book on orchestration has quoted copiously from both Stanford's concerto and Mozart's by way of showing among other
things how the essentials of clarinet-playing remain the same
to-day as they were in Mozart's time. It is interesting to compare the orchestra of the two works. It stands to reason that in
neither of them will clarinets be present in the background, but
Mozart's solo clarinet is in a different relation to its background
from Stanford's, for Stanford relies upon oboes as a contrast to his
solo instrument in wind tone, whereas Mozart has only flutes,
bassoons, and horns. He thus surrounds his clarinet with no strong
contrasts of tone at all, and yet there is no lack of relief. The softness
of the flutes rather enhances the vitality of the clarinet. I quote
three of the many themes of the first movement.

Ex. 1.
1st Subject.

Ex. 2.
Transition.

Clarinet.

Ex. 3.

The slow movement will be recognized as well known by many
listeners who have never before realized where it came from. I
have heard it as a horn solo and as a violin solo, and in almost any
form except that in which Mozart wrote it.

Ex. 4.

The finale is a full-sized rondo of which the following are the
main themes:

A point as fine as any in Mozart's chamber and orchestral music is
the freedom with which the second subject (Ex. 6) is treated in its
recapitulation before leading to the spacious coda.

XCV. VIOLIN CONCERTO IN D MAJOR
(KÖCHEL'S CATALOGUE, NO. 218)

1 *Allegro.* 2 *Andante cantabile.* 3 RONDO. *Andante grazioso, alternating with Allegro ma non troppo.*

Of Mozart's violin concertos the fourth, in D, and the fifth, in A, show the style of his adolescence at its wittiest. The fourth is in higher animal spirits and therefore has less leisure for meditation than the A major; but it is not less witty, and, like the A major, it has its surprises in dramatic incident and form.

As the orchestra is without trumpets the opening theme imitates those heraldic perquisites with great vigour.

Ex. 1.

The main theme of the second group is graceful, with the peculiar tang of Mozart's style at the age of nineteen.

Ex. 2.

There are as many other themes as there are musical sentences, so that this opening tutti contains at least four more that would deserve quotation. And the solo violin has many more of its own. But the most interesting matter is the question of how it can deal with Exx. 1 and 2. To those who do not know this concerto I will not divulge the secret of how the solo violin, like the sonnet in Milton's hands, becomes a trumpet; but there is no harm in remarking that it delivers Ex. 2 in a deep bass voice.

The slow movement is serious in manner, but not less inveterately witty in detail. Its main theme is grave.

Ex. 3.

Its second group is heralded by an ornate theme.

Ex. 4.

Mr. Fox Strangways, in an interesting analysis of certain criteria of melodic beauty, crowned his argument with a gesture of humorous despair induced by a phrase in the coda of this movement, where the violin (like the Duke of York with his 20,000 men) simply walks up a scale and then walks down again. But Mr. Fox Strangways knew all the time that this phenomenon was the surface of a harmonic process without which it would have no meaning. Still wittier is the way in which the movement ends with a phrase that had hitherto always appeared to be merely medial.

The contredanse of Mozart's time was a dance with abrupt alternations of tempo; and there were also minuets *mit eingelegten Contredansen.* From such origins arises a special kind of rondo, to be found in more than one of Mozart's violin concertos, and also in his D major Violin Sonata, the rondo of which is twin brother to that of the present work.

The main theme asks wistful questions in a slow tempo (*Andante grazioso*).

And the questions are answered quizzically in a quick movement (*Allegro ma non troppo*)—

which leads to the dominant, where a second group begins with the following theme—

The two tempi alternate in consequence of the rondo form. But the second episode, beginning in B minor, leads to another change of tempo in the shape of a slow gavotte in G major—

which is continued with a delicious theme over a drone-bass.

56   MOZART. K. 218

When Ex. 5 returns, it is worked out in regular recapitulation
with Exx. 6 and 7, and the concerto ends, like its middle movement,
with a sudden dying away in mid-phrase.

XCVI. VIOLIN CONCERTO IN A MAJOR
(KÖCHEL'S CATALOGUE, NO. 219)

1 *Allegro aperto.* 2 *Adagio.* 3 *Tempo di Menuetto.*

Mozart's five authentic violin concertos were all written in Salzburg
in 1775 when he was nineteen years of age. The Concerto in E flat,
which is the most frequently played, and which purports to be
the sixth, may be based on genuine material, but no competent
musical scholar believes that it can possibly be genuine in the
form in which it is known to us. The seventh concerto was discovered early in the present century, and has been often played
with success. It is not in a perfectly satisfactory state of preserva-
tion; but, if it is a forgery, it is an exceedingly clever one, and it
does not make the mistake of imitating a generalized Mozart of no
particular period. No composer has had so many forgeries foisted
upon him as Mozart. There are five spurious masses, including
the celebrated Twelfth Mass; a concertante for four wind instruments and orchestra, purporting to be the lost work known to have
been written in Paris for a rather different combination; a number
of spurious songs; several sonatas and smaller pieces; to say
nothing of the peculiar disaster of instrumental parts added to
genuine works so unskilfully that the authenticity of the whole
seems questionable until the additions have been removed. What
is known, then, about Mozart's violin concertos is that in 1775 he
made a brilliant beginning in this most difficult art-form, and never
afterwards followed it up. It is noteworthy that the three greatest
violin concertos in existence are all peculiarly happy but solitary
efforts of their composers: Beethoven, Mendelssohn, and Brahms.
It is not so remarkable that Mozart produced five violin concertos
in one year as that he produced them early in his career. It was
natural to produce several, since the scale of the form at that
period was not large. I have had occasion, in commenting upon
the flute concertos which belong to the same period, to call attention to the special vein of epigrammatic comedy which characterizes
Mozart's style up to the age of twenty-three. In the A major Violin
Concerto it attains its height, and is also combined with a specially
fantastic kind of childlike beauty. Mozart's form at this period
was almost as full of experimental features as Haydn's, and the
work is full of surprises.

The opening theme as given out by the orchestra seems to
be merely a formal assertion of the chords of the key in the

usual eighteenth-century style, but I quote together with it a
totally new idea which the solo violin is eventually going to build
upon it.

Ex. 1.

The theme which afterwards becomes the second subject is one
that could walk into the House of Lords with the same friendly
self-possession as into its own kindergarten.

Ex. 2.

And who would have thought that the formula which ends the
orchestral tutti—

Ex. 3.

could so coolly become an important transition theme when the
solo violin takes it up?

Ex. 4.

The entry of the solo violin itself is one of the greatest surprises
ever perpetrated in a concerto. We expect it to begin either

directly with a statement of the opening theme, or else, if Mozart
is inclined to anticipate Beethoven, with some preliminary running
passages. We certainly did not expect that the violin would begin
with a sustained arioso in a very slow adagio time with a running
accompaniment. There is a childlike grandeur in this gesture,
which almost overawes the sense of humour to which Mozart was
undoubtedly appealing. You may take this as a measure of the
poetic power underlying all the fun. For the rest of the movement our four quotations will suffice. It was surprising enough
when Ex. 3 developed into the solid structure of Ex. 4, but it is
still more surprising when it turns out to be the absolutely abrupt
end of the whole movement.

The slow movement is not less notable for the terse and epigrammatic character of its themes. The essentials of them are all stated
in the opening tutti, the substance of which is expanded by the
solo violin much on the lines of the first movement in sonata form.
I quote the two figures in the stream of melody which become
articulated into first and second subject.

Ex. 5.

Ex. 6.

The finale is, like most concerto finales, a rondo. In a moderate
tempo di menuetto it begins as if it was going to pass all its existence
in graceful ease. I quote the first theme with its codetta.

Ex. 7.

Ex. 8.

The first episode on the dominant presents just the kind of contrast
one would expect; and the return to the main theme follows in due
course. The second episode, beginning in F sharp minor, with
darker colouring and a somewhat wider range of key, is again just
what the situation seems to require; and in the second return of
the main theme the attentive ear may note that there is a little more

detail in the accompaniments, whereby the design is unobtrusively
kept alive. The next thing to expect would be a recapitulation of
the first episode in the tonic, with some slight modification of the
transition leading to it. But suddenly we have a contredanse in
A minor (2/4 time), scored with the grotesque effects characteristic
of the real dance-music of the Viennese public ball-rooms in 1778.
Mozart gives this full scope to express itself with all manner of
repeats and alternating sections. It enlarges the range of the finale
as triumphantly as that impressive adagio arioso enlarges the range
of the first movement. After this the rondo theme returns and
leads to the orthodox recapitulation of the second subject and to
a final return, the accompaniments naturally varying in detail each
time; and to crown all, this broadly designed movement ends with
the simple abruptness of the codetta to the theme (Ex. 8).

It is not surprising that this work was a great favourite with
Joachim, who wrote cadenzas for it that are among the most
perfect that have been written for any concerto.

XCVII. ADAGIO IN E, FOR VIOLIN WITH ORCHESTRA
(KÖCHEL'S CATALOGUE, NO. 261)

This broad and dignified aria for violin was produced by Mozart
as a substitute for the more kittenish slow movement of his A
major Violin Concerto, on an occasion when that work was played
by a violinist named Brunetti, who, we may infer, wanted an
opportunity of displaying his full range of tone. We need not
infer that Mozart wished the new adagio to remain permanently
as a part of the A major Concerto, the childlike humour of which
it would only embarrass. Public performances of concertos, even
as late as Chopin's time, were given in conditions that make it a
marvel that the great composers showed any sense of unity of
mood and style; and Mozart had more to gain than to lose by
pleasing Brunetti in a performance where the first movement was
to be given in the first part of the concert and the rest in the second
part after several other items. On the other hand, we gain a rare
addition to the small number of single movements for violin and
orchestra; a piece at least as important as the violin romances of
Beethoven, and, for all its seemingly automatic handling of forms
already highly conventionalized, far more distinguished in style.

The orchestral violins (but not the lower strings) are muted, and
the wind-band consists of two flutes and two horns. The A major
Concerto has oboes instead of flutes, and thus Mozart seems to be
taking special measures to throw the solo violin into higher relief
in this movement. With this tiny orchestra he achieves many
remarkable tone-colours by a few unexpected holding-notes and
by sforzandos in the inner parts.

Ex. 1 shows the main theme; Ex. 2 a characteristically pregnant connecting link; and Ex. 3 is the beginning of the second subject.

XCVIII. CONCERTO FOR FLUTE AND HARP (KÖCHEL'S CATALOGUE, NO. 299)

1 *Allegro.* 2 *Andantino.* 3 RONDO: *Allegro.*

In 1778, during Mozart's visit to Paris, the Duke of Guines commissioned him to write a concerto for flute and harp. Mozart shows no great respect for dukes as such in his family letters, and so we may believe him when he writes that the Duke plays the flute incomparably and the daughter plays the harp '*magnifique*'; the resources of the German language apparently failing him as English avowedly failed Dr. Johnson when he was '*pénétré* with His Majesty's goodness'. Accordingly, though these instruments were precisely the two that he could not abide, he soon began to luxuriate in the fun of writing for them. The possibilities of the single-action harp of the eighteenth century he exhausted in this work. Nothing could be done for it but to proceed on the lines of very sketchy pianoforte music with an anxious avoidance of cantabile; but the flute reconciled him so far that after his Paris visit he produced five by no means uncharacteristic works for it, of which the three with orchestra (two concertos and an andante) are discussed in this volume.

It is not necessary to quote more than four of the sixteen themes which Mozart sends streaming out in festive processions throughout and around this work. Although a developed style for the harp cannot be said to exist within fifty years of Mozart's death, this concerto is no exception to the rule that Mozart's imagination for combinations of instruments and harmonies is infallibly accurate and incomparably vivid. He has here to reckon with the fact that the harpists in 1778 were preoccupied with making their instrument speak a language it could not properly pronounce; and he makes no miscalculations. Even the daughter of a duke could not, in spite of her *magnifique* playing, prevent the mischievous Mozart from twice asking the harp to say 'shibboleth' at the end of the finale. (And, by the way, the will to play practical jokes is distinctly discoverable in Mozart's works. I, for my part, feel absolutely certain of his intention of getting the choir to mock the pronunciation of some friend of his in a certain Mass, once well known, where the word 'Osanna' is set in close stretto to a syncopated rhythm, and a fortissimo mark is placed under the third syllable in all the voices and instruments at every single one of the forty or fifty repetitions of the word.)

The technique of the flute, unlike that of the harp, was not only essentially mature in 1778, but had already reached a second period of development. For Bach and Handel the flute was a cantabile instrument well suited for principal melodies or polyphonic threads played in its lower registers among an ensemble of soft instruments. But already in Mozart's time the habits of the flute had changed in order to enable it to assert itself in the new styles of symphonic and dramatic orchestration, and he never loses an important feature by writing low for the flute in a tutti, as Haydn, who also developed the new technique, continued often to do in his latest works. This being so, it is interesting to find that the Duke of Guines had a flute provided with holes (possibly also keys) for the low D flat and C; which Mozart evidently could not count upon in any of his later flute works, as he never wrote those notes again. This, at all events, indicates that it was not ducal stimulus that induced him to write his remaining five solo works for the flute. (It was 96 ducats.)

Those extra low notes for the flute will be heard by the alert listener about half-way through the first movement, during its development, where they are used as a bass to the harp! For the rest it will suffice to quote the opening themes; of the first movement—

Ex. 1.

and of the luxurious slow movement, in which the style of the harp is at its best within the possibilities of 1778, and the string orchestra is throughout enriched by division of the violas into two parts—

Ex. 2.

and the opening and closing themes of the five which are poured out in the first tutti of the rondo.

Ex. 3.

Ex. 4.
Oboes and Horns.
3 times.
2nd Vlns. and Viola.

The viola and second violin of this last theme contain one of the shibboleths with which Mozart worries the harp on the last page, a passage in which the hands and strings are brought into mutual interference. There is no reasonable doubt that this is malicious; and so is the other passage, in which Mozart goes out of his way (altering, in recapitulation, a perfectly safe theme) to introduce some chromatic steps for which even the modern harp is not conveniently suited. Of course there is nothing embarrassing in these jokes, which the composer expects to turn against himself in either of two possible events; for the passages will either be played with success, or something appropriate and more effective will be substituted for them.

HAYDN

XCIX. VIOLONCELLO CONCERTO IN D MAJOR

1 *Allegro moderato.* 2 *Adagio.* 3 *Allegro.*

The concertos of Haydn all date from his Esterhazy period, and are on a small scale, like the horn concertos of Mozart. Their forms hardly deviate from those of the vocal aria on a large scale; but, even before the modern editor has enjoyed himself over them, they give remarkable scope for the art of the virtuoso player.

At present the only orchestral parts available for this concerto

are those of the venerable and voluminous Gevaert, whose reign
over the Brussels Conservatoire and whose treatises on ancient
music and modern orchestration sufficed in themselves to make
an epoch in musical education.

The worst of such thoroughness is that, where it re-scores the
classics, the results are like the leg that was so beautifully suited
for a top-boot—'Same size all the way up, sir!'

Haydn's scoring of this concerto was probably primitive, possibly
for strings alone, and certainly the better for a pianoforte to exercise
the obsolescent function of the continuo. That function being now
exercised by Gevaert with a wind-band in the style of a full swell-
organ, the orchestra must do its best to play the accompaniments
gently.

The first theme surprises us by being based on a *cliché* we would
have thought peculiar to Mozart. My knowledge of the lesser
contemporaries of Haydn and Mozart is severely limited by my
patience, and I have not found this *cliché* elsewhere.

Ex. 1.

But in the slow movement the same *cliché* is followed by one
equally peculiar to Haydn.

Ex. 2.

Nobody can tell me the exact notes of the tune of 'Here we go
gathering nuts in May'; but everybody agrees that the finale of
Haydn's 'cello concerto is suspiciously like it.

Ex. 3.

And perhaps the wicked people who, with the late Mr. Rudyard
Kipling among them, persecuted the miso-auto-bureaucrat squire,
J.P., and M.P. for Huckley, may have reverted to the Haydn
archetype when they turned this innocent tune into *The Village
that Voted the Earth was Flat*. At all events, bars 5 and 6 of Ex. 3
irresistibly remind me of

Flat as my hat,
Flatter than *that!*

But we digress. And so does Haydn. [But see Addendum, **p. ix**,
supra.]

BEETHOVEN

C. PIANOFORTE CONCERTO IN C MAJOR, OP. 15, WITH BEETHOVEN'S CADENZA

1 *Allegro con brio.* 2 *Largo.* 3 RONDO: *Allegro.*

The first three pianoforte concertos of Beethoven show, in the opening tuttis of their first movements, a phenomenon almost unique in his works. In other branches of music we may find signs of a struggle with stubborn material, and Beethoven himself sometimes admitted that for this or that problem of vocal and dramatic music he had 'not studied enough'. But in the first two pianoforte concertos all is facile and spacious, while in the third, in C minor, which he declared, before he wrote it, 'will be the best of the three', he not only made a great stride in the direction of his 'second style', but set the model for the orthodox concerto form of his younger contemporaries and later theorists. Yet in all three concertos the nature of the opening tutti is radically misconceived; and that of the C minor Concerto (as is pointed out in my analysis of it) is an advance upon the other two only inasmuch as Beethoven seems to discover the error at the moment of committing it, with the result that its tutti executes a charmingly dramatic *volte-face* in mid-career, as if to say 'But no!—I must not be the beginning of a symphony'. In his later concertos Beethoven realized and carried out the purpose of Mozart's opening tutti, one of the subtlest and grandest art-forms ever devised; but no sooner was he able to do this than he was able to transcend Mozart in every line of instrumental and harmonic form, so that contemporary and later orthodoxy blundered far more grossly about his concerto form than any early failure of his to see the purport of Mozart's.

The composer or theorist may imagine that because Mozart's tutti is voluminous and flowing it is also discursive and can indulge in passages of development. Or he may imagine that it can be throughout like the exposition of a symphony, and that it should accordingly display its first subject, transition, and second subject, so that the listener knows beforehand exactly what the solo instrument is going to do. The first misapprehension is shown by Beethoven in his first two concertos; the second appears in the C minor Concerto and is instantly corrected, but not until its impression has been made with such force that, until Brahms came to the rescue, the opening tutti of the classical concerto remained a mystery to composers and theorists alike.

Now the C major Concerto (which is later than the B flat Concerto published second to it as opus 19) seems to have been an

object of more interest to Beethoven than he admitted. At all
events he wrote no less than three cadenzas to its first movement,
and the third of these cadenzas is one of his most splendid successes
in recording the style of an extemporization. It is fully in his
'second manner', and the compass given to the pianoforte shows
that it must have been written at least as late as the published score
of the C minor Concerto; that is to say, later than the Kreutzer
Sonata, and not much earlier than the Waldstein Sonata, which
it closely resembles in pianoforte technique. It is a wonderful
exception to the general style of the cadenzas Beethoven wrote for
his own concertos (he also wrote two for Mozart's D minor Concerto); and indeed I have not a word in favour of what he called
a *cadenza per non cadere* for the Concerto in G, or of the curious
pianoforte version he made of his Violin Concerto. I remember that a
distinguished English pianist played the G major Concerto in Berlin,
in 1900 or 1901, with Beethoven's cadenzas, not having announced
the fact. The critics really hardly deserved their fate; but it was
unfortunate that they went so far as to call these cadenzas *geradezu
unmusikalisch*, though they might well think them hopelessly inadequate and frivolous. There is another set which is not bad.

But the case of this third cadenza to the C major Concerto is
utterly different: it affords a noble pretext for reviving a neglected
early masterpiece which it harmoniously lifts to a higher plane of
musical thought. I cannot help wondering whether Beethoven
could not have made something almost as great out of his first
cadenza, which he left unfinished just after it had developed on
lines calculated to bring certain discursive passages of the tutti
into closer organic connexion with the whole. The speculation is
interesting, because the point, if achieved, would have anticipated
what he does in the coda of his last concerto (the great E flat, called,
to his profound if posthumous disgust, 'The Emperor').

The C major Concerto begins with quiet and martial energy.

Ex. 1.
(a)

A *forte* counterstatement leads to a grand pause on the dominant, upon which a fragment of the second subject appears in a
remote key, and is carried through other keys in rising sequence.

Ex. 2.

III

This is very beautiful; but processions (or concerto tuttis) will get into difficulties if they often thus digress in search of the picturesque; and it is this passage which Beethoven worked up bodily into his, unfortunately incomplete, first cadenza. The next passage, founded on Ex. 1, is also discursive—

Ex. 3.

and forms the opening text for all the three cadenzas.

At last the orchestra settles down to a cadence theme in Beethoven's most British-Grenadiers style—

Ex. 4.

and with a final paragraph on figure (a) of Ex. 1 the orchestra comes to a formal close. Not until the G major Concerto did Beethoven follow the example, twice set by Mozart, of letting the solo enter on the dominant chord with an introductory passage. On the other hand he follows several examples of Mozart in beginning with an entirely new theme—

Ex. 5.

though, unlike Mozart, he omits to develop it later, not even finding room for it in any of his cadenzas. The orchestra intervenes with figure (a) of Ex. 1, and the dialogue now follows the orthodox course of a concerto, the pianoforte working out a broad transition to G major, where Ex. 2 appears as a regular and complete melody by way of second subject. After a short digression, Ex. 4 follows, and brilliant passages then run an easy course, though some energetic staccatos markedly anticipate a prominent feature of the E flat Concerto. The anticipation becomes still more noticeable at the end, and amounts to more than coincidence, formal as the

passage is in both cases, and deeply rooted in the organization as
it is in the later work.

The development is, as usual in concertos, largely episodic, the
pianoforte beginning grandly with another entirely new theme
which I need not quote. Perhaps one reason why Beethoven
abandoned his first cadenza was a feeling that if he once began to
pick up loose threads there would be no end to the task; and that
the true course was to accept the pleasure that the Mozartean Angel
of All Art-Forms allows to those who Really Can Extemporize.

The return to the recapitulation is gravely dramatic in Beethoven's best 'first style'; the pianoforte taking its final plunge there-
into by an octave-glissando; at which the modern pianoforte jibs.
The recapitulation itself is adroitly curtailed as to the first subject
and unaltered as to the second.

And now comes the pause for the cadenza. Beethoven's third
cadenza storms away in magnificent Waldstein-sonata style, at first
apropos of Ex. 3, then apropos of figure (a), which starts on a voyage
round the solar system. The second subject (Ex. 2) appears at last
in vastly remote keys, and drifts sublimely from the style of *La
Clemenza di Tito* to the style of *Fidelio*. Thunderous further
developments of figure (a) burst forth, and at last the usual final
shake is heard; but surely rather too much on the dominant of G?
Quite so; we have something to say in G major about Ex. 4; please
don't interrupt! This being said, the shake arrives again and
develops with great excitement—while the orchestra waits for the
final turn. Instead of which the shake trails off into runs. And at
last the cadenza ends without any shake at all.

The difficulties of the classical concerto form are almost entirely confined to the first movement, and especially to its ritornello. In slow movements and rondos Beethoven was from the outset as great a master in concertos as in other instrumental forms; and a quotation of themes is all the commentary required for the rest of this unjustly neglected work. The largo begins with a three-strain melody (A, B, A), of which Ex. 8 is the first clause.

Ex. 8.

A broadly designed transition to the dominant gives an impression that the whole may be developed into full sonata form with Ex. 9 as second subject.

Ex. 9.

But Beethoven prefers to keep space for a less crowded scheme, and he brings back his whole first melody with rich ornamentation and new scoring (in all his early orchestral works there is no other example showing such appreciation of the clarinet), and, without any allusion to the middle portion, concludes with a long-drawn coda full of solemn new ideas.

Beethoven never wrote a wittier paragraph with more Haydn-esque irregularity of rhythm than the main theme of the rondo of this concerto.

Ex. 10.

The various transition themes need not be quoted. The first

episode, which is treated (as in all full-sized concerto-rondos) like
a second subject—

Ex. 11.

gives rise to a romantic digression in E flat and G minor, such as
has made the second subject of the first movement of Beethoven's
First Symphony famous; and it is remarkable in how many points
the First Symphony follows cautiously the steps this rondo had
already taken firmly and boldly.

The returns to the main theme are effected by the following
Schubertesque transformation:

Ex. 12.

The middle episode alternates two superb themes in contrast,
the one spirited (compare the corresponding theme in the Triple
Concerto)—

Ex. 13.

and the other quiet, chromatic, and polyphonic.

Ex. 14.

The rest of the movement arises naturally out of these materials,
and the coda is full of Haydn-Beethoven surprises, being (with the
addition of several small undeveloped cadenzas) a glorified version
of the later and less elaborate comic wind-up of the First Symphony.

CI. PIANOFORTE CONCERTO IN C MINOR, OP. 37

1 *Allegro con brio.* 2 *Largo.* 3 RONDO: *Allegro vivace, Presto.*

Beethoven's third concerto was projected at the same time as his
first and second; neither of which, as he openly avowed, was so
important as this, for which he was reserving his best efforts. It
is one of the works in which we most clearly see the style of his

first period preparing to develop into that of his second. The main theme—

Ex. 1.

is a group of pregnant figures which nobody but Beethoven could have invented. They would rank as important themes in his latest works; but he here states them, quite successfully and unselfconsciously, in the tonic-and-dominant symmetries that still interested him for their own sake in his first period. With the transition theme—

Ex. 2.

he emphasizes the barest harmonic formulas with a youthful sententiousness peculiar to an artist who has grown conscious that these formulas are still necessary but no longer interesting, and that until some totally new light can be shed on them they are best left undecorated. (Two other works in the same key, the C minor Quartet, op. 18, No. 4, and the C minor Violin Sonata, show the same drastic simplicity at this juncture.)

Now comes a turning-point in the history of the classical concerto. The opening orchestral ritornello of the first movement in the concerto form had been developed by Mozart on a scale that has not to this day been surpassed; with the result that the entry of the solo instrument must, if it means anything at all, mean an event impressive because long delayed. If, then, long delayed, it must be long expected; and the expectation must be roused by the music and not merely by the title of the item on the programme. Mozart's opening tuttis are among the highest triumphs of art in their command of expectant exposition; no two examples are identical in their own plan, or in relation to the solo. Nor can Mozart's forms be correctly said to have a restraining influence on Beethoven's early work. To him these forms were no more orthodox than the forms of Richard Strauss were to the young composers of 1900. Nor indeed have Mozart's concerto forms been codified even yet with any greater accuracy than that of a child's hieroglyph of the human form as a disk supported on a triangle with two five-pronged forks attached as hands.

At all events Beethoven had something better to do than to consult text-books on the subject of concerto form. He did not immediately achieve Mozart's solution of the problem of the opening tutti; indeed it is arguable that he did not at first grasp what the problem really was. In his first two concertos the orchestra enjoys itself in ruminating developments which, like so many of the happy thoughts in Schubert's large instrumental works, stray away from the purpose of exposition. In the C minor Concerto, Ex. 2 takes direct dramatic action and leads to a long passage of preparation for the second subject in its destined new key. This is sheer symphonic exposition; it rouses no expectation of the entry of a solo instrument, and, as we shall find, leaves nothing essential for the pianoforte to add when its time comes. The second subject enters—

Ex. 3.

a cantabile midway between a Mozart heroine and the heroine of Beethoven's *Coriolanus* overture. Suddenly the orchestra seems to realize that it has no right to take the drama into its own hands; that its function is not drama but chorus-like narrative; and with a modulation in itself dramatic, the melody calmly turns round to C major and is followed by a series of cadence-phrases in the tonic minor (including derivatives of Ex. 1) which bring this, the longest of all Beethoven's concerto tuttis, to a massive formal close.

The works of Beethoven that have had the most influence on later composers are rather such transitional compositions than the compositions which Beethoven himself based on the experience he gained therein. It is the C minor Concerto that has ever since been taken as the normal classical example, and not the G major and E flat Concertos, which are supposed to introduce bold innovations. Yet it is only in these later works, and in the violin concerto, with the voluminous preparatory exercise of the Triple Concerto, op. 56, that Beethoven achieves Mozart's methods of handling the opening tutti, plus his own methods of setting the solo free. Spohr, Hummel, Chopin (in his F minor Concerto), and even Joachim in his Hungarian Concerto, all took Beethoven's C minor Concerto as their model for concerto form; and they all regarded as an inimitable and individual stroke of genius the one feature (the sudden shift back to the tonic during the announcement of the second subject) by which Beethoven rectifies something that dangerously resembled a mistake. This stroke being thus regarded as unorthodox, the 'classical' opening tutti henceforth became accepted as an ordinary symphonic exposition, prefixed, for reasons impious to inquire, to a sonata for a solo instrument with orchestral accompaniment. No wonder the easy common sense of Mendelssohn abolished this convention; but the possibilities of concertos with no scope for orchestral organization became fascinating to the virtuoso jerry-builder; and until Brahms tackled the true problem again, the vitality of concerto forms was becoming the vitality of undesirable things.

Beethoven, then, has in this C minor opening tutti recognized and saved a dangerous situation in the nick of time. The pianoforte can now enter and restate the exposition that the orchestra has given. Beyond two introductory bars of scales, dramatically useful in later entries, and a slight expansion of the passage of preparation for the second subject, the pianoforte follows the opening tutti, bar for bar, until the second subject (Ex. 3) has arrived. Here there is of course no need for the *volte-face* made in the original tutti: the pianoforte is now at last free to expand the material into a brilliant group of new phrases. These consist mainly of developments of figure (*b*) in Ex. 1 with running accompaniments, culminating in a long shake, below which clarinets and horns enter with a triumphant version of the whole theme. Then the full orchestra bursts out with its cadence phrases, and soon proceeds to shed new light on the long passage of preparation for the second subject (between Ex. 2 and Ex. 3) by giving it in G minor.

This is a genuine and important innovation, which Beethoven uses with powerful effect in the E flat Concerto, and in the Violin Concerto. Mozart never lets his second tutti modulate, and always brings it to a full close. Beethoven's new experiment goes far to set his form free. The pianoforte enters with its introductory scales, not as a formula on a tonic, but as a dramatic intervention on a dominant. It then settles down to a pathetic cantabile development of Ex. 1, the figure (*b*) unifying the whole design by persisting as an accompaniment. In broad and distinct steps the threshold of C minor is reached, and, after suitable preparation, the first subject begins the recapitulation fortissimo. After the close of the second subject (the triumphant clarinets beneath the final shake now becoming trumpets), the orchestra enters in the minor and soon leads to the usual pause for a cadenza, which Beethoven leaves to the player to compose or extemporize. After the cadenza it was usual for the orchestra to conclude the movement formally with the last few bars of the opening tutti: but Mozart had already found ways of using the solo instrument in the coda, notably in his C minor Concerto, a work which influenced Beethoven profoundly and conspicuously both as a

whole and in detail. And so here the final trill of the cadenza leads
to an unexpected turn of harmony which, together with the quiet
entry of the drums with figure (*b*), is one of Beethoven's most
typical strokes of genius. The pianoforte retains the whole conduct of the coda, and ends the movement with scales recalling
its first entry.

The largo is the most highly developed slow movement in all
Beethoven's concertos, and *a fortiori* in any concerto. In his later
concertos the slow movements lead into the finales; gaining thereby
various dramatic subtleties and depths by release from the necessity
of completing their own design. But in the C minor Concerto we
have one of the great independent symphonic slow movements,
reaching the climax of Beethoven's powers of solemn expression
in his first period, and indeed quite in keeping with all that he
found to say in his second. The shock of the first chord, in its
remoteness from the C minor of the rest of the work—

Ex. 4.

is in itself a feature of Beethoven's second period, though his
earlier works show some preoccupation with things of the kind.
The impulse came from Haydn, whose later works contain
examples of every possible key-relation. The example of the slow
movement of Beethoven's C minor Concerto has had a direct and
obvious influence on later composers, e.g. Brahms's First Symphony
and Third Pianoforte Quartet.

An ornate transition theme leads to a well-defined second subject
in the dominant.

Ex. 5.

This is followed in due course by a sombre episode in dark keys,
with cloudy pianoforte arpeggios accompanying a slow dialogue
in the winds. The episode, which has the function of a development, drifts steadily towards the tonic, E major, and so returns
in its own good time to the first subject. Instead of recapitulating
the transition and the second subject, Beethoven makes a broad
coda out of the orchestral pendants to the first subject, having
already redistributed the dialogue as between solo and orchestra.

The shock of E major after C minor is chiefly concentrated in
one note, G sharp, the major third of E. This is so near in pitch to
A flat that on keyed instruments the same note has to serve for

both. Haydn, in the last and greatest of his pianoforte sonatas, had
ventured upon this shock in a still more paradoxical form, as
between the keys of E flat and E natural (equivalent in this case
to F flat); he accordingly began his finale with a theme which
first taps rhythmically at G natural, and, having duly explained
this as third of E flat, proceeds to show that the next step is A flat.

The first two notes of Beethoven's finale are a more immediate
and drastic summary of a similar process. Like Haydn, Beethoven
has taken care that the last chord of the slow movement shall
display his Berkeleyan G sharp. Which Dr. Johnson refutes *thus*—

Ex. 6.

This great rondo is an admirable study in temper, worthy of
the wisdom that inspired the tragic style of the other movements.
Among the works with which this concerto is always provoking
comparison by reason of its singularly direct influence on later
composers, three finales are conspicuous—those of Joachim's Hungarian Concerto, Brahms's First Pianoforte Concerto, and Mendelssohn's C minor Trio. It is astonishing how closely both Brahms
and Joachim have followed the scheme of this finale, even in such
details as the structure of the transition passages and the fugue
passage of development after the second episode. The interest in
comparing Mendelssohn's C minor Trio finale is different; it is a
warning against giving tragic weight to emotions which in real life
relieve themselves in a gust of temper. Mendelssohn's first theme
is in much the same temper as Beethoven's, and promises a not
less spirited career. His second theme is in an enthusiastic mood
which would be rather shocked by an apparent lack of moral
indignation in Beethoven's energetic second theme.

Ex. 7.

And for the consolatory middle episode and triumphant end of his
finale Mendelssohn unfortunately bursts into tears and a chorale.
Beethoven's way of sounding the depths is more religiously
consistent with his opening.

Ex. 8.

This comfortable and leisurely tune is followed by a little fugue
on the main theme (Ex. 6), beginning in F minor. The pianoforte

intervenes dramatically and carries us to a remote key which is the more impressive in that it happens to be that of the slow movement. From this the steps back to C minor are broad and firm, and the anticipation of the return to the rondo theme is duly exciting. The recapitulation of both main theme and second subject (Ex. 7) is complete and regular.

But the coda is utterly unexpected. In the tuttis of the main theme the oboe had already made a splendid point by appearing with the theme in the major, transforming its initial G–A♭ into G♯–A♮. Now the pianoforte, entering after an ornamental cadenza, takes up this idea in the following new tempo and rhythm:

Ex. 9.

The rest of this presto is a brilliant series of fresh cadential phrases, the last of which—

Ex. 10.

is a transformation of Ex. 7.

CII. PIANOFORTE CONCERTO IN G MAJOR, OP. 58

(Meiningen Programmes, 1902, with alterations.)

1 *Allegro moderato.* 2 *Andante con moto; leading to* 3 RONDO: *Vivace.*

The G major Concerto is a work of a particularly prolific time in Beethoven's career. Its opus-number places it between the so-called 'Appassionata' Sonata and the three enormous string quartets dedicated to Count Rasoumovsky; but Beethoven was always at work on so many things at once, and so often allowed one work to wait for years before completing it from sketches, that his opus-numbers give little clue to the chronology of anything but publication. In almost any four consecutive years of Beethoven's life the chronology of his works is inextricable. The first idea for a finale to this concerto was a graceful theme in semiquavers, which, a year later, became the principal figure of the prisoners' chorus in *Fidelio*. The present slow movement of the third Rasoumovsky Quartet supplanted a wonderful idea in the same key which could hardly have been developed properly by a string quartet, and which eventually became the allegretto of the Seventh Symphony. Nottebohm's *Beethoveniana* and *Zweite Beethoveniana*, consisting of

copious extracts from Beethoven's sketch-books, will almost impel
one to believe that Beethoven's whole life's work was as connected
as a single composition. We even find the theme of his last sonata,
op. 111, appearing in connexion with early sketches for the Violin
Sonata in A major, op. 30, no. 3.

So much, then, for the chronology of this concerto. Beethoven
himself took the pianoforte part in its first public performance (on
December 22nd, 1808); and, we are told by eyewitnesses and
critics, played very impulsively and at a tremendous pace. This
seems at first startlingly out of character with the first movement,
but the explanation of Beethoven's 'tremendous pace' is simply
that, the tempo being allegro moderato, the rapid passages are
written in triplet semiquavers and demisemiquavers, and are thus
nearly twice as fast as any that had been written before.

All three movements of Beethoven's G major Concerto demonstrate the aesthetic principles of concerto form with extraordinary
subtlety. In the first movement Beethoven lets the pianoforte state
the first phrase—a quiet cantabile which is immediately taken up
by the orchestra entering softly in a bright, remote key, a wonderful stroke of genius.[1]

Ex. 1.

Here the orchestra (a small one without trumpets and drums)
has the next sixty-eight bars to itself, and gives in rapid succession, with beautiful variety of crescendos and *fortes* and *pianos*,
the following themes—

Ex. 2.

A development of No. 1.

leading through a broad crescendo to another quiet theme belong-
ing (as we afterwards learn) to the second subject, and modulating
through a considerable range of keys—

Ex. 3.

---

[1] Mozart's interesting early Concerto in E flat (K.V. 291) anticipates
Beethoven in allowing the pianoforte to share the first theme with the
orchestra, but only in a jocular fashion with results no more than formal
and witty.

followed by mysterious rising sequences on (*a*) and other figures

Ex. 4.

(*a*)

culminating in—

Ex. 5.

a very important theme, which leads to the final figures of the ritornello; viz.—

Ex. 6.

and a new derivative of Ex. 1—

Ex. 7.

on which the solo enters with a meditative, long-drawn development of figure (*a*) which broadens and quickens into brilliant running passages.

Fifteen bars (no less) of this broad expanse lead to the restatement of the material of the opening tutti, with the co-operation of the solo instrument. The restatement begins with Ex. 2, and the pianoforte interpolates a series of brilliant new figures while the orchestra holds the thread with the rhythm ♩ ♪♪♩ | ♩ of (*a*), and the bassoon and other wood-wind take up the theme in dialogue.

Suddenly the pianoforte becomes contemplative in a dark key—

Ex. 8.

and in a few bars of the highest beauty modulates to the dominant, where there is a passage of preparation for the second subject. This soon appears, beginning, to our surprise, with a new melody of which the opening tutti had not uttered a note.

Ex. 9.

Strings.

This is answered by the pianoforte in a playful variation; and another brilliant solo, in which again the orchestra holds the thread with ♩ ♪♪ ♩, leads to Ex. 3, beginning in D minor, and soon enriched with an ornate flow of semiquavers in the pianoforte. This leads through Ex. 4 (as in the tutti) to Ex. 5, all with the most brilliant pianoforte accompaniment. These pianoforte figures seem, as they have already done before, to force their way through the structure till they emerge in a broad open expanse, and we hear the long trill which classical composers have generally found the most convenient way of ending the first solo in the exposition of the first movement of a concerto. Beethoven, however, does not end with the trill; he makes it lead gently to another repetition of Ex. 5 by the pianoforte, beginning this time *piano* (so as to reveal the innate tenderness of this majestic theme), but with a crescendo that brings in the orchestra in triumph with the rest of the ritornello (including Exx. 6 and 7) just as in the opening tutti.

Beethoven has now well and truly laid the foundations of his concerto form and is free to raise his edifice to heights undreamt of in earlier music. As the first essay in this volume shows, the composer's main difficulties in the classical concerto are concentrated in the opening tutti and the solo exposition of the first movement, the rest of the concerto presenting no special problems. Unless appearances have misled me (the chronology of Beethoven's Opp. 53–60 being so inextricable), the voluminous Triple Concerto, Op. 56, is the technical exercise by which Beethoven experimented with dry material in correcting the errors which he recognized in his first three concertos. The obvious stroke of genius by which the pianoforte opens the G major Concerto and gives the orchestra occasion to enter in a foreign key is not more wonderful than the art with which the sequel retains and enhances the processional character of the classical tutti; avoiding alike the dangerous symphonic action which in the C minor Concerto threatens to make the pianoforte an intruder, and the not less dangerous discursiveness which in the C major and B flat Concertos leaves the tutti at a loose end with matter almost more improvisatorial than that of the solo. Contrast those expensive luxuries with the wonderful modulating single theme (Ex. 3) which quietly takes its place in the procession and yet covers a wide range of keys, only to confirm the home tonic more strongly.

Again, note the complete freedom of the solo exposition in expanding in brilliant or ruminating passages and in introducing new matter such as Exx. 8 and 9. Yet the material of the tutti is quite as exhaustively used as in the C minor Concerto, where the pianoforte was rigid in its translation of it. Every allusion to it increases by reflection the cogency of the original orchestral statement.

Imagine the solo version of Ex. 3 as it would sound if we had not heard the opening tutti: brilliant ornamentation for the pianoforte, with a melody on an oboe; beautiful in itself, but no contribution to the balance of forces. But the opening tutti has taught us to associate that theme with the orchestra, and its appearance on a single oboe now gives us the feeling that the orchestra is being properly represented by its most pathetic member; so we listen to the ornamental pianoforte part with worthier feelings than admiration of personal display.

The development begins with the pianoforte interrupting the quiet close of the ritornello (Ex. 7) by striking the rhythmic figure ♩ ♫♩|♩ on the minor third, F natural. Then follows a series of mysterious modulations, with an entirely new figure (x) springing out of (a) as if by accident.

Ex. 10.

(a)   (x)

Suddenly the pianoforte awakens to an energetic mood, which lasts for a considerable time, while the orchestra quietly works out (a) in combination with the new figure (x). At length we come to an impassioned climax in the extremely distant key of C sharp minor, and another mysterious process begins. Figure (a) is worked out again, from its rhythm ♩ ♫♩ ♩ in the basses, to the following extraordinary transformation (the original tonic, G major, having been reached in two steps of a simple sequence)—

Ex. 11.

(y)

The new figure (y) will be seen to be a free diminution of the two bars of (a) that preceded it. It is now worked out very quietly as a fugue with a running countersubject. Beethoven does not expect us to recognize that we are in the home tonic, but the fact adds much to the mysterious effect of this very unexpected development. A short crescendo with the rhythm of (a) reasserting itself, first in its usual form, and then diminished (♩♫♩), soon brings us in triumph to the recapitulation of the first subject.

This development is the most complicated passage in all Beethoven's concertos; yet it is perfectly typical of concerto style. Its breadth of sequence and its copious use of episodic matter that has not been heard in the exposition are natural results of the principles we have already seen in operation. The relation between solo and tutti has made the repetition of material in the exposition specially impressive and characteristic, and the recapitulation and coda will make it still more so; and therefore the development needs to be more simple and more contrasted than it would be in a symphony or sonata, apart from the enormous difficulties of balancing solo against tutti in a development on ordinary lines. Accordingly we find that in classical concertos the develoment may be based either on the least weighty of the themes of the exposition, or on one that the solo had omitted (a brilliant device of Mozart's), or it may transform the themes almost beyond recognition (as here), or may have much episodic matter (as here also).

Beethoven's recapitulation here follows the opening tutti much more closely than did the first solo; but Ex. 2 is interrupted by a sudden modulation to E flat, where a lofty contemplative passage, corresponding to Ex. 8, leads to the second subject (beginning of course with Ex. 9) exactly recapitulated in the tonic. Where the ritornello bursts in, taking up the thread of Ex. 5, we have a pause on a 6/4 chord, as in all classical concertos; and the whole responsibility for the greater part of the coda is thrown upon the solo player, who is supposed to extemporize the long cadenza that comes at this point. Here we have the only really conventional element in this much-maligned art-form; for obviously a bad cadenza is the very appendicitis of music; and unfortunately Beethoven himself subsequently scribbled some astoundingly bad cadenzas to this most ethereal work. Clara Schumann's cadenzas are better, but feverishly Schumannesque; and a good musician is justified in doing his own best. Fortunately Beethoven has a wonderful way of designing his movement so that a long spell of uninterrupted solo, in a style of development modified by the impulsive manner of an extemporization, shall seem necessary and effective, whether it be actually extempore or not.

Beethoven, knowing that some pages of solo will intervene, repeats Ex. 5, the theme he has just written before. Very quietly it floats upward, and is followed by the final cadence theme Ex. 7 (thus omitting Ex. 6). As this dies away in the upper ether, we are roused by a rapid crescendo, with the rhythm (*a*) and its diminution (as at the end of the development) surging up till it pervades the whole orchestra, and the movement ends triumphantly.

If I am not mistaken, it was Liszt who compared the slow movement of this concerto to Orpheus taming the wild beasts with his music. This is so apt that it is almost free from the general objection that such comparisons tend at first to substitute their own vividness for that of the music and then to lose their vividness in the necessity for tiresome qualifications of detail. But here the comparison is remarkably spiritual and free from concrete externals. Note, in the first place, that, as in Liszt's own symphonic poem *Orpheus*, it refers to the taming of wild Nature, not to the placating of the Furies, though Liszt tells us that he was inspired by the experience of conducting Gluck's *Orfeo*. But the spiritual, or, if you prefer popular scientific jargon, psychological depth of the analogy is best shown in the one point of resemblance between this unique movement of Beethoven's and a very different one, Orpheus's first sustained address to the Furies in Gluck's opera. The pleadings of Orpheus are met phrase by phrase with a thunderous *No* from the Furies in unison, until the last *No* is a chord which shows that they will at length yield. In this andante the orchestra does not imitate wild beasts or nature, and the pianoforte does not imitate a lyre or a singer. But the orchestra (consisting of the strings alone) is entirely in octaves, without a vestige of harmony, so long as it remains stubborn and rough in its share of the dialogue with the quiet veiled tones of the solo. After its first soft pizzicato note it melts into harmony. In the supreme moment of darkness at the end, the orchestra and solo join in the same material (the chords in this rhythm ♩. ♪ │ ♩), whereas they had hitherto been totally contrasted.

The finale breaks in, pianissimo, with an intensely lively theme in that prosaic daylight by which Beethoven loves to test the reality of his sublimest visions. The daylight is the more grey from the strong emphasis the theme gives to the subdominant chord, almost producing the impression of C instead of G major.

Ex. 12.

The treatment of rondo form does not differ much in concertos from its ordinary treatment on a large scale in other works. For the main body of this movement, it will suffice to summarize its form, and devote the rest of the analysis to the enormous coda which (if we take it as beginning after the recapitulation of the second subject) is exactly five-twelfths of the whole movement, not counting the cadenza.

The first theme, after a variation by the pianoforte, has a counter-theme.

Ex. 13.

III   G

The orchestra resumes Ex. 12 fortissimo, with trumpets and drums appearing for the first time in the concerto. A transition theme—

Ex. 14.

leads to a very broad passage in triplet quavers on the dominant of D—taking its own time to bring us at last to the second subject.

This begins with a leisurely and serene melody for the pianoforte in extremely wide three-part harmony, of which the bass is a deep tonic pedal. It intends to repeat itself.

Ex. 15.

&c.

The self-repetition impatiently breaks off, saying 'and all that!' The orchestra urbanely gives a completed counterstatement, with intricate polyphony.

Then comes the lightest and simplest possible formula, in brilliant arpeggios. We begin to think it unaccountably simple; when suddenly we wonder to find ourselves on the dominant of C. The orchestra explains, with these rhythms ♫ | ♩ ‖ | ♪꜖ ♪꜖ | ♩ recalling (*a*) and (*d*) of the first theme (Ex. 12); and, after keeping us in suspense an enormous time (nearly forty bars) on this dominant of C, Beethoven brings us back with a long rhythmless run to our first theme. This and all its accessories are repeated unaltered, but Ex. 14 is made to lead to E flat. Here we begin the central episode with a new theme, consisting of nothing but energetic arpeggios of tonic and dominant chords. But this is made to alternate with rich developments of the first three figures (*a*), (*b*), and (*c*). (Note especially the drums as a bass to the wind, with figure (*a*); and the treatment by the pianoforte of figure (*c*) in triplets.)

This leads, through various keys, to the dominant of our tonic G, where a brisk chromatic passage for pianoforte brings us to the broad expanse of dominant preparation that culminates in the second subject, which we thus reach without having again returned to the first. The recapitulation is exact until the end of the humorous arpeggio-theme, which this time lands us on a chord of E flat, where, as before the first return of the main theme, we seem to be dwelling a long time while the orchestra hints ♫ | ♩. But it gradually dawns on us that we are listening to the whole first theme in B flat on the violas.

Ex. 16. (Compare Ex. 12.)

The wood-wind become witty over figure (*d*); and suddenly the full orchestra enters in a rage on a strange chord, working round to the dominant of C, our old position for a return. The pianoforte turns figure (*b*) into a slow arpeggio on that chord, taking, as before, an unconscionable time in getting back to our first theme in its original key. This time we have it in a new variation, and the orchestra comes blustering in with yet another, leading to the transition theme (Ex. 14). Now the real business of the enormous coda begins. Figures (*a*) and (*d*) seem to be settling down in a leisurely tonic-and-dominant stride, when the dominant chord seems to overstay its time and slowly changes to the vastly distant key of F sharp major. Here we have the placid second subject, Ex. 15, which calmly turns round to C major, and thence back to G, where it is gradually taken up by the whole orchestra with a crescendo, leading to a 6/4 pause for a cadenza. The cadenza (which Beethoven says must be short) is followed by more witticisms on figure (*d*) (augmented) in the horn; and then we settle down comfortably to another variation (like Ex. 16) of the first theme, which I quote in its still more delightful form as repeated in a remarkably close and persistent canon. It does not defeat its aim by pedantic exactness.

Ex. 17.

The music dies away in that upper ether which it has never left; but all the while we hear more witticisms on figure (*d*), which suddenly quickens into presto quavers, with a crescendo. On the top of this the full orchestra storms in with the principal theme, more lively than ever in this quicker tempo. Of course, when it reaches figure (*d*), the irrepressible wood-wind and pianoforte have a little more to say before ending this audacious masterpiece of gigantic and inexhaustibly varied proportions with that astronomical punctuality which gives solemnity to Beethoven's utmost exuberance of high spirits.

CIII. PIANOFORTE CONCERTO IN E FLAT, OP. 73

1 *Allegro.* 2 *Adagio un poco mosso, leading to* 3 RONDO: *Allegro.*

From the history of the 'Eroica' we know how Beethoven would have appreciated the vulgar title by which this concerto is known in the British Isles. So we will say no more about that, but attend to the music.

The fifth concerto has a majestic introduction, in which the key of E flat is asserted by the orchestra and pianoforte in a rhapsodic outburst. This introduction reappears once at the beginning of the recapitulation, and plays no further part in the narrative. As in the first movements of all classical concertos, including Brahms's, the main threads of the story are set forth very broadly, but with explicit avoidance of anything like development or combination, in the opening tutti, which is best called by its primitive title of ritornello. In this concerto the ritornello is specially formal and voluminous; but we must be content with two quotations, though there are at least five distinct themes, and any number of important derivatives. Most of the derivatives come from the groups here marked (*a*) and (*b*).

Ex. 1.

Ex. 2.

Obviously enough, Ex. 1 is the beginning of the 'first subject'; and it so happens that Ex. 2, which sounds exactly as if it were going to become the principal theme in the 'second subject', does not deceive that expectation, as many an equally important theme has deceived it elsewhere in Mozart, Beethoven, and Brahms. In fact the whole procession of contrasted themes which this great tutti reviews, in severe monotony of key, gives an unusually faithful summary of what the pianoforte is going to discuss. The severe monotony of key provides a firm basis for the marvellous richness of the distant keys of B minor and B major (*alias* C flat), in which the pianoforte is hereafter to present two variations of Ex. 2 before the orchestra turns it into a rousing march in the orthodox key of B flat. The general plan of the whole movement is as follows:

I. Introduction.

II. Opening tutti or ritornello, containing all the themes.

III. First solo, entering quietly with a chromatic scale, and turning the whole opening ritornello into a vast exposition of a 'first' and 'second' subject: with such devices as the modulations just mentioned.

IV. Close of the exposition by resumption of last stages of the ritornello, in the key of the 'second subject'. By a device first introduced by Beethoven in his Violin Concerto, the end of the ritornello is now diverted into a remote new key. Here in due course the pianoforte again enters with its quiet chromatic scale. (No concerto that boasts a modern or Mendelssohnian 'emancipation from the conventional classical ritornello' can achieve such impressive entries of the solo part.)

V. Development, dealing entirely with Ex. 1. The pianoforte part is, for all its beautiful colouring, at first no more than an accompaniment to the whispered dialogue in which the orchestra discusses Ex. 1, chiefly from the point of view of the turn which I have marked with the letter (*a*). By degrees, the rhythmic figure marked (*b*) becomes more insistent, till it arouses the full orchestra, and sets the pianoforte off into a furious passage of octaves, descending in dialogue with the strings, while a solitary bassoon keeps the rhythm (*b*) mysteriously threading its way in the bass. I have called these octaves 'furious', but must take the opportunity of pointing out that the modern pianistic martellato effect is utterly useless here. Not only could Beethoven's pianoforte not produce it, but no first-rate composer has ever wished for anything remotely like it; and I for my part do not believe that Liszt himself, who inculcated it, ever really did it as it is understood nowadays. He may have *looked* as if he were committing all manner of awe-inspiring pianistic crimes, but he had acquired a perfect touch at too early an age for any superb gestures to damage it. (The best evidence is that he sat immobile as a rock, but that his long arms caused him to sit on a high stool and make his chords seem to fall from a great height.) At all events, what Beethoven wants here is the fury of a hail-storm; and you can see daylight through hail-storms, and hear the bassoon through the right sort of octaves in this passage. On the other hand there is no fury in the fall of a ton of coals.

The curtain of hail is lifted away into blue sky, and we find ourselves in the very key in which the development started. The calm closing theme of the ritornello reappears; and in the bass the turn (*a*) of Ex. 1 moves in slow steps up through distant keys to the threshold of home; and the quiet excitement becomes breathless until at last a crescendo leads to—

VI. The introduction, followed by the recapitulation of II. The modulations at the 'second subject' become still more wonderful, the key being now one of those 'contradictory keys' (C sharp minor and D flat) of which such subtle dramatic use is made at a similar point in the Eroica Symphony.

VII. The Coda. The saddest chapter in the story of the concerto is the classical custom of leaving all but the orchestral wind-up of the coda blank, and trusting to a display of the solo-player's powers of improvization to fill up the blank with a cadenza. Here Beethoven has, for the first time, forbidden extemporization, and written out in full a coda that begins like a cadenza, but soon settles down to what turns out to be a final glorified recapitulation of the whole ritornello, from the entry of Ex. 2 onwards. Gradually the orchestra joins in, beginning with the horns, until the full band is in dialogue with the pianoforte. At last we hear a chromatic scale. It was of this passage that Schumann said that 'Beethoven's chromatic scales are not like other people's'. No wonder! This quiet scale and the following trills have now borne the Atlas burden of the whole mighty structure for the third time— first, at the outset of the first solo; then at the outset of the development; and now, leading unswervingly to the glorious close.

The slow movement needs no quotation. It is in B major, the first remote modulation in the first movement, and it has two themes—the serene, devout melody of the muted violins (it is a misprint in the band-parts if the lower strings are muted); and the meditative theme with which the pianoforte enters and moves into a rather remote key on the shaded side (D major) of the harmony. Here the pianoforte seems to be settling down in a cadence with a trill, but the trill rises and rises until it breaks over into the tonic key again. Thus the pianoforte comes to deliver its ornamental version of the main theme. As its close fades into a cloud of wavy light, three wind instruments, led by the flute, give out the whole theme again, the pianoforte accompanying with the wavy figure which the admiration of Berlioz has made familiar to all students of orchestration. At last the waves die down, and nothing is left but a cold grey octave. This sinks a semitone, and becomes glowing. As it continues, the pianoforte whispers a strange new

theme with a mysterious rhythm and, finding itself already in
E flat, after a moment's hovering, plunges into the finale.

Ex. 3.

No further quotations are necessary for the enjoyment of this
most spacious and triumphant of concerto rondos. Lovers of
Schumann's *Carnaval* will easily recognize in the second part of
Beethoven's main theme a phrase that enlisted in Schumann's
army of Davidites marching against the Philistines. Equally obvious
is the great part played by the rhythmic figure ♩♩♩ ♩♩♩ from
its first formal appearance as part of the orchestral group of themes
to its final mysterious domination in the person of the drum.

What gives this rondo its chief impressiveness is the immense
breadth of its middle episode, in which the main theme has three
separate escapades, firstly fortissimo in C major (a bright key in
this connexion), secondly piano in A flat (a sober key), and thirdly
pianissimo (breaking into forte) in E major, a remote key. The
subsequent exciting return, where the violins remind us of what
the pianoforte said at the end of the slow movement, will not escape
notice. The drum passage at the end reveals the sublime depths
from which all these outbursts of hilarity spring.

CIV. VIOLIN CONCERTO IN D MAJOR, OP. 61

1 *Allegro ma non troppo.* 2 *Larghetto, leading to* 3 RONDO.

The autograph of Beethoven's Violin Concerto is a lesson in the
correct attitude of a composer towards a player. It was written for
a virtuoso of the name of Clement, and is inscribed to him with a
vile pun on his 'clemency' towards the poor composer. The score
assigns four staves to the violin solo, in order to leave room for
alterations; and in many places all the four staves have been filled.
The violinist whose criticism Beethoven took so much pains to
meet produced (or, as he perhaps called it, 'created') the concerto
under conditions of his own making that were not considered
unusual in those days. The first movement was played in the
first part of the programme, the slow movement and the finale in
the second part. Among the items which took place between these

divisions was a sonata of Clement's own composing, to be played on one string with the violin upside down. Clement survived this performance for many years, and as an old man was seen by a young violinist of very different calibre, who became perhaps as inseparably identified with the Beethoven concerto as any player can be identified with a great work. Joachim's cadenzas earn the right to be treated as integral parts of the composition, instead of as necessary evils. I heard them from him only in an abbreviated form; but he included the full version in one of his last publications, the volume of concertos in his Violin School; and it is interesting to note that in this form the cadenza to the first movement still contains a certain famous chromatic scale in octaves which made a tremendous impression when he played the concerto in London as a boy of twelve, though the cadenza as a whole is very much more important than the already extraordinarily ripe achievement of his boyhood. I believe that in its full form it dates from the same period as his Hungarian Concerto, where, by the way, the same chromatic scale occurs.

Beethoven's Violin Concerto is gigantic, one of the most spacious concertos ever written, but so quiet that when it was a novelty most people complained quite as much of its insignificance as of its length. All its most famous strokes of genius are not only mysteriously quiet, but mysterious in radiantly happy surroundings. The whole gigantic scheme is serene. The only two definitely pathetic passages, the G minor episode in the development of the first movement, and the G minor episode in the finale, are (in spite of the immense solemnity of the horns and the trumpets in the first instance) in a childlike vein, and show how Beethoven in his ripest middle period had far more command of Mozart's special resources than he possessed in those of his early works which imitate Mozart. One might be inclined to say off-hand that the most mysterious stroke of genius in the whole work is the famous opening with five strokes of the drum which introduces the peculiarly radiant first subject on the wood-wind; but in truth there is still more mystery in the astounding D sharp which follows the second strain, for which reason I quote the whole first paragraph.

Ex. 1.

In Beethoven's first sketches he thought of the D sharp as E flat, a distinction which, unnoticed on tempered instruments, is really important here. E flat means something harmonically clearer, but the point about the D sharp is that it indeed is D sharp, though Beethoven leaves it unharmonized and carefully avoids letting it move in the direction which would explain it away. We shall see the explanation in one of the later phrases. The remaining themes I quote as they occur in the opening tutti. First there is the important scale theme—

Ex. 2.

which the solo violin is eventually to work out as a transition theme. The orchestra, however, does not as yet think of it in that light, but makes it lead quietly to an unexpected crash in a foreign key.

Ex. 3.

This energetic outburst leads more or less in the manner of a symphonic transition to the second subject, but, as is usual in classical concertos, leads to it in the tonic, so that there has been no radical change of key. The second subject, given in the characteristically radiant colouring Beethoven extracts from the woodwind throughout this work, is, as given by the orchestra, accompanied by that all-pervading rhythmic figure which the drums announced at the outset.

Ex. 4.

Broad as this melody is, it becomes still broader as the strings take
it up softly with a flowing triplet accompaniment in the minor.
This leads eventually to a smiling phrase in the major in which the
mysterious D sharp of Ex. 1 is now explained away.

Out of this arises a crescendo which brings the full orchestra to the
last and in some ways the grandest of this great procession of
themes.

Suddenly the orchestra dies away in the basses, as if warned of
the advent of its master, and the solo violin arises in one of the
most spacious introductory passages to be found in any concerto.
This entry is quite unforgettable; which is well, because it recurs
in a very subtly dramatic way. The solo violin, with the aid of the
orchestra, now proceeds to work out the whole procession of
themes *seriatim*. Ex. 2 becomes a symphonic passage of transition, leading with great breadth to the dominant of A major, and
there preparing for the second subject. (Ex. 3 is held over for
another purpose.) The second subject (Ex. 4) enters in the clarinets,
while the violin trills on the dominant until it is ready to take up
its second phrase. One of the most significant subtleties in the
structure of the whole work is that, under the guidance of the solo
violin, the second subject is no longer accompanied by the rhythmic
figure of the drums.

Mr. Cecil Forsyth, in his book *Orchestration*, remarking on the
difference between the tone-colour of a number of orchestral violins
in unison and that of a solo violin, says very truly that

in a violin concerto it undoubtedly gives the soloist a somewhat greater
chance of 'standing out' from the string ensemble, though, on occasion,
the repetition of a simple solo phrase by the orchestral violins has had an
almost comic effect, as if they were saying 'this is how it ought really
to sound'.

The Beethoven concerto is a sublime object-lesson on this point,
inasmuch as that contingency never happens. Here, for instance,
the solo violin takes up the theme from the clarinets, and gives it
in a region to which the orchestral violins do not happen to mount.
(In the recapitulation Beethoven gives it an extreme height and

brings it down to normal regions with an impressive swoop essentially the gesture of a solo player.) Now comes the expanded counterstatement in the minor. This is, indeed, entrusted to the orchestral violins, and a wonderful background they make with their melody to the ornamental figures of the solo violin, which does not take up the melody until we reach Ex. 5, where it has the A sharps (as they have now become) and some ornamentations of its own. After this has been expanded to a brilliant conclusion, the orchestral strings have Ex. 6 very quietly; and here again the solo violin, instead of competing with them in sustained melody, soars aloft in vast ramifications of ornament, while the great melody which was originally so short and terse expands in rising sequences. A climax is reached, and the solo violin broadens out on the basis of harmonies forming a cadence, which appears to be ending in the conventional shake that in practically every one of Mozart's concertos ushers in the re-entry of the orchestra. But below this shake the rhythmic drum figure appears with the most mysterious modulations that have yet occurred.

Ex. 7.

Above this profound harmonic cloud the shake rises, and eventually gathers itself into a rush downwards and upwards over a long penultimate chord, leading to the re-entry of the orchestra. And now the orchestra bursts in with the crashing theme (Ex. 3) which, it will be remembered, began in a foreign key, and accordingly now begins in F. With a sublimity which certain lewd fellows of the baser sort would reduce by cuts, the orchestra calmly proceeds with the whole of the original tutti from this point onwards. Hence we have once more the whole second subject, this time with its drum-taps in the violins, followed by its expanded counterstatement in the minor. As if to emphasize the spaciousness of all this repetition, this counterstatement is given fortissimo, and continues unabridged through the appearance of Example 5, still fortissimo. Here, however, there is a sudden twist in the harmony which produces one of those dramatic consequences that are true only when the ground has been thus thoroughly prepared. The rest of the tutti finds itself diverted into the key of C major, a key utterly paradoxical in relation to the D major of the concerto. Accordingly in C major the last theme (Ex. 6) enters, still fortissimo, until, as at the end of the opening tutti, there is a sudden hush; and in this paradoxical key of C major the solo violin mounts upwards with its immense introductory passage. Just when it ought to be closing into the first theme, it pauses on a solitary expectant note. A vast distance below it the basses enter, and suddenly we are in B minor beginning a development of the first subject. The fourth bar of the theme is passed through several keys, always accompanied by the drum figure, until at last both it and the drum figure diminish to quavers, bringing us to a very deliberate settling down in G minor. And here, accompanied by no theme except the drum figure (given in succession by the horns and the bassoons, and lastly by the trumpets and drums), the violin has an entirely new cantabile in a vein of the tenderest pathos. With the entry of the trumpets and drums the key of D minor is reached, and the phrases of the violin become shorter and more and more wistful, while the trumpets and drums turn their rhythmic figure into a solemn steady tread. At last even this ceases; and there is nothing but a holding-note of breathless anticipation as the solo violin mounts upwards in chromatic arpeggios, until the rhythmic figure reasserts itself in different parts of the orchestra, which suddenly bursts out in full and gives the whole first sentence in the tonic, fortissimo. It continues triumphantly with the transition theme (Ex. 2), which the violin takes up and now carries through some new harmonic regions in such a way as finally to settle down upon its preparations for the second subject. From this point the recapitulation is quite regular, until the re-entry of the orchestra with its crashing theme in a foreign key (Ex. 3). This last orchestral tutti leads to the cadenza. Many a clever cadenza occupying the place of a symphonic coda has ruined the work into which its virtuoso perpetrator had introduced it; but Joachim's cadenzas are the work of a classical composer, and they combine the extempore quality, which the cadenza ought to have *ex hypothesi*, with the structural features which its position in a symphonic design demands. Joachim begins his cadenza with the rhythmic drum figure; continues with the transition theme (Ex. 3), and contrives to make a very effective development of the second subject in the triplet rhythm of the accompaniment, which the solo violin had given to it while the orchestra was playing it in the minor. This treatment secures it against any effect of forestalling its quiet appearance after the cadenza, on the third and fourth strings of the instrument when the orchestra re-enters. The sublime calm of the first movement of the concerto reaches its serenest height when the last theme (Ex. 6) is given out quietly by the bassoon, and is answered in its highest regions by the solo violin, bringing the gigantic movement to an end in five bars of a terse crescendo.

In the slow movement we have one of the three cases of sublime inaction achieved by Beethoven, and by no one else except in certain lyrics and masterpieces of choral music. The other two cases are the slow movements of the Sonata Appassionata and the Trio in B flat, op. 97. The form is that of a theme with variations; and in the present instance the theme, in spite of the rich modulations between its third and sixth bars, is practically a single strain, with a characteristic expansion produced by echoing its last two bars.

Ex. 8.

There are other differences between this movement and the two other examples I have mentioned; but the point in all three cases is that a strict set of variations, confined to a melody with none but its own local modulations, and with no change from major to minor and no change of time, constitutes a scheme in which there is no action; or, at all events, which is in so dreamlike a state of repose that it is impossible to bring the movement to any conclusion except that of a dramatic interruption. Wit or humour might explain it away, but the more natural style of such inaction is sublime, and only in songs or choral music can solemn things of this kind be brought to a natural end. Beethoven in his later instrumental works, notably the last quartets, was able to design complete slow movements in this mood by means of certain devices, which are equivalent to just enough action to allow the design to complete itself. In other words, he found that a set of variations on a slow and solemn theme could, without radically or dramatically changing its rhythm, develop the kind of energy that would enable him to construct a coda. At present this was not his intention, and the whole point of this slow movement is that it cannot end. The theme, with its touching broken rhythms and its rich local modulations, is given out by the muted strings. Then the solo violin enters with a dreamlike accompaniment to the theme in the wind instruments. This constitutes a complete variation. In a second variation the solo violin continues the accompaniment with an increasingly florid movement, while the theme is heard in a lower octave. Then the full orchestra (as reduced and muted throughout the slow movement) restates the theme very simply but with the fullest possible tone and harmony. This constitutes the third variation. And now occurs something unique in the history of musical form. The violin re-enters on the last chord with some dreamy arabesques, and without the slightest change of key settles down to an entire new melody, a single broad phrase beginning as follows—

Ex. 9.

which slowly comes to the final trill of a long-drawn cadence. This trill behaves like all the cadential trills in this concerto; that is to say, instead of ending conventionally, it mounts aloft and leaves us awhile in doubt about what is going to happen. And what does happen is true to the nature of dreams, for the main theme re-enters, and we listen in peace to a fourth variation as if nothing had interrupted the normal course of the form. Yet the interruption is not without its results; for with the last bar of this variation another and still calmer new theme appears, connected with the main theme only by the rhythmic figure in the horns.

Ex. 10.

This new theme leads back to the other one (Ex. 9) with still more serene colouring. Then again Ex. 10 sets the rhythm swinging in its own impressively final way, until at last, as the violin slowly mounts aloft, fragments of the main theme (Ex. 8) are heard in the muted horns and strings, while the violin in extreme heights dreams of the figure of the first variation. Nothing can be really final in a movement so ethereal and so static as this larghetto has been from the outset: there is only one way to prove that the vision is true, and that is to awaken in the light of common day and enjoy that light with the utmost vigour and zest. Accordingly the orchestra breaks in with a purposely conventional modulation to the dominant of D. The violin extemporizes a cadenza and plunges into a finale, beginning with one of those drastic rondo themes with which Beethoven loves to shock the superior person (or would if he had time to think of him).

Ex. 11.

With all its light-heartedness and comparative simplicity of form, the finale is the truthful outcome of its sublime antecedents. To complain that it is not the finest movement in the concerto is to make the mistake exposed a considerable time ago by Plato, when he derided the argument that 'since purple is the most beautiful colour, and the eyes the most beautiful feature, therefore in every statue the eyes ought to be painted purple'. In no art-form is it so constantly a mistake to expect the last part to be the 'finest' as in the concerto form. To find the *right* finale to a scheme so subtle and delicate as that of a classical concerto is of itself a crowning stroke of genius. And there is no finale which more boldly and accurately gives the range, so to speak, of the whole, than this most naïvely humorous of rondos. Besides its first theme, we must quote the transition theme with the pendulous introductory notes from which witticisms are to arise on its later occurrences (e.g. the only two pizzicato notes for the solo violin in the whole concerto)—

Ex. 12.

the main theme of the first episode or second subject in dialogue between the violin and the orchestra—

Ex. 13.

and the pathetic childlike second episode with its fully formed melody in two parts, each of which is repeated by the bassoon.

Ex. 14.

As in many of Beethoven's finales, the main form of the movement is carried through with a certain economy of development, in order to throw into relief the full proportions of his coda, which in some cases is as long as the whole of the rest of the movement. In the present case the main form, though simple, takes up a good deal of room; but the coda, even if we did not allow for the cadenza which Beethoven has left to the player to extemporize, is considerably larger than any other section of the movement. It begins by working the most surprising of all the miracles Beethoven produces from the cadential trill, which in this case actually modulates to A flat, the most remote of all possible keys from D. Naturally it is only through a very wide and remarkable sequence of harmonies that the figures of the first theme can work their way back to the tonic. This done, there is a delightful dialogue on the first theme between the oboe and the violin, and a glorious final climax, in which the violin shows its command of the whole orchestra by being able to silence the fullest and most irrepressible outbursts again and again with its light arpeggios and scales.

CV. TRIPLE CONCERTO FOR PIANOFORTE, VIOLIN, AND VIOLONCELLO, OP. 56

1 *Allegro.* 2 *Largo, leading to* 3 RONDO: *alla Polacca.*

Once or twice in the middle of Beethoven's career we meet with what is usually described as a reversion to an earlier style. This description generally means that certain works make a less powerful and less definite impression on us than others. A close study and a sympathetic hearing of such works is a valuable experience not obtainable from greater things. Without the Triple Concerto Beethoven could not have achieved the Pianoforte Concertos in G and E flat, nor the Violin Concerto. It is in some sense a study for these works; and if it were not by Beethoven, but by some mysterious composer who had written nothing else and who had the romantic good fortune to die before it came to performance, the very people who most blame Beethoven for writing below his full powers would be the first to acclaim it as the work of a still greater composer. Let us take it on its own terms, and see what it can tell us.

None of Beethoven's three previous concertos had satisfied him as to the treatment of the opening orchestral ritornello. In the first two he had allowed the orchestra to develop themes and sequences in a rather discursive way; in the third (in C minor) he had frankly begun like the exposition of a symphony, and had allowed the orchestra to change its mind abruptly just after that impression had been irrevocably conveyed. He is now going to solve the real problem of stating the vast procession of themes on the orchestra in such a way as to prevent any group from seeming to mark a separate development of dramatic action. If the procession can thus be kept, so to speak, on one plane, then the solo instrument or instruments can produce the grandest dramatic effects by spacing all this material out and adding their own material so as to build up a gigantic sonata form, with a second group in a suitable foreign key. But the opening tutti, in maintaining its processional movement, must also have its own dramatic character, and must arouse in more than a negative way some expectation that the orchestral crowd is going to be addressed and dominated by an individual.

The true solution of an art problem is often first achieved on the largest possible scale. Beethoven thoroughly enjoyed spacing out this first solution of his mature form of concerto on the huge scale required by three solo instruments, of which the pianoforte will generally demand its separate statement of each theme, and the violin and 'cello (as a pair) their own statement. The dimensions of nearly everything except the opening tutti in this work are thus at least twice those of any normal concerto, even on Beethoven's scale. Moreover, he is so profoundly interested in the elements of trio-writing against an orchestral background, that his pianoforte part is very light, and his violoncello has, in virtue of its opportunities and position, quite the lion's share of the ensemble. Lastly, the material both of ornaments and themes is severely simple. Players and conductors who are not satisfied with art for art's sake, put all this more shortly and say that the work is dull. Beethoven cannot be thus lightly dismissed, even in a work which is a stepping-stone to greater things. Sometimes, as in the second subject of the finale, its themes descend to dryness. Throughout it is extraordinarily severe; and it demands from performers and listeners the fullest recognition of the grand manner in every detail.

The statement of the opening theme pianissimo in the basses—

Ex. 1.

is one of those mysterious simplicities peculiar to great works. If the composer were Cherubini, every history of music would refer to it as epoch-making; and indeed the continuation is in its severe formality not unlike what Cherubini might have made it. The ensuing crescendo is in Beethoven's grand style, but not beyond lesser powers of invention. I quote its climax for reasons which will appear later.

Ex. 2

Suddenly the unapproachable Beethoven shows himself very quietly in the calm entry of what is afterwards to become the second subject.

Ex. 3.

Formal as this theme appears, it gives us that Greek combination of simplicity and subtlety which is the highest quality in art. It appears here in G major, but under circumstances which make it impossible for the ear to take that key seriously. We simply accept it as the dominant of C, and are not surprised when the theme continues in that key. A beautiful purple patch—

Ex. 4.

asserts for a moment a note of romantic solemnity, but leads to another tonic-and-dominant tributary theme in the same nonchalant marching rhythm as Ex. 3.

Ex. 5.

Then there is a formal and emphatic process of 'presenting arms' in G major, which again cannot possibly be taken as an established key. There is something mysterious in the way in which this passage lets fall an unharmonized cadence figure; but it seems quite natural that, this being so, the cadence figure should go a step farther and end emphatically in C.

Ex. 6.

Evidently we are waiting for something or somebody.

The violoncello enters quietly with Ex. 1 as the main theme; the violin answers it in the dominant; and the two move back to the tonic with great breadth, gracefully ushering in the pianoforte, which, with its third statement, rounds off the theme in trio dialogue with proportionate brilliance and climax. The orchestra then surprises us by bursting in with a new military march.

Ex. 7.

The solo trio takes this up calmly, and proceeds to shed an unexpected light upon the whole past and future of the movement by modulating towards a key of which no hint has been given, the key of A, the submediant. The preparations for this are laid out on a huge scale; and we have the full power of Beethoven revealed in the radiant effect of the entry of Ex. 3 as second subject in A major. The violoncello and the violin have divided its two phrases between them; and the orchestra begins vigorously with a counter-statement, which, however, the solo trio instantly catches up as a variation, carrying it through the purple patch shown in Ex. 4. The variation now develops on a large scale, and comes to a deliberate close in A minor. Or rather, just as it is going to do so, the violin and the 'cello rush in with an energetic new theme.

Ex. 8.

f marcato.

The first four bars of this they turn into an expanded variation, and then they join the pianoforte in a vigorous counterstatement, presenting it in yet another variation, and expanding and delaying the close in the grandest style. Indeed, the close is interrupted by a sudden *piano*, and the approach and building up of the characteristic trill is an intense pianissimo unsurpassed even by the closely similar passages in the Violin Concerto. The orchestra bursts in with the new transition theme (Ex. 7), in the unexpected key of F major. From this it passes back to A minor, in which key it concludes matters with the passage of 'presenting arms' at the end of the opening tutti. And now is revealed the mystery of the unharmonized cadence which this otherwise formal passage let fall (Ex. 6). That cadence is made once more to swing round to A major, while the violoncello embroiders a beautiful cantabile upon it and passes straight on to an immense restatement of the opening theme in A major. The solo trio works this out at complete leisure as at the outset, as if there were no such things as modulating developments to trouble about. But when at last the trio chooses, it has no difficulty in starting the development with a sudden plunge into B flat. Indeed the trio seems rather to have been storing energy for this very purpose, and pursues a simple and direct course of dialogue in staccato triplets, while the wood-wind accompany with the quaver figure of Ex. 1. Soon the dominant of C is reached; the violoncello and the violin, joined in due course by the

pianoforte, call for the recapitulation in an expressive cantabile,
followed by provocative references to Ex. 1 in a diminuendo that
reaches an exciting pianissimo, until suddenly the anticipatory
scales gather up strength and bring back the orchestra with the
first theme in full harmony and full scoring.

In the recapitulation Beethoven shows an appreciation of a point
established by Mozart, in that he follows this time the course of the
original tutti, breaking the fortissimo so that the solo trio can
participate in Ex. 2, which is now so developed as to lead to the
solo transition material on the dominant of C. This brings the
second subject with all its solo accessories into C major; and fresh
light is shed upon the vigorous new solo theme, Ex. 8, by the fact
that after the first four bars it is continued throughout in the major.
In due course the orchestra bursts out again with Ex. 7 in the key of
A flat. This is so worked as to lead easily back to C; and we are
now surprised by a huge symphonic coda in which the solo trio
calmly takes up a phrase which has not been heard since the
opening tutti (Ex. 5), and follows it up by making something very
brilliant and full of colour out of the passage of 'presenting arms'
(Ex. 6). This broadens out and makes, for the last time, one of
Beethoven's characteristic pianissimo climaxes, which settles down
to a beautiful cantabile for the solo trio, while the orchestra has
fragments of the main theme in the bass. Then the orchestra
wakes up (*più allegro*) pulling the figure of that theme into a livelier
form; and so the huge movement comes to a brilliant end.

It is doubtful whether a large architectural design can be combined with a severe study in pure colour, if the themes are such as
to attract attention to themselves. Beethoven's Triple Concerto
is rather like Mozart's writings for wind-band, in which Mozart
actually goes the length of avoiding any theme which is not
purely a formula. In no case of this type will any sensible person
suppose that the composer's invention is at fault. It may be significant that the great composer does not often restrict himself to
problems of the kind. He leaves it to pedagogues like Reicha to
turn out by the hundred perfect solutions of such a problem, for
example, as that of writing for five wind instruments that by no
human possibility can blend. But when a composer of Beethoven's
or Mozart's calibre does give us solutions to an extraordinary art-
problem, it is well to listen with some idea of the points at issue.

The indiscretion of Beethoven's Triple Concerto consists in combining a problem that makes for dryness of matter with a problem
that makes for exceptional length.

The slow movement foreshadows that of the E flat Concerto in
the dark and solemn tone colour of its opening melody with the
muted violins.

Ex. 9.

The melody is severely reserved; though here, as elsewhere in the by-ways of Beethoven's art, it would have become famous for its warmth and breadth if it had been ascribed to Cherubini. After the fourth bar the violoncello lifts the whole continuation to a higher octave. As the melody comes to its close the pianoforte enters with a florid accompaniment, and the whole is restated, the first four bars being given by the wood-wind, and the rest continued by the violin and violoncello in the heights. The resulting impression is that of a very large opening indeed; and this impression is strengthened by the broadly dramatic sequel which swings slowly round to the dominant of C, whereupon the solo trio proceeds to make preparations in an intense pianissimo. What it is preparing for turns out to be not a central episode but the finale.

The style of the Polonaise was not uncommon for rondos and finales in Beethoven's time (an example may be found in the slow movement of one of Mozart's pianoforte sonatas); but Beethoven has left us only three polonaises, one in the middle of the Serenade trio, op. 8, one a solitary pianoforte piece, op. 89, dedicated to the Tsarina, and the finale of this concerto. None of these shows any of the formidable temper of Chopin's Polonaises; nor is it overdressed or in any other way similar to the polonaises of Spohr and Weber, who, when they write a *polacca brillante*—which is the only kind they ever do write—are inclined to make a very smart-society person of it indeed. Otherwise all three of Beethoven's polonaises are eminently aristocratic and charmingly feminine. The genius and romance of the main theme lie in its exquisite modulation to E major and back again, for which reason I quote ten bars.

Ex. 10.

Violoncello.

Violin.

There is a crowd of orchestral and transitional accessories which will turn up at the end of the movement in the coda. They and the very formal second subject do not require quotation; but the listener should look out for the characteristic way in which the second subject lands on its subdominant and thereon seems to

evaporate, until the chord flutters down among the three solo
players as a tonic chord and so leads back to the first theme. The
second episode fills the middle of the movement with two contrasted
themes which no one but Beethoven could have written. Against
the athletic energy of the first—

Ex. 11.

we have a note of reproachful pathos in the second.

Ex. 12.

espressivo.

This leads to a very dramatic passage of preparation on the dominant of C; and when the placid main theme returns it is accompanied by one of the most Beethovenish of thunderous trills in the
pianoforte. A full recapitulation of the first episode ensues, which
in due course evaporates on the subdominant chord. This chord
the solo trio now turns into something rather more mysterious,
which instead of leading to the first theme, delights us by drifting
into Ex. 12. This leads melodiously back to the dominant of C, but
instead of a thunderous trill we have a more matter-of-fact pause of
anticipation. Then the first theme astonishes us by trotting away
at a brisk pace in duple time—

Ex. 13.
Solo variation.
8*va*

a version which, after due statement and following up, the orchestra
transforms into the following—

Ex. 14.
Orchestral variation.

The orchestra stops abruptly on a 6/4 chord; whereupon the solo
trio executes a written-out cadenza accompanied with occasional
chords on the orchestra, and suddenly dropping into a pianissimo at
its climax. The final trill swells out and fades away; and then the
full beauty of Beethoven's design is revealed in the fact that instead
of ending brilliantly in this double-quick tempo, the polonaise

theme returns in its original rhythm, broken up into dialogue for the solo trio, punctuated by acclaiming chords from the orchestra, and finally settling down in calm triumph to the unquoted accessory themes before the transition. These rise to an end the brilliance of which lies in its formal and ceremonial fitness.

CHOPIN

CVI.   PIANOFORTE CONCERTO IN F MINOR, OP. 21

1 Maestoso. 2 Larghetto. 3 Allegro vivace.

Chopin's F minor Concerto, op. 21, is really earlier than that in E minor, which is numbered op. 11. Both works belong to the period of his triumphs as the young Polish pianoforte virtuoso whose opus 2 (Variations for pianoforte with orchestra) was greeted by Schumann with the expression, 'Hats off, gentlemen; a genius!' It was necessary for Chopin to compose works with orchestral accompaniment in order to assert his position as a composer; otherwise the public, which is not easily persuaded that an artist can accomplish anything besides the first object that happens to have attracted attention, might have regarded him as a mere pianist. As it was, excellent pianoforte composers like Moscheles remained to the end of their days convinced that their own musicianship was more solid than Chopin's. To demonstrate the sense in which they were right is a theoretic possibility. But it is not interesting.

There is some interest in the fact that Schumann's enthusiastic recognition of Chopin's genius was elicited by just the works in which he is hampered by forms for which his training had given him no help. Some critics would go farther, and say that he had but little talent for the sonata style; but no judge of composition would say this of Chopin's Violoncello Sonata, nor can any serious critic explain away the masterly and terse first movement and scherzo of the B flat minor Sonata. The concertos need more indulgence. The first movement of the E minor is built on a suicidal plan which Chopin's adored master, Elssner, must have at least approved if not actually taught, since it is to be found in two earlier works and can hardly be conceived to have resulted from natural instinct. The F minor Concerto, though not a powerfully organized work, has no fatal flaw; and its style is the perfection of ornament. The chief subject of orthodox objection has been its orchestration; but nowadays we can take a simpler view of this matter. Klindworth, a very masterly and masterful pianist with an excellent all-round musicianship, could never contemplate a line of standard pianoforte music without showing how much better it might have been arranged. When he

had tidied up Chopin's pianoforte technique he turned his attention to Chopin's orchestration. This he found thin, and so it is.
We may frankly concede that Chopin knew nothing about the
orchestra—at least, not much more than Sir Michael Costa. But
Klindworth seems to infer that the only alternative to thin is thick.
At all events he reorchestrated the F minor Concerto really very
cleverly, in the style of a full-swell organ, with a beautiful balance
of tone. In order to penetrate this, even the tidied-up solo part
had to be rewritten in a heavier style. Klindworth duly points this
out, and remarks that those purists who wish to confine themselves
to Chopin's original pianoforte part must accordingly abstain from
using the improved orchestration. In other words, Chopin's
orchestration, except for a solitary and unnecessary trombone
part (not a note of which requires replacing), and a few rectifiable
slips, is an unpretentious and correct accompaniment to his
pianoforte-writing. We may be grateful to Klindworth for taking
so much trouble to demonstrate this.

Chopin begins with an orthodox opening tutti. The quiet first
theme—

Ex. 1.

is followed by an accessory used in the development.

Ex. 2.

Bassi 8va.

The second subject, though (as in Beethoven's C minor Concerto) it appears in its destined complementary key instead of in
the tonic—

Ex. 3.

does not, in the manner of its entry, unduly forestall the broader
statement it is to receive later from the pianoforte. Altogether
Chopin shows far too fine a gift for design in this opening tutti to
justify the prevalent custom of cutting it short. The impatient
dramatic entry of the pianoforte needs all the delay Chopin has
given before it.

One other theme must be quoted, a passage in C minor, which

key Chopin (striking out on unusual lines first found in Beethoven's Coriolanus Overture) adds to the scheme of his second subject.

Ex. 4.

In the development the orchestra accompanies the pianoforte with figures from Ex. 1 and Ex. 2. After a certain amount of dramatic expectation, the first subject returns in F minor. But the pianoforte promptly changes the topic and brings back the second subject not in the tonic, but in its old complementary key, a singular but not unsuccessful experiment in form. Chopin may have had in mind certain rare procedures in Mozart. The continuation is expanded in a different harmonic direction, which brings Ex. 4 in F minor, so that from this point Chopin is able to work up to a final climax. The short closing tutti alludes to Ex. 2 and the opening theme.

Schumann's enthusiasm for the slow movement, voiced through the persons of his imaginary Florestan and Eusebius, was boundless. I quote the main theme, divested of its ornaments. The listener will thus gain a clearer notion of Chopin's art than can be given by the sight of a mass of detail, which only long practice can bring into shape as intelligible phrases.

Ex. 5.   8va...loco.

The unornamented portion stands out in relief as a haunting refrain.

Ex. 6.
8ves......................................

The middle episode is a dramatic recitative, accompanied by an orchestral tremolo with pizzicato double-basses. This is as fine a piece of instrumentation as Berlioz could have chosen to quote in his famous treatise. In the final return of the main theme Ex. 5 is more elaborately adorned than ever. Ex. 6 remains in its perfect simplicity, but a bassoon imitates it at the second bar, continuing in counterpoint of an adroit simplicity worthy of Bach or Mozart. The movement ends with the same passage that served as its short orchestral introduction. Like the romance of the E minor Concerto, it is a masterpiece in a form and a mood which neither Chopin nor any other composer reproduced later.

The finale is a delightful example of the long ramble through picturesque musical scenery, first straight up a range of keys and then straight down again, which Chopin, for reasons unknown to history, called a rondo. I quote the main theme—

Ex. 7.

an orchestral accessory—

Ex. 8.

the first item of the surrounding scenery—

Ex. 9.

and the important mazurka-like main second subject, accompanied *col legno* (i.e. with strings played with the wood of the bow), an effect rather in vogue in the concertos of Chopin's young days. The respectable Hummel uses it, and Chopin revered him.

Ex. 10.

This, when Chopin is comfortably home again in F major, is reduced to a horn-call inscribed *Cor de Signal*; upon which invitation the pianoforte perorates with fairy-like brilliancies, for the most part new, alluding only at the last moment to one of the sequels of Ex. 10.

JOACHIM

CVII. HUNGARIAN CONCERTO FOR VIOLIN WITH ORCHESTRA

1 *Allegro un poco maestoso.* 2 ROMANZE. *Andante.* 3 *Allegro con spirito.*

The Hungarian Concerto illustrates nearly, but not quite, every aspect of Joachim's music. To the violinist it is a complete revelation of what Joachim's playing must have been when his physical powers were at their height. To students of composition and of musical history it is one of the most important documents of the middle of the nineteenth century. It is the second of three concertos that stand in direct line of descent, and that each cost their composer great efforts concerning fundamental matters of musical form. Joachim's model is Beethoven's Pianoforte Concerto in C minor, the work in which, without as yet perfectly solving his problem, Beethoven realized that his first and second concertos had misconceived the purpose of the long opening tutti. In the Hungarian Concerto Joachim begins by following Beethoven's C minor Concerto in organizing his first tutti on purely symphonic lines which give no hint that the work is going to submit to the dominance of a solo instrument at all. But Joachim finds a simpler way to explain the entry of the solo violin than the drastic stroke with which Beethoven diverted the course of his C minor tutti. He evidently did not trust himself to take Beethoven's later works as models: indeed to the end of his life he always had a smile of pity for the inexperienced composer who will not learn from any Beethoven earlier than the last quartets. And so the Hungarian Concerto accepts, as a definite principle, the element of conflict between symphony and concerto in the first movement. Within a few years of his meeting with Joachim, Brahms took up this problem with drastic power, and forced its extremest terms into a chemically indissoluble combination.

The process was accompanied, like many chemical experiments, with formidable eruptions of light and heat. Beethoven's Ninth Symphony and Wagner's *Tannhäuser* did not cost their creators greater agonies than Brahms's D minor Concerto. Joachim helped with advice and criticism at every stage of its growth, from its beginnings as a symphony drafted in an arrangement for two pianofortes, to its final perfection. When it was ready for orchestration, Joachim's relation to Brahms was practically that of master to pupil. In the handling of form Brahms was from the outset a bold and resourceful inventor who needed Joachim's criticism only as the painter needs to see his work reversed in a mirror. But in orchestration he was not only inexperienced but actually untaught. Moreover, orchestration had already come to be regarded as the special province of the progressive party in musical politics. Brilliant scoring was like brilliant playing; it was suspected of having a taint of virtuosity. Brahms would probably have worked out his own salvation even if he had not found a friend who believed in him. But in Joachim he found not only a believer, but a composer whose qualities were exactly fitted to complete his education. Joachim's artistic outlook was already becoming highly conservative, but his alienation from Liszt was a revolt, not a prejudice. At the outset Joachim had been as ready to revolutionize musical traditions as any of the groups who gathered round Liszt at Weimar. His objection to Liszt's compositions was based on no orthodoxies as to musical form, but was as fundamental and insurmountable as Wagner's objection to Meyerbeer. But he was in no danger of letting himself and Brahms miss the means to classical ideals because other composers used these means to purposes he did not approve. On his own instrument he was as great a player as Liszt; and Wagner alone had a greater command of orchestration. This estimate of Joachim's orchestration will surprise those who have never heard or read his scores, or whose judgement is at the mercy of ready-made effects such as harp-glissandos and prominent celesta passages, or, to use Brahms's gibe, 'Tam-tam *divisi*.' All competent judges of orchestration will agree with Stanford in regarding Joachim's mastery of this art as on a level with his mastery of the violin. Nothing more fortunate could have happened to Brahms than that his most whole-hearted admirer should possess not only an exceptionally fastidious ear, but also the most highly developed technique for satisfying that ear in composition as well as in playing.

And so the two composers worked together. Their motto was '*Frei aber einsam*', and its initials, F, A, E, form several themes in Brahms's early works. They invert into the notes G sharp, E, A, which may be read in a mixture of German and sol-fa terms, as Gis-e-la, the name of Joachim's beloved Gisela von Arnim, afterwards Gisela Grimm. Brahms pulled his mighty D minor Concerto into shape with the united strength of his own impulse and Joachim's advice. The orchestration did not get beyond the first page before Joachim showed Brahms that its whole basis of orchestral tone-production was wrong. Brahms was quick to learn, and it is no exaggeration to say that he learnt orchestration from Joachim. It would be a mistake to seek in the first two movements of his D minor Concerto for the influence of Joachim in matters of form and dramatic content. But Brahms's finale clearly shows the influence of the finale of the Hungarian Concerto. Both, indeed, are closely modelled on that of Beethoven's C minor Concerto; but it is from Joachim that Brahms has derived the main points in which his form differs from Beethoven's.

The great length of the Hungarian Concerto results mainly from the composer's determination to achieve clearness. Joachim told me that soon after he had finished the concerto he thought a certain passage too long; but that when he recast it the result came out longer. Few are the young composers who have escaped damage from well-meaning advice to shorten for shortness' sake. Horace knew better, and so did Joachim and Brahms. If a young composer is not a mere epigrammatist, he needs space in which to move freely. By the time he is nearer sixty than fifty he may be trusted to calculate rightly the force of the half-statement and to express in it the experience of a life-time. But when we advise young artists to move like old ones, we tell them not only to ape a sententiousness that is unnatural to them, but actually to say things which they do not believe. The young Joachim believed everything which Beethoven uttered in his last works; but the Hungarian Concerto represented Joachim's experience at twenty-three, not Beethoven's at fifty-six. The young Joachim's experience was extraordinarily rich, and he had had enough of his own efforts at what I have heard him call 'psychological' music, such as his unpublished overture to *Demetrius*. The form of the classical concerto gave him exactly the opportunity he needed both to find himself and to learn how to help Brahms. Both to him and to Brahms the principal danger of their reaction against Liszt was that their music, in aiming at consistency, might become schematic. With Brahms one security against that danger was his constant preoccupation with the setting of words on a basis consistently lyric instead of loosely declamatory. He never accepted the dogma that sustained melody was contrary to the true declamation of words; and his instrumental melodies all show the freedom which comes only to composers who are accustomed to handle poetry. Joachim also made a deep study of the art of song. But the concerto form gave him his freedom on a larger scale. The first effect of his reaction against Liszt was to make him diffident about the more improvisatorial features of musical art-forms. Thus, both he and Brahms were eminently capable of designing an impressive or mysterious introduction. But the tendencies of progressive music in the 'fifties were all for works consisting of introductions to introductions to introductions, without any prospect of a clear answer to the question which Beethoven put to a famous *improvisatore* after twenty minutes of stimulated expectancy: 'When will you begin?' And so Joachim and Brahms formed the habit of always beginning at once; and the few examples of an introduction in Brahms's works make us inclined to regret that he did not more often take the risk of rousing expectation.

Now it is a fundamental necessity of concerto form that it should have large spaces of discursive interlude for the solo instrument. Joachim's character made any frivolity in such interludes unthinkable; his enormous powers as a violinist gave him freedom to develop the full resources of his instrument, and he had an inexhaustible inventiveness in ornamentation, inspired by instincts akin to those of Bach and Beethoven. Accordingly his own classical conservatism set him free in the spacious interludes which are as necessary to the concerto as parks to large towns and lungs to the human frame. The Hungarian Concerto thus became a composition from which Brahms was proud to learn. The forms, in their general aspect, are four-square and youthfully weighty in their completeness. To ask for compression would be to fall into the commonest of donnish errors. It is obvious that these large forms lay an enormous burden on the function of ornamental detail that is to fill them out. But herein Joachim's mastery is neither youthful nor middle-aged; it is absolute. Nowhere outside Bach and the last works of Beethoven is there to be found any such ornamentation as that of Joachim's violin works. There are plenty of good schools and formulas in this matter; but with Joachim, as with Bach and Beethoven, the ornaments are only in small part formulas, and are mostly individual inventions as pregnant as any theme. Brahms himself never attempts such a style. Still less does it come within the imagination of the mere virtuoso player. Virtuoso ornamentation, even when it is as good as Liszt's, consists in knacks which, if more difficult than harp-glissandos, are hardly more intellectual. The ornaments of the Hungarian Concerto (quite apart from the Hungarian formulas which I purposely refrain from quoting in the musical examples) are like Bach's. Play them slowly and you will find them to be living melodies with real harmonic meanings.

One by-product of this style is that Joachim's violin-writing is almost always, even in his smaller works, extraordinarily difficult. He had a large hand, and extensions were easy to him which give great trouble to most players. He retained his left-hand technique in full efficiency to his last days, long after he had given up playing works that depended on staccato bowing. The Hungarian Concerto shows, especially in the finale, that in his physical prime his bow-arm was as wonderful as his left-hand. Above all, the concerto shows that he had the greatest of all technical gifts: the staying power without which Beethoven's Violin Concerto is inaccessible to players who think nothing of its individual passages. Beethoven writes no such difficulties as turn up in every passage in the Hungarian Concerto; but he demands the same kind of staying power. The difficulties of a big piece of music cannot be measured by the mere fact that its passages correspond to exercises of such and such a grade. Violinists, for example, usually defer the practice of harmonics in double-stops until they have mastered more necessary things. There are no double-stop harmonics in the Hungarian Concerto. But pieces that have room for such follies are easier to play, though they may be harder to practise at first. Most violinists will probably agree that the Hungarian Concerto is the most difficult work ever written for the violin. Its difficulties all have the double quality of being the work of a composer who could play them, and of being the most straightforward and economical expression of his thought.

The concerto opens with the following grave theme, typically

Hungarian in its minor mode with raised fourth, and also in its later cadences.

Ex. 1.

The orchestra works this up in a broad symphonic exposition which soon comes to a grand forte modulating deliberately to F major, where a second group begins with a theme rhythmically derived from Ex. 1, but continuing in a vein of its own.

Ex. 2.

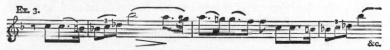

An important new theme is given to the oboe, an instrument which it suits to perfection, though it afterwards comes with new meaning from the solo violin.

Ex. 3.

Then with an impatient gesture—

Ex. 4.

the orchestra seems about to rouse itself to action; but with subtle dramatic purpose it soon comes to a series of dying cadences in F; and the solo violin makes its entry in a way not to be found in any other concerto. It begins quite quietly on its middle strings with dreamy meditation over the dying cadences, which have moved back to the home-dominant; but it soon gathers energy and in due course reaches a climax from which it descends to take up the first theme.

And now Joachim shows a freedom and truth of form that place him far above any epigonoi of the classics. The violin immediately follows Ex. 1 by Ex. 3 in tragic D minor harmony, and thence proceeds to a new theme which is to have the function of leading to the second group in F major.

Ex. 5.

The solo exposition has thus entirely avoided the effect of a transcription of the opening tutti, and by this very freedom welds the whole movement into a more highly organized unity. Other unorthodoxies are to follow; but at present the transition leads to a quite regular reproduction of the whole second group (Exx. 3 and 4) suitably expanded in terms of the solo violin. After this the orchestra bursts in with the first forte of the opening tutti in F minor. This leads to a sustained development of Ex. 2 passing through several keys with beautiful changes of orchestral tone. This is another unorthodox feature, which gives the orchestra more freedom than the normal scheme would allow. But here again the purpose is classical in its dramatic truth. The abrupt entry of the solo violin with a new counterpoint to Ex. 2—

Ex. 6.

reveals itself as the explanation of the previous development and lays the foundation for the coda. The violin takes the rest of the development into its own control, making energetic use of Ex. 5. In a few decisive steps it leads to the home-tonic and so to the recapitulation, of which solemn warning is given by the whole orchestra playing pianissimo below the climax of the violin passages.

In accordance with Mozart's principles the recapitulation follows rather the course of the opening tutti than that of the first solo. One of the most ingenious details is the passage of chromatic octaves with which the violin accompanies a quiet version of the first forte. Joachim himself compared this to a neighing horse. It is not the only striking feature in a recapitulation admirably free from anything like mechanical stiffness.

The coda is largely occupied by a cadenza, beginning, like the usual extemporized cadenzas, with the violin alone, but joined at intervals by a flute and an oboe, each of which intervenes with Ex. 6. Thus the cadenza sums up the development. When the orchestra re-enters, the violin once more gives Ex. 3 in the tragic D minor of its first solo; and then rounds off the whole structure with Ex. 5.

After a meditative introduction the slow movement (entitled *Romanze*) begins with the following theme—

Ex. 7.

The second part of this melody is worthy to rank, like Matthew Arnold's 'touchstones of poetry,' among those things in great

music which we may keep in mind as standards of beauty. I quote
the whole strain:

The typically Hungarian figure of its cadence becomes the main
figure of a square-cut but agitated middle section in E minor.
When this is completed, a short passage leads to the return of
Exx. 7 and 8 in the violoncellos accompanied by a most gorgeous
ornamental counterpoint in the solo violin.

The cadence-figure of Ex. 8 is used in fresh ways in the quiet
coda, which also resumes the features of the introduction.

The finale begins by taking up the last notes of the *Romanze* in
the full orchestra as a call to action. After some dramatic questionings the orchestra settles down to dance-rhythm over which the
violin plays a theme in perpetual motion. (Note again the Hungarian minor scale with its sharp fourth.)

This is worked out as a rondo on the largest possible scale. The
transition passages are again admirably free and unexpected in
their digressions and in the deftness of their returnings. Their
influence on the finale of Brahms's D minor Concerto has already
been mentioned. A detailed analysis of the whole movement
would be well worth the trouble of writing or even of reading it;
and experienced composers will not underrate the difficulty of
inventing and developing a *perpetuum mobile* theme. Such stiffness as may be imputed to Joachim's phrase-rhythms disappears
in the finale. The other main themes are: the first episode—

the middle episode—

Ex. 11.

and the entirely unexpected new presto theme of the triumphant coda.

Ex. 12.

Presto.

The drastic simplicity of such themes is deceptive: there is drama behind and around them.

BRAHMS

CVIII. PIANOFORTE CONCERTO IN D MINOR, OP. 15

1 *Maestoso.* 2 *Adagio.* 3 *Allegro non troppo.*

With this work the genius of Brahms shook itself free alike from formalism and vagueness. Not even Beethoven's Ninth Symphony cost its composer more titanic struggles, and few works of art can have undergone stranger transformations. It began as a sketch for a symphony, written for convenience as an arrangement for two pianofortes to be scored later on for orchestra. Brilliant pianoforte writing, however, had an irrepressible tendency to break in on the one hand, while on the other hand the most important themes were clearly orchestral in conception.

The final result was inevitably a classical concerto, but one of unprecedented tragic power. There is no vestige of immaturity or inconsistency in the style and form. Everything that happens in this gigantic work is as much a *locus classicus* as anything in the last two pianoforte concertos and the Violin Concerto of Beethoven. The storm of disapproval which greeted its first performance at Leipzig had origins of partisan opposition as disgraceful as the row organized by the Jockey Club of Paris when Wagner produced *Tannhäuser* there. But all this tale of storm and stress must be mentioned in order to guard ourselves against letting it at this time of day lead us to think that what is still unfamiliar in the work is

immature. Brahms attained maturity in it at every point; and
neither in performance nor in listening can we afford to shirk its
difficulties as if they were crudities with no artistic justification.

The first danger of misconception rises at the beginning. It is
possible and natural to play so powerful an opening with a highly
effective and orchestral-sounding fortissimo on the pianoforte; and
Brahms undoubtedly at first thought that this fact would represent
the real orchestral possibilities. When Joachim (who, at the time,
had far more orchestral experience) saw his first attempt to score
this opening he burst out laughing; and the scoring as we now
know it shows (like many other important works of Brahms at this
period) the result of Joachim's advice. What is not always understood by conductors is that the opening now does not represent
a fortissimo at all. Nothing could be shallower than the criticism
that it is now, what it was at first, an unsuccessful attempt to
score pianoforte music for an orchestra. Brahms, whether on
Joachim's direct advice or on his own initiative, has abandoned all
effort to force the tone and has reduced his orchestra to a sound of
distant menace, growing thunderously nearer whenever the harmony changes. All that is needed in performance is to attend to
his markings as they stand in the score, instead of deserving the
blame, wrongly imputed to the composer, of remaining under the
spell of the pianoforte. I do not claim that the scoring is fool-proof.

The first theme of the opening tutti is one of the mightiest
utterances since Beethoven's Ninth Symphony.

Ex. 1.

Its climax subsides into a mournful cantabile, accompanied by its
ubiquitous main figure (*a*).

Ex. 2.

In three slow swoops of wheeling flight this rises to a remote key,
in which appears a new theme destined later to form part of the
second subject.

Ex. 3.

In spite of the foreign key this has not been introduced in an unduly
symphonic manner, and we have not lost the sense of introductory
style which the opening tutti of a concerto should have. Hence, the
abruptly dramatic return to the main key and main theme is well-
timed. With tragic irony the tutti rises to a note of triumph.

Ex. 4.

This dies away pathetically, and the pianoforte enters with no
bravura display, but with a touching theme worthy of Bach's
ariosos in the *Matthew Passion*.

Ex. 5.

From this the pianoforte drifts into a passionate development of
Ex. 1 (beginning with the trills at the 8th bar), and passes on to
Ex. 2, which it carries into the orthodox 'complementary key' of F,
there to give out Ex. 3 as the beginning of the second subject. And
now it asserts the function of the solo player in developing dramatically on symphonic lines, and introduces an entirely new cantabile
in a vein of noble consolation.

Ex. 6.

This continues with an impassioned development of Ex. 4 into a
long flowing paragraph. Brilliant and sonorous as is the pianoforte

writing, it has none of the habits or ambitions of virtuoso display, but the paragraph dies away in gentle pathos, and the orchestra concludes the matter with an elegiac epilogue on Ex. 3.

The development starts unexpectedly with a fierce note of triumph (from Ex. 4) on the pianoforte. This turns out to be but a tragic plunge into developments of Ex. 1, which assumes more transformations than can be quoted here. But they will not prove difficult to follow. First, however, Ex. 2 appears in the basses, and modulates grandly into distant keys, as if there to seek Ex. 3. Quite unexpected is the change of mood in Ex. 3, when the pianoforte bursts out with it angrily in 'diminution'.

Ex. 7.

This, combining with figure (a) of Ex. 1, becomes quite light-hearted in a graceful passage which eventually moves to the dominant of D, thereby preparing for the return to the main theme. The recapitulation begins with one of the grandest surprises in music since Beethoven. The orchestra has crashed on to its unison D; the drums are rolling, and this time it is the pianoforte that will deliver the theme. It does so; but instead of taking it on the dark chord of B flat, it blazes out on the chord of E major (dominant of A minor). The rest follows in normal position. Magnificent new harmonic vistas are revealed when the orchestra, after bursting out with the pathetic solo-theme (Ex. 5) in high rage, modulates with it to E minor, and again to F sharp minor, where the pianoforte resumes it, leading to the recapitulation of Ex. 3 in that key with exquisite new ornamentation. A slight change in the following harmonic conduct brings the rest, the recapitulation, from Ex. 6, into the tonic D major; and there is no further change until the final dying away of Ex. 4, which descends to the drums.

From this the pianoforte rouses itself to the tragic issues of the coda. No cry of triumph, such as that which began the development, breaks in here. The pianoforte takes up Ex. 7, beginning quietly and proceeding in a short crescendo till it calls forth the orchestra, with Ex. 1, this time on the chord of D major with an effect of tragic irony. The stormy antecedents of Ex. 4, as at the end of the opening tutti, are worked up to a passionate conclusion of the movement.

It is known that the tragic mood of this first movement was inspired by the catastrophe of Schumann's illness, on the terrible day when he threw himself into the Rhine. The slow movement is a Requiem for Schumann; and that is why in one of

the sketches for it Brahms inscribed its quiet devout theme as a
Benedictus; a fact that gave rise to an erroneous impression that he
at first intended it for a choral work.

Ex. 8.

The phrasing throughout the movement is very broad and free.
The pianoforte enters with a kind of meditation on the main theme,
without binding itself to follow the lines of the whole melody more
than allusively. In a quiet dialogue with the orchestra it modulates
to B minor, where a spacious middle episode alternates two themes
(a long 8-bar paragraph and a short phrase) in binary form.

Ex. 9.

Ex. 10.

The return to the main theme is effected by one of Brahms's
master-strokes of harmonic poise (Mendelssohn was the discoverer
of the device, which is emphatically not a mannerism). The meditative pianoforte development of the theme now rises to a grand
climax, and the ensuing dialogue dies away into a simple but
exquisitely poetic cadenza, after which the orchestra concludes with
its *Benedictus* in a line of austere beauty. The entry of the drums
(silent throughout the rest of the movement) completes the solemnity of the last chords.

The rondo of Beethoven's C minor Concerto has had an extraordinarily strong influence on the form of two concerto finales
powerfully independent in their styles. One of these is the finale of
Joachim's Hungarian Concerto, a great work which, if it will never
be widely popular, will also ever remain one of the major events in
the history of the form. The other is the finale of this concerto.
There is a superior prejudice to the effect that an orthodox rondo
cannot be an adequate finale to a work with so tragic a first movement; but this is not borne out by the immense energy of Brahms's
main theme (Ex. 11), with its impassioned second part which arises
from its 7th and 8th bars and modulates with romantic depth into
C sharp minor, to return in a kind of cadenza evidently modelled
on Beethoven's procedure in the C minor Concerto.

Ex. 11.

Nor is there any loss of symphonic power in the immensely broad transition and in the gorgeous paragraphs of the second subject, from which I quote the beginnings of two themes.

Ex. 12.

Ex. 13.

The spacious returns to the main theme are again modelled on Beethoven's C minor Concerto; and so, in spite of its greater richness of phrasing and variation, is the middle episode—

Ex. 14.

including its development in a fugue—

Ex. 15.

in which Brahms shows himself a contrapuntist of the calibre of Bach and the lightness of Mozart. The main theme (Ex. 11) also enters into combination with this fugue subject, which is moreover treated by augmentation (i.e. given in notes of twice the length) and by diminution.

In due course the rondo theme returns again in D minor, and now the movement strikes out on independent lines. The normal recapitulation is represented by an abridgement of the calm theme of Ex. 12 in a towering passion in D minor, and the coda grows

grandly and slowly into triumph by a development of Ex. 14 in D
major, leading through a pastoral passage on Ex. 11 to a great final
stretto on its first bars, the pianoforte becoming an integral part of
the symphonic orchestra, with complete maintenance of its own
independence.

CIX. PIANOFORTE CONCERTO IN B FLAT MAJOR, OP. 83

1 *Allegro non troppo.* 2 *Allegro appassionato.* 3 *Andante.*
4 *Allegretto grazioso.*

Of all existing concertos in the classical form this is the largest. It
is true that the first movement is shorter than either that of Beethoven's E flat Concerto or that of his Violin Concerto; shorter also
than that of Brahms's own first concerto. But in almost every
classical concerto the first movement is as large or larger than the
slow movement and finale taken together, and there is no scherzo.
Here, in his B flat Concerto, Brahms has followed the first movement by a fiery, almost tragic allegro which, though anything but
a joke, more than fills the place of a symphonic scherzo: the slow
movement is the largest in any concerto since Beethoven's C minor,
while the finale, with all its lightness of touch, is a rondo of the
most spacious design. We thus have the three normal movements
of the classical concerto at their fullest and richest, with the
addition of a fourth member on the same scale.

This stormy extra allegro appassionato rather puzzled Brahms's
friends at first. Like Beethoven, he was apt to answer questions
according to the insight shown by the questioner; and so, when he
was asked why he inserted that movement, he said, 'Well, you see,
the first movement is so harmless' (*simpel*).

Perhaps the music itself may give us more light.

The first movement, in spite of appearances, does *not* (with due
respect to the text-books) 'abolish the conventional opening tutti'.
It simply begins with an introductory statement of the first theme
in dialogue between a horn, the pianoforte, and the wood-wind.

Ex. 1.

Then the pianoforte bursts out alone with an energetic figure, and
follows it with an impassioned and melodious cadenza preparing
the way for the orchestra, which begins the 'conventional opening
tutti' or (as it is better called) ritornello with a triumphant version
of Ex. 1, passing rapidly on to a review of several themes. One of
these—

Ex. 2.

mp espress.

with its vigorous sequels, the pianoforte will later on show to be the
principal part of the second subject. Here it is given in D minor,
a key not used in the rest of the movement, and concludes with
a majestic short cadence-theme fortissimo for full orchestra, derived
from the figures (*a*) (*b*) and (*c*) of Ex. 1.

From this foreign key the pianoforte brings us back to the tonic
in three powerful chords (figure (*a*) of Ex. 1), and then proceeds to
a broad and leisurely discussion of the first theme in dialogue with
the orchestra. By degrees the design reveals itself as the real
sonata-form exposition of first subject and transition to second
subject; that symphonic exposition for which all that we have
hitherto had is but an introductory pageant. Several new themes
and derivatives appear, and the drift is steadily towards F major
or minor, the normal key for the second subject. One important
new theme needs quotation—

Ex. 3.

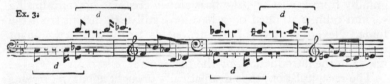

for the quiet rhythmic figure (*d*), here marked with brackets,
underlies the whole of the development-section. At present it leads
up a long straight avenue to the second subject itself (Ex. 2). It
was easy to see that there was passion therein when we heard it in
the orchestra; and the usual experience in concertos is that the
orchestra can deliver with massive force what the solo-player can
make subtle and delicate with eloquence and ornamentation. But
here Brahms surprises us: there is ornamentation indeed, but the
orchestral version of the second subject was mild compared with
the version given by the pianoforte. To the continuation a new
theme is added (which clever speculators may, if they choose,
derive from figures (*a*) and (*b*)—Brahms will not care), and a furious
climax is reached, figure (*a*) booming in the bass beneath cataracts
of trills, until at last the pent-up orchestra bursts through with the

fortissimo cadence-theme that closed the ritornello. (Yes—'you see, the first movement is so harmless.')

The orchestra continues with an angry allusion to Ex. 2; at last there is a high wail from the clarinets, and, answering from the darkness, the horn gives out the first theme (Ex. 1) sadly in F minor. The pianoforte carries on the dialogue as at the beginning of the work. When it reaches the energetic continuation which it formerly had as an introductory solo, the orchestra takes the lead. (This device, of giving to the orchestra what formerly belonged to the solo, is another of Brahms's new resources; hitherto it had always been the solo that borrowed from the orchestra; and the composers who 'abolish the ritornello' have done less than nothing towards this other side of the balance.)

Soon the key shifts to an immense distance (B minor), and we are in the full swing of the development. This now settles down to a witty dialogue on the rhythmic figure (d) from Ex. 3. The smooth melody that binds Ex. 3 together does not appear here, the foreground being occupied by a quite new theme given to the pianoforte. But in the background you will find the steps shown in Ex. 3 systematically carried out in sequence through many rich modulations, all of which, however, group round and revert to B minor, their starting-point. The details crowd closer, and the action, which started in comedy, becomes serious. At last the figure (a) of the first subject crashes in, and, while smoky arpeggios rise in the pianoforte, that figure and its continuation (c) move grandly from key to key, the bass slowly creeping upward, until a solemn calm is attained on a harmony still very distant from the tonic. Nevertheless this harmony yields easily to the dominant of B flat, our tonic, and in sails the first subject on the horn taken up, as in the introduction, by the pianoforte.

The recapitulation, thus dramatically brought about, represents the first subject only by its first two phrases, and passes thence immediately to Ex. 3 in (or rather, *about*) the tonic. From this point all is exactly reproduced in the tonic, until we reach the furious cascade of shakes which revealed the 'harmless' character of this gigantic movement. Here a momentary deviation into a foreign key gives a point of departure for the coda. The tonic is restored with a sudden plunge into extreme darkness. Out of subdued mutterings the first theme again arises and hovers, while the air seems full of whisperings and the beating of mighty wings. Suddenly the sunlight breaks through, and the movement ends with a triumphant summary, in broad melodious flow, of those topics arising from the main theme that were left unaccounted for in the exposition and recapitulation.

The second movement, a scherzo in form if not in mood, is no

less powerful than the first; and if it were a finale instead of being
(as it obviously is by nature as well as position) a middle movement, we might be in two minds about calling it tragic, in spite of
its jubilant central episode (or trio) and its elemental enjoyment of
its own rage. Of its three principal themes the first two—

Ex. 4.

Ex. 5.

are presented like a first and second subject in a terse sonata-form
exposition. This exposition is repeated. Then a development
ensues; but we are surprised to find it soon veering round to the
tonic (D minor), where, after a tremendous orchestral climax, there
enters a jubilant new theme in the tonic major—

Ex. 6.

which, with an important sequel, has much the effect of a trio.
After this trio has thus been grafted on to the development, we
naturally have no mere da capo of the scherzo, but a free sonata-
like recapitulation of its materials (Exx. 4 and 5) in the tonic. Then
there is a tremendous coda. Brahms has blended the solo and
the orchestra on quite new principles, with perfect freedom and
adequate scope for both, in this unique movement.

If there ever could be any doubt as to the purpose of that stormy
second movement, the first notes of the andante should settle it.
The key is B flat, the key of the first movement, and its emotion
is a reaction after a storm, not after a triumph. Thus both in
harmony and mood it would be fatally misplaced immediately after
the first movement. After the second its emotional fitness is perfect, and is enhanced by the harmonic value of its being in the
tonic of the whole work. It gives this slow movement a strangely
poetic feeling of finality, though the slow tempo and lyric style
make it obviously unlikely that it can really be the end. The first
movement had its storms; the second movement was all storm,
and here we are not only enjoying a calm, but safe at home again.

The orchestra begins with a broad melody for a solo violoncello.

Ex. 7.

Later on an oboe joins the violoncello in dialogue; and in the last
two bars the pianoforte enters with a new figure (*b*) and delivers
a free monologue suggested by the first two bars of the theme
(see especially figure (*a*)).

Ex. 8.

(*b*) continued in bass.

No composer has ever surpassed Brahms in the art of making a
closely-woven passage seem as if it was extemporized whereas it
really carries the communicating threads of a whole vast organization. Compare the slow movement of the Violin Concerto.

The time of storms and anxieties is not yet past: the orchestra
breaks in with much agitation, and the pianoforte transforms the
calm figures of its first solo (Ex. 8) into matter for a very impassioned dialogue with the orchestra. This is worked out on
a large scale and with an energy which goes far to make this slow
movement as difficult as the finales of ordinary concertos. At last,
however, it comes to a mournful end in the tonic minor; there is
sudden modulation, and then, in F sharp major and in slower
tempo, an entirely new melody rises. The pianoforte is accompanied by two clarinets. The melody consists of few notes spaced
out like the first stars that penetrate the sky at sunset. When the
strings join in, the calm is as deep as the ocean that we have
witnessed in the storms of this huge piece of music. To crown all,
the solo violoncello enters, still in F sharp major, with the main
theme. A slight digression at the end of the first phrase brings the

continuation round into the tonic, B flat; and then the rest of the movement is simply a recapitulation of its orchestral opening with the addition of an ornamental pianoforte part, until the original entry of the pianoforte is reached (first two bars of Ex. 8). To this the pianoforte and violoncello add a close, with a simple chain of shakes, a slow arpeggio, and soft final chords.

And now we have the finale. What tremendous triumph shall it express? Brahms's answer is such as only the greatest of artists can find; there are no adequate words for it (there never are for any art that is not itself words—and then there are only its own words). But it is, perhaps, not misleading to say here, as so often of Beethoven's finales, something like this: 'We have done our work —let the children play in the world which our work has made safer and happier for them.'

There are no trumpets and drums in this finale. Neither are there any storms. There is abundance of young energy and grace, and there is all that greatness of design which, as Mozart and the Greeks have proved, is unfailingly sublime, whatever the ostensible range of the subject. Here the emotional reaction is so convincing that, with all the 'roaring cataracts of nonsense' that were poured out on the subject of Brahms's concertos when they were new, it has, as far as I know, never been suggested that this finale was too light-hearted for the rest of the work. In the same way it has never been suggested by even the most sacerdotal Wagnerians that *Die Meistersinger* is in any way a slighter work than *Tristan*. Such cases are really well worth noting for the light which they throw on the relation between the 'subject' of a work of art and the emotions which the art itself calls forth.

I will leave this great and childlike finale to call forth the right emotions without further analysis in words; but the listener may perhaps find some use in a specially full budget of quotations, as there is a very large number of themes. I therefore subjoin the six principal ones in the order in which they occur, marking, as usual, with letters those figures which are used in derivative themes.

Ex. 9.

First Theme.

Ex. 10.

Second strain of First Theme.

Ex. 11.

First Episode or 'Second Subject' I.

Ex. 12.

First Episode continued, II.

Ex. 13.

First Episode continued, III.

Ex. 14.

From middle Episode, or Development.

simile.

Ex. 14 alternates with meditations on Ex. 10, which eventually returns in the tonic without waiting for the main theme.

CX. VIOLIN CONCERTO IN D MAJOR, OP. 77

1 *Allegro non troppo.* 2 *Adagio.* 3 *Allegro giocoso, ma non troppo vivace.*

This work is of the same period as Brahms's Second Symphony in the same key. It is his second work in concerto form, the first being the gigantic D minor Pianoforte Concerto, op. 15. Mr. Huberman summarizes a whole essay on the aesthetics of this and of all concertos in the following correction of a famous epigram of Bülow's. Bülow said that Max Bruch had written a concerto *for* the violin and Brahms a concerto *against* the violin. Mr. Huberman says that 'Brahms's concerto is neither *against* the violin, nor *for* violin *with* orchestra; but it is a concerto *for* violin *against* orchestra—and the violin wins'. One of my earliest recollections of a great musical scholar, A. J. Hipkins, is his delight at discovering that the etymology and musical history of the words 'concertanto' and 'concerto' originate in 'certare', to strive.

I give, with slight changes, the analysis I wrote for the London concerts of the Meiningen Orchestra in 1902.

Brahms's opening tutti states all except one of the themes of the first and second subjects, with such terseness that the first three sound like a single theme, being, in fact, absolutely continuous.

Energetic as Ex. 3 is, in contrast to the quiet beginning, we are much surprised to find that in three more bars the whole orchestra crashes out in a grand fortissimo, with (a) in the bass, imitated by the treble, and treated in diminution. We may already realize that this is no symphony that we are hearing, but the true headlong single outpouring of manifold material by an orchestra, to be worked out by a solo instrument in classical concerto form. The outburst leads to the themes of the second subject, another series of three themes, all stated in the same continuous style. These are—

with its derivative—

and a mysterious variation thereof which must rank as an important separate theme, so much is it changed by the division of (*f*) among the instruments and the conjunction of a new figure (*g*).

This leads to an energetic cadence theme in the minor, beginning thus—

Ex. 7.
(h)

and followed by a running figure in semiquavers which may speak for itself. Suddenly the solo violin enters, with rolling drums and a solemn sustained tonic pedal on the deepest notes of the horns. The violin begins with a fiery transformation of the quiet first theme (Ex. 1 (a) (b)) in the minor—

Ex. 8.

(a)

(b)

&c.

while the string band throws in the strong rhythm ♩ ♪♩ ♩ of Ex. 7 (h).

Soon, through the flaming arpeggios of the solo violin, we hear the original form of (a) in broad sequences of minor harmonies on the oboe, answered by clarinet, bassoon, and flute, always with the tonic pedal in horns and drum. Gradually the sweeping arpeggios of the violin become more gentle; until in a moment the flame burns softly and steadily, the harmony brightens to major, the tonic pedal gives place to a 6/4 chord, and the rhythm expands, as the orchestral colouring seems to drift away in clouds, leaving the pale tone of the string-band as the background to the solo violin that soars calmly into the quiet heights above, there to begin its song.

The solo restatement of Ex. 1 must be quoted, as the new quaver accompaniment (i) of the viola is very important.

Ex. 9.

(i) &c.

Between Exx. 1 and 2 the violin interpolates a meditative passage with that sublime calm which only the greatest artists have learnt to call their own. Ex. 2 is made to pass into the dominant. It will be heard in the violoncellos, with a wonderful counterpoint for the solo violin. Ex. 3 appears first in the deep basses and is then repeated in canon by the other strings, the solo violin having another new and independent theme.

The second subject follows Ex. 3 in the orthodox dominant, beginning with Exx. 4 and 5. When we reach figure (g) of Ex. 6 the violin turns it into a lovely new theme, beginning thus—

Ex. 10.

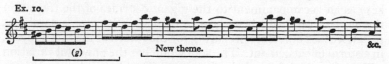

This is worked out at some length, before we reach the rest of Ex. 6, which we find at last much enhanced by the new contrast just gained, and still more mysterious from being placed in a firm position on the tonic instead of on a secondary chord as in the tutti. The effect of the double-stops on the solo violin is unique.

Ex. 7 follows, and its continuation is expanded so as to bring the exposition to a stormy close. The orchestra bursts in—with the ritornello, as in all previous examples of concert-form? No; Brahms hits on the grand idea of giving it that stormy trans-formation of (a) Ex. 8, with which the solo made its first sudden entry.

As in Beethoven's Violin Concerto at the same point, the orchestra modulates simply and broadly to C major, the key that is most of all opposed to our tonic D. There it groups the solo violin's additional theme in the second subject, Ex. 10, into eight-bar phrases together with (f) as in Ex. 6. This closes in C minor; and the solo violin re-enters with the following intensely plaintive development of (f), a landmark in the musical experience of many a Brahms-lover.

Ex. 11.

True to those principles of balance and variety which have led the great classical concerto-writers to make their developments decidedly episodic in character, Brahms not only dwells long on this without change of key, but enriches it with an entirely new counter-subject (x).

Ex. 12.
tranquillo.

K

After some time the violin awakens angrily to an energetic mood, and the orchestra takes up the new theme (*x*) and works it out independently in a few stormy sequences, till suddenly there is a bright flash of trumpets. The solo violin re-enters in high rage with an extraordinary new figure on the dominant of D (our main key) as an accompaniment to the gigantic strides of the transition theme, Ex. 3 (*e*), which we hear in the bass. Soon, on a dominant pedal, we find ourselves preparing for the return of the first subject, in a storm of excitement. The solo violin has the powerful variation of (*a*) with which it made its first entry (Ex. 8), and the winds have that figure of accompaniment (*i*) which we saw in Ex. 9. The rhythmic figure (*h*) ♩ ♪ ♪ ♩ . ♪ also plays a prominent part in this tremendous passage, which at last ends in the appearance of the first subject in grand triumph on the full orchestra. The counter-point (*i*) is given to the violins in their most brilliant register, while the theme is trumpeted forth by all the wind-band.[1]

The violin re-enters with sublime calm, and we have Ex. 2 so placed as to lead to an exact recapitulation, in the tonic, of the whole of the rest of the solo exposition. An amazing new light, however, is thrown on the point at which the violin introduced its own new theme, Ex. 10. The omission of one step in the sequences just before brings it unexpectedly into F sharp major, the brilliant major mediant used by Beethoven in the Waldstein Sonata and the Leonora overtures.

The return to D is easily managed without greatly enlarging the ordinary course of the melody, and the rest of the recapitulation is again quite exact, until the fiery climax which is crowned by the inrush of the orchestra.

And now, will the orchestra enter with Ex. 8 as it did at the beginning of the development? Brahms has something in store which, in this context, is yet more grand. In the unexpected new key of B flat (admirably chosen, as it exactly counterbalances that startling change to F sharp in the middle of the recapitulation) we have that splendid blaze of full orchestra which, in the opening

[1] Note how the trumpets themselves alter the first two bars in order to avoid the note B, which is not in their natural scale. Brahms has the modern trumpet, with a complete scale, at his disposal, but he detests any use of the instrument that audibly contradicts its character as a 'natural' instrument whose scale is the harmonic series that exists in the very nature of musical sound itself. Beethoven shows the same fastidious taste in the finale of the Ninth Symphony, where in giving the great choral theme to trumpets he distorts two bars in the second part to avoid a note which, though actually in the natural scale of the instrument, is so harmonized as to sound as if it were not. Such subtleties are among the things which, even more than matters of noise or economy, distinguish the great com-poser's treatment of brass from the vulgar abuse of it.

tutti, had followed Ex. 3 with the suddenness of a tropical sunrise. This quickly returns to D major, and Brahms actually makes the time-honoured pause on a 6/4 chord, and leaves it to the player to furnish something like half of the coda in an unsupported, quasi-extempore cadenza. Brahms could afford to risk this, since he had dedicated this concerto to the player and composer of the most ideally appropriate cadenzas that have been produced since those grand inspirations that Beethoven extemporized (and so signally failed to write down).[1]

The short conclusion, after the cadenza, begins with a quiet resumption of the first theme with sublime harmonies, and a development of the second figure (b) into sequences crowned by some of the tenderest notes ever drawn from a violin. Faint suggestions of the rhythm of Ex. 7, ⅂ ⅂ ♪ ♩, in the horns, are answered by triplets in the solo violin, that recall, in a far-off way, the triplets of Ex. 8, transformed into something infinitely touching and gentle. Then, with astonishing speed, the air becomes full of life and energy; the rhythm ⅂ ⅂ ♪ ♩ ⸢ is insisted on sharply by trumpets and drums; the pace quickens; the solo violin has an extremely brilliant version of the counterpoint-figure (i), divided between it and the wood-wind—

Ex. 19.

and the grand movement is ended in triumph before we have regained our breath.

The slow movement is very highly organized on a remarkably broad melody; and the treatment, though thoroughly classical in spirit, is in detail so unlike anything else that a little technical knowledge is apt to be a misleading preparation for its enjoyment.

---

[1] The hypothesis of the concerto cadenza nevertheless implies that a new cadenza may be produced on each occasion. The problem of cadenza-writing is extremely interesting. In the case of the violin it is complicated by the fact that a composer writing (like Bach) for unaccompanied violin invents themes that require no accompaniment; whereas the cadenza-writer has to make the violin produce an unaccompanied coda-like fantasia on themes that have been conceived as supported by harmonies which they need not have the power of implying in themselves. I append my solution of Brahms's problem at the end of this essay. Two points may be taken as essential to any cadenza for this concerto; namely, the first bar and the final close, where any other plan than Joachim's would be unthinkable. Elsewhere the possibilities, on the right general principles, are incalculable.

The opening theme must be quoted at some length, as the whole
subsequent solo is best followed from it.

I number the bars of the melody for reference. The closing strain
of this great tune must also be indicated.

The strings make their entry with the initial chords (*a*), and the
solo violin appears with phrases that on a first impression seem to
be freely declamatory. If that was all that could be said, they
would not have the wonderful and touching effect that we experience in them. As a matter of fact the violin is giving us an
exact and systematically expanded variation of the whole opening
melody. I quote the three bars that correspond to those numbered
1 and 2 in Ex. 14.

With this hint we can follow the rest by fixing our attention on
Ex. 14, making two of its bars correspond with three or four of
the violin solo. When we come to figure (*e*), bars 9 and 10, there
is a sudden change to the key a semitone higher; one bar being
still systematically expanded into two. The time slackens; (*e*) is
given by 'diminution' (i.e. in semiquavers instead of quavers), and
in the extremely distant key of F sharp minor the violin begins an

impassioned central episode. This consists of a highly ornate
melody, containing two new figures (g) and (h)—

Ex. 17.

(e) diminished.

(h), it will be seen, being accompanied by (e) diminished. As soon
as this has formed a regular eight-bar melody, it is given again in
an expanded counterstatement. (g) is assigned to the violoncellos
in a form which I give here, as it is important that it should not
escape notice.

Ex. 18.

(g)

(g) varied.

The counterstatement follows the lines of Ex. 16 on a larger scale
with more and more elaborate ornamentation, especially as regards
figure (h), while the diminution of (e) is treated in splendid rising
modulations in the accompaniment. Three bars of these modulations bring us back to our tonic, F; the clouds drift away leaving
the violin singing peacefully in the blue vault, and the oboe returns
with its world of melody. The violin, which now has a rich accompaniment, interpolates, after the second bar, three bars of its
augmentation, Ex. 16, after which the melody proceeds as at first,
till we come to the twelfth bar. Here the violin gives us a new
development of figure (b) in dialogue with the horn, crescendo.

Ex. 19.

Horn.

This comes to a climax, and as it dies away, we are thrilled to
hear the lovely codetta, Ex. 15, for the first and last time since its
original appearance. The initial chords (a) entering again on the
bassoons and horns, followed by a beautiful closing change of harmony, round off this wonderful organization so perfectly that even
the vast range of key and contrast through which we have been
carried cannot dispel the impression that the whole movement

is a single unbroken melody. Thus the reason why some critics have thought it too slight is the very reason why it is gigantic.

The same inexhaustible variety and resource in unexpected alternations and correspondences in melodic grouping that we find in the slow movement appear in the extremely spirited and humorous finale. This is a rondo; like many of Beethoven's finales, rather terse in its formal body, but with an enormous expansion in the coda.

The first theme is given by the solo violin—

Ex. 20.

in alternation with the full orchestra. The last figure (c) should be specially noted. The tune has a second part on the same material, which must be quoted independently here to facilitate reference later on.

Ex. 21.

This leads, with a short crescendo (listen to (a) in the basses), to a resumption of Ex. 20 by the full orchestra, with a characteristic tightening of the sequences of (a), bringing the cadence-figure (c) into the tonic.

A transition passage founded on (c), first augmented and then diminished, leads playfully by a devious path to a very stormy and wayward second subject in the dominant. The scales that precede it should be noted, but I need only quote the beginning of the second subject itself.

Ex. 22.

Like many second subjects in Beethoven's finales, this soon shows a tendency to drift back from its key. It dwells on the chord of F sharp minor, till it overbalances itself and falls straight back into the first theme in the tonic as at the beginning. But the orchestral counterstatement does not continue to recapitulate this after the third bar. Figure (*b*) is broken up into rising sequences, and the violin enters with placid arpeggios in the quiet key of the subdominant, while (*a*) is worked out by the orchestra. The violin arpeggios merge into a graceful new theme in a totally unexpected rhythm.

The arpeggios and figure (*a*) intervene for a moment, in their own 2/4 time in B major. The new 3/4 theme returns in E major, a key strongly opposed to our tonic, D, and then in C major, the one key that is still more opposed. Then the orchestra breaks up these new figures (*f*) and (*g*), giving (*g*) by augmentation, while the violin has expressive counterpoints, all in the key of G minor (in the major of which this episode began).

Suddenly the gentle theme is brushed impatiently away. We hear an expanded version of the scale passages that led to the second subject, and the second subject itself inevitably follows in the subdominant. And Brahms gives us a perfectly regular recapitulation of it, as if this were quite a normal position for its reappearance, instead of being a unique combination of two formal peculiarities that had hitherto always stood alone; the appearance in a foreign key, and the omission of the first subject. When he comes to the point where it overbalanced itself on the chord of F sharp minor, now of course B minor, we naturally expect the return of the long-lost first theme. Instead, we are surprised and delighted to hear its still more long-lost second part, Ex. 21. The listener will readily appreciate its powerful effect in pulling the whole structure together. It has not been heard since the opening; it reminds us of the first part of the theme, which was last heard before the paradoxical middle section, that so tersely combined the qualities of a melodious and independent central episode with those of a solid piece of thematic development. Then we had the unexpected recapitulation of the second subject in the subdominant. Now we return, not to the tonic, which would not be bright enough to give relief immediately after so unusual an expanse of subdominant, but to the key of this second part. And

Brahms now expands it, making it cover other keys, such as the
dominant of F. And as he proceeds, we understand yet more.
That second part did originally lead to a final restatement of
the first theme, which of course now returns with greater force
than ever. It takes its fill of expansion and climax; and its closing
figure (c), augmented, becomes the text for a great accompanied
cadenza by the solo violin.

Ex. 24.

As the violin settles down to a trill that gradually becomes a chain
of modulations, we hear (a) in the strings; and when, after the
modulations, the tonic is re-established, the whole phrase (a) (b) is
heard in the basses (a fine point that should be watched for). Then,
on a dominant pedal, the rhythm of (a) ♩ ♫ ♩ is, to borrow
Sir George Grove's happy phrase, *blown at the hearer*, in answer
to the sequences of the violin. We reach a climax and a pause.
Then the time quickens, to a stirring march rhythm, in which
we have a new version of the principal theme, with laughing
gruppetti on the wind instruments, and a lively tread of drums
and trumpets.

Ex. 25.

This rapidly rises to a climax, especially through the aid of its new
version of (b). No less suddenly does each successive climax (they
are several and short) give place to the following transformation of
the second subject (Ex. 22).

Ex. 26.

With a running fire of unexpected variations on (*a*) and (*b*), the
gigantic work ends in a glory that is intensified by the sudden
alternations between *forte* and *piano* which, while they take our
breath away, preserve the balance between solo and orchestra up
to the last moment.

Cadenza for Brahms's Violin Concerto by D. F. Tovey.

cres.

largamente.

f

decres.

p espressivo.

&c.

CXI. CONCERTO FOR VIOLIN AND VIOLONCELLO, OP. 102

1 *Allegro.* 2 *Andante.* 3 *Vivace non troppo.*

An important work for an unfamiliar combination of instruments
is always at a disadvantage; mainly for the reasons which make the
combination unfamiliar. One *chinoiserie* by Ravel does not make
an art-form of duets for violin and violoncello; and the sound of
this combination of extremes is inherently strange without a
middle part to bridge the gap. But the strangeness is not an
absurdity, such as the combination of a violin and a double-
bass would be. It is, when properly handled, a powerful stimulus to the musical imagination alike of listeners, players, and

composers. When Brahms brought the resources of his ripest experience to the handling of this combination together with an orchestra in the last of his orchestral works, the novelty for many years completely puzzled even those critics who took an official attitude of apostleship towards his music. The explanation of the difficulty is simple enough. Brahms did not make the new work a systematic display of the charms of the new combination, but simply expressed some of his most powerful and dramatic ideas for all the world as if the combination of instruments was perfectly familiar. His critics and his admirers had, in short, to deal with Brahms's most powerful ideas as well as with the unfamiliar combination, and it is pathetic to see the struggles of such a critic as Hanslick with this excursion beyond the lines laid down by him in his apostleship. The most familiar features of Brahms's way of developing themes, as for instance in the middle of the finale, where the phrases of the heroic middle episode are in their restatement dramatically interrupted by echoes through which the solo instruments are heard with their own ornamentation, similar devices in the middle of the slow movement, and the terseness of the slow movement as a whole—these and other equally normal features impressed Brahms's friends as well as his hostile critics just as if they were technical immaturities. There is no other explanation for this than the fact that everybody expected in a modern double concerto to hear as much of the violoncello as if there were no violin, and as much of both as if there were no orchestra. In the meantime Brahms did as Mozart and Beethoven always did—he treated his orchestra symphonically. Accordingly the orthodox complaint became, first, that the solo parts were enormously difficult; secondly, that it was impossible to hear them; and thirdly, that there was not nearly enough of them. As for the pathos and the poetry of the work, all this general disappointment made it out of the question to speculate whether such qualities existed at all.

It is to be hoped that at this distance of time there may be less difficulty in taking the work as it really comes. Any one who has made a study of musical first impressions in general and of concertos in particular, knows at once that the complaints described above are illusions. If the work is of a loosely-knit texture, the composer can thicken his score almost with impunity. For instance, the Dvořák Violoncello Concerto (over which Hausmann on his last visit to Brahms found him boiling with generous admiration) is, on a moderate computation, twice as heavily orchestrated as this, the most difficult of Brahms's concertos; and the truth is that Brahms's thickest accompaniments in this Double Concerto are written with scrupulous economy, whereas Dvořák's are alarmingly reckless. But with a loosely-knit work many points may escape the

listener without much damage to the sequel. In works such as this
of Brahms, every theme and every inner part has its results in later
chapters of the story. Therefore it is as well for us to have a good
number of quotations for our present analysis.

The dominance of the solo violin, the still greater dominance of
the violoncello, and finally, the wonderful solidity of harmony and
wide compass of the united couple, are demonstrated in the introduction. First the orchestra throws out a challenge in the shape
of the figures of the first subject on the dominant (that is to say,
the threshold of the key).

Ex. 1.

The last three notes of the orchestral phrase are instantly taken up
by the violoncello, entirely unaccompanied, in a most impassioned
kind of recitative. Then the wood-wind enter gently in the major
with the first phrase of the second subject, one of Brahms's
tenderest themes.

Ex. 2.

This time the solo violin takes up the last three notes, at first
meditatively. It is soon joined by the violoncello and works up to
a climax of extraordinary fullness of harmony, ending in an uprush
of scales and chords which leads to the entry of the whole orchestra
with the first subject launched full on the tonic into the course of
a mighty concerto ritornello.

Ex. 3.

Brahms proceeds simply and broadly, but in a style which does not
make any confusion between the lines of a concerto and those of
a symphony, though he boldly strikes out into a foreign key in
preparation for his second subject. The passage of preparation

with its fierce syncopations is the most impassioned theme in the whole work.

Ex. 4.

And when the theme of the second subject bursts out in F major (a different key from that for which it is destined in the solo), it continues in a storm of passion. No worse mistake in interpretation could be made than for this orchestral version to be treated in the style of the solo. Again I must quote the theme as it occurs here, on account of its continuation.

Ex. 5.

Very soon it has passed back to A minor with abrupt questionings, and a new theme bursts out which will be heard again in the coda.

Ex. 6.

With this the orchestra comes to its conclusion, and the violoncello impetuously enters with a new development of the first theme—

Ex. 7.

answered after four bars by the violin. (Always it will be found that the original first bar of Ex. 1 (a^1) is answered sooner or later by the second bar (a^2) whatever new developments have happened in between.) The two instruments develop this idea rapidly and passionately to a climax in which they discuss the second phrase of Ex. 3 (those very striking minims in its fifth bar), and after this

they settle down to a spacious and entirely new transition theme
in dialogue.

Ex. 8.

Starting with the utmost energy and drifting towards the orthodox
key of the second subject (C major), this yields to a melting mood;
and the preparation of the second subject, with the figures of the
first theme tenderly reiterated in the oboe and flute through the
interlacing arpeggios of the solo instruments, broken by an impressive silence in the middle, would be the most pathetic passage
in the concerto, but for the fact it leads to the still more pathetic
expanded version of the second subject announced by the violoncello and eventually taken up by the violin. I know no more powerful instance of the dramatic possibilities of concerto form than the
way in which this melody changes its character according as it is
stated in the ritornello or expanded in the solo. Suddenly however it breaks into a stormy passage, leading to what in the ritornello
appeared to be the transition theme (Ex. 4). The violin and
violoncello have but to state the first two bars of this (which they
do with extraordinary fullness of sound) for the whole orchestra to
burst in at the same height of passion as it had reached in the ritornello; and it comes to an even greater climax, being under the stress
of plunging into a somewhat distant key for the development. In
the midst of the storm the two solo instruments enter together with
the first theme, and proceed to work out the figure of triplet
crotchets which characterizes its third bar. This becomes a mysterious figure at twice the pace with a characteristic change of
accent in the wood-wind.

Ex. 9.

(I may mention, as a sample of the intelligence which is sometimes
brought to bear upon the interpretation of Brahms, that at a performance by a good foreign orchestra, I found that some one had
corrected this 'discrepancy' of rhythm in the band-parts!) Soon the
syncopated theme reappears in a pathetic calm in the orchestra,
while the solo instruments weave round it a network of trills.
Before long the calm becomes a stiff breeze, and the breeze a
storm, through which the first theme cries out angrily in the
wood-wind. Suddenly the storm ceases, and the syncopations of

Ex. 4 soar upwards in the violoncello and violin through remote modulations in a pathetic passage, which the most disappointed detractors of this work on its first appearance admitted to be sublime. We are on the threshold of the tonic, and the violin and violoncello come back to the uprush of scales and chords (the chords now alternating with the orchestra) with which they ended the introduction.

And so the recapitulation now begins in the tonic in the orchestra, just as the big ritornello did. Its second sentence, however, is delivered by the solo players, and leads straight to the solo transition theme of Ex. 8. Slight changes in the course of the harmonies keep the music in the key of A. There is the same pathetic passage of preparation, with its impressive bar of silence. Then the expanded version of the second subject is given out high up by the violin, the violoncello having a new flowing accompaniment. In due course the fatal syncopated theme evokes the stormy orchestra, which now carries the latter part of the ritornello to its greatest climax. This owes much of its power to the fact that its last theme (Ex. 6, which has not been heard since its first appearance) is now combined with the figures of the first subject (Ex. 1). This brings the violin and violoncello back upon the scene in tragic passion with the same statement as that of their first entry after the ritornello. There is something extraordinarily sonorous in their appearance here in octaves, and still more in their boldly coalescing in unison as the passion yields to a tragic calm with a ritardando. From this they rouse themselves with the syncopated figure (Ex. 4), and the tragedy is consummated by the transformation of the second subject itself into a final outburst of indignation, the theme being given in pizzicato chords in the minor, while the solo instruments emphasize the bass of the harmony by a stormy figure of their own. With a final allusion to their transition theme (Ex. 8) the solo instruments bring down the full orchestra upon the last chords.

The slow movement begins with a signal of two notes on the horns answered in the upper part of the scale and in a high octave by the wood-wind. On the four notes thus delivered, the solo violin and violoncello immediately build one of the broadest and most swinging melodies ever written.

Ex. 10.

This is worked out as a complete tune in two parts with repeats. The second part is peculiarly gorgeous in its deep harmonies, and its climax is heightened on repetition. Then without further development or pause the middle episode enters in the somewhat remote key of F. It begins with a very quiet melody for the wood-wind scored with a highly-seasoned reedy tone.

Ex. 11.

The violin and violoncello answer this with a new theme in rather wistful dialogue which modulates richly.

Ex. 12.

Then the reedy theme (Ex. 11) returns unaccompanied, with semi-quaver movement by the solo instruments, and expanded by very characteristic echoes of the last two notes of each phrase in pizzi-cato chords. A quite short but far-reaching passage moves in a few steps through remote keys, when suddenly the first two notes of the introductory signal are heard in the trumpets. The solo instru-ments respond to them, and in a notoriously difficult but very majestic passage float down again to the whole first melody, which on repetition they expand in a simple but surprising way which will not escape notice. When the great melody has come to an end, there is a short and peaceful coda in which the two middle themes (Exx. 11 and 12) are heard simultaneously. As this reaches an exquisite dying fall, the figures of the first theme come surging back again until the solo instruments rise up on to the answer to the opening signal (that is to say, the second bar of Ex. 10), to which the trumpets reply quietly with the first bar; and so, with the majestic and difficult returning passage on the tonic chord, the slow movement ends in a golden glow.

From the point of view of first impressions, the finale of this double concerto commits the most deadly crime possible to a great work—it shows a sense of humour. Let us admit this, and let us accept the still more serious fact that the first theme is playful, which is not always the same thing as humorous. This does not prevent it from giving rise at the end of the movement to one of the most pathetic passages in the whole work. Apart from the humour and the unusual combination of instruments, the chief difficulty in contemporary appreciation of the finale arose from the fact that, like the slow movement, it is very terse, and therefore failed to impress the listeners of the 'eighties and 'nineties with the true

breadth of its proportions. (It is an odd thing that the critics who
are loudest in their denunciations of unnecessary length are always
the first to grumble that a terse statement is inadequate.) The form
of this broadly designed but short finale is the clearest of rondo-
types. In Ex. 13 I give the first phrase, calling attention to the
figure I have marked (*a*), for the sake of its extraordinary consequences in the coda.

Ex. 13.

The first episode or second subject is a full-toned aspiring melody—

Ex. 14.

the rhythm of which expands in a remarkable way in its counterstatement, compelling Brahms temporarily to change his time to 3/4
and 4/4, until he abruptly breaks it off and leads back to the first
theme. This now gets no farther than its first phrase, after which
it is playfully laughed into evanescence until nothing is left
but rhythmic fragments amid a silence. Suddenly out of these
rhythmic fragments arises a fiercely triumphant new theme in a key
compounded of F major and D minor with a preponderance of
D minor.

Ex. 15.

With the aid of an angry alternating second part, which I do not
quote, this leads to a counterstatement by the orchestra, interrupted by characteristic echoes of the last two notes of its phrases.
(These echoes form the only discoverable ground for the allegation
that the structure of this very spacious middle episode is disjointed.
As a matter of fact, the device is one of those bold simplicities
which give the scale of design, and secure that it shall continue
to surprise by its breadth and flow long after we have known the

whole work by heart.) Then follows a calm swinging tune in
F major given by the wood-wind, with a delicate accompaniment
of rising arpeggios in the solo instruments derived from those
echoes.

Ex. 16.

The solo instruments work it up vigorously on their own account,
till it leads to a gorgeously bright and soft version of Ex. 16 in D
major with the syncopations smoothed away. Then Ex. 15 bursts in
again. Its angry sequel is now used to lead us back to the tonic, and
the rondo theme (Ex. 13) re-enters in due course, followed by all
its accessories. This now goes through a wide range of key before
alighting upon the second subject (Ex. 14) triumphant in the tonic
major. The second subject now leads immediately to the coda,
which is in the major throughout. It begins in a slower tempo
with a calm version of the first theme (Ex. 13), from the third bar
of which arises a most touching stream of melody in dialogue
between voices of different octaves outlined in arpeggios by the solo
instruments.

Ex. 17.

It is the privilege of works in sonata form that they can, without
weakening or falsifying tragic issues, bring their finales to a happy
ending. The tragedy of the first movement has been told without
flinching, but told within the quarter of an hour which contains
symphonic movements on a large scale. Within that quarter of an
hour we have not time to see enough of the world in which such
tragedies take place; and we are allowed to see its glorious melodies,
its humours, and its capacities for happiness, in the other movements. And so the whole concerto leads up to the wonderful
tenderness of this last page which finally breaks into joyful triumph,
and brings the great work to an end.

DVOŘÁK

CXII. VIOLONCELLO CONCERTO IN B MINOR, OP. 104

1 *Allegro.* 2 *Adagio ma non troppo.* 3 FINALE: *Allegro moderato.*

The superstition still survives in some quarters that Brahms, because of his own consciousness of supreme mastery and fastidious taste in form, must have been a pedantic critic of composers whose style was less disciplined. It still passes for orthodox criticism to compare Brahms and Dvořák as composers of opposite schools. The historic facts are that Brahms and Joachim were the two first to recognize and acclaim the genius of Dvořák. This does not mean that either of them pledged himself to regard all Dvořák's output as worthy of him, and still less does it imply that either thought his most popular works his best. Among friends Brahms could be generously indiscreet, and at this time of day there can be no harm in publishing one of his indiscretions, which was told to me by Hausmann. On perhaps the last occasion on which Hausmann called upon Brahms in Vienna he found him reading a score that had just been sent him. Brahms, before he would talk of anything else, must first give vent to his grumble: 'Why on earth didn't I know that one could write a violoncello concerto like this? If I had only known, I would have written one long ago!' This is all the more remarkable as Brahms had in fact given the violoncello the lion's share in one of his most recent and greatest works, the Double Concerto for violin and 'cello, op. 102; a work which, then violently abused by all the critics, is now coming into its own. The Violoncello Concerto of Dvořák is not without its composer's more amiable weaknesses; nor is it possible to say that all the weak points are, as in some other great works by Dvořák and Schubert, suggestive of new types of form. But it is permissible to plead that the weaknesses do not matter. Both the slow movement and the finale relapse into Charles the Second's apologies for being such a unconscionable time in dying; but it is impossible to grudge them their time, and as a matter of fact none of the three movements of the concerto is of unreasonable length. Dvořák developed in his later works a curious habit of planting his harmonies firmly on to the tonic of whatever key he had drifted into, and giving thereon a series of short phrases, each of which comes in the manner of an afterthought suggested by the one before. There are not many forms of instrumental music where this kind of construction is dramatically effective; but it has its claims where the style can inspire affection, and it goes far towards explaining itself when the means of expression is a solo instrument to which a large orchestra appears to be listening with rapt attention.

In the first movement there is no feeling of diffuseness or redundancy, though the construction is by no means close-knit. Dvořák is, as throughout the work, peculiarly full of invention; and, to begin with, he abandons the modern position adopted by him in his comparatively slight and sketchy violin concerto, and states the main themes of the movement in a full-sized classical orchestral tutti. He even goes so far as to put the second subject into its own foreign key; a device which Beethoven in his C minor Concerto contradicted at the very moment of suggesting it, because it makes the opening tutti too like the beginning of a symphony. I quote the two main themes of the first subject and the second subject as they occur in the opening tutti.

Ex. 1.
(a)

Ex. 2.

Clar.

The second subject is one of the most beautiful passages ever written for the horn. I purposely quote more than its first phrase, as its highest merit lies in the simple originality of the continuation. In the opening tutti this leads to a naïvely perfunctory new theme for the full orchestra which I do not quote. It gets Dvořák out of the difficulty of concluding a tutti which might otherwise just as well have done for the exposition of a symphony; and we need not trouble ourselves about its unpolished manners, since, having done its duty and declined in a dramatic diminuendo, it is never heard again. Then the violoncello enters, quasi improvisando, and pours out an inexhaustible flow of splendid developments of the first theme, leading (in dialogue with the orchestra, on lines quite different from those of the opening tutti, but equally naturally) to the second subject. The second subject is now followed by a large variety of new accessory themes with some very rich changes of

key, and eventually comes to a climax, upon which the orchestra
re-enters grandioso and begins the development with a dramatic
transformation of the first theme, modulating to the distant key
of A flat minor (= G sharp minor). In this key the violoncello
re-enters and, instead of carrying the development through further
wanderings of key, settles down to a sustained episode in which
the figure of the first theme is worked out in a cantabile. Soon the
violoncello takes to a rippling arpeggio figure, while the cantabile
is carried on by wind instruments. This drifts easily towards B
minor, and thus we feel that we are returning, perhaps unexpectedly soon, to the tonic. The entry of a drum with an impressive
low roll is dramatically ominous, and the violoncello swiftly rushes
to the crisis. The event paradoxically justifies the shortness of its
preparation and the suddenness of its accomplishment, for the
theme which enters in the tonic is not the first subject but the
second subject, triumphant in the full orchestra. Dvořák has, to
put the matter briefly, brought this great loosely-knit first movement within surprisingly moderate dimensions by 'short-circuiting'
its development and recapitulation. The success is brilliant, both
in form and in dramatic expression; and the total impression left
by the movement is unequivocally that of a masterpiece, whatever
theorists may say.

The slow movement has either two themes or five or six, according as you choose to single out any of the numerous afterthoughts
tacked on to each of its sentences. I compromise by indicating its
material in two composite quotations, one from the quiet main theme
and the other from the tragic central episode.

In both groups of material there is the persistent tendency to come time after time to a close on the tonic, as I mentioned at the outset. This is accentuated when the violoncello in the recapitulation turns the first theme into a sort of cadenza in dialogue with the orchestra, where every phrase is so explicitly of the nature of an ending that it is not easy to separate the coda from the rest of the design. The listener will be materially helped in his appreciation of the whole by the following quotation. It shows that the extremely quiet passage which follows the quasi-extempore recapitulation of the theme is really a transformation of the stormy first phrase of the middle episode (Ex. 4).

Ex. 5.

We shall do injustice to such a piece of music if we imagine that its habit of perpetually closing in the tonic is merely a weakness. It is obviously essential to the point of the music; nor is the point really difficult to appreciate when every moment is an outstanding example of euphony.

The finale, a short-circuited rondo, begins with a dramatic marching introduction for the orchestra, foreshadowing the main theme, the gist of which is then given out by the violoncello.

Ex. 6.

From the large number of other themes I quote the transition with its continuation for the violoncello (which continuation elsewhere brings about a return to the tonic)—

Ex. 7.

and (overleaf) the theme of the first episode, which never recurs—

Ex. 8.

with the first theme of the second episode in rather slower time—

Ex. 9.

which eventually surprises us by short-circuiting the whole structure (compare the similar case in the first movement) and appearing on a solo violin in the tonic major. Here, then, Dvořák settles down to another glorious series of epilogues in a steady progression of picturesqueness and calm. Eventually, in quite a slow tempo, the ghost of the first movement (Ex. 1) appears seraphically in the clarinets. But at last the orchestra rouses itself. The trombones give out the figure of the rondo theme (Ex. 6) in solemn big notes; and, after all, the work ends allegro vivo in high spirits.

ELGAR

CXIII. VIOLIN CONCERTO IN B MINOR, OP. 61

1 *Allegro.* 2 *Andante.* 3 *Allegro molto.*

Elgar's Violin Concerto, like the *Enigma Variations*, and probably like many other of its composer's finest inspirations, is a character study. This is attested by its dedication to some one unnamed, in the words prefaced in the score: '*Aquí está encerrada el alma de* ...(1910).'

Of all external subjects for music the illustration of human character is the most purely musical; if indeed it can be an external subject at all. Music either has character, or it is meaningless, and the character either has human interest or none. We nourish our interest in the characters of animals by describing them in human terms; and if there is such a thing as 'cosmic emotion', it is nourished by contrasting the vastness of the universe with the insignificance of man, while at the same time we pride ourselves in the fact that it is the human mind which recognizes the contrast. The blank space which stands for the name of the person whose soul is enshrined in this concerto shows that nothing is to be gained by inquiring into the private affairs of Sir Edward Elgar and his friends. The soul of the music is musical, and we need no further external programme. My analysis, therefore, will have nothing but musical facts to present to the listener. I give as nearly as possible a complete list of the themes, a policy which saves many a difficult paragraph of description. But the quotations, though numerous, are very short; and the listener will be grievously misled if he infers from this that the melodies represented by them are short. There is in fact the same danger here as there is in the orthodox discussion of Wagnerian leitmotiv, and such famous examples of the use of an all-pervading figure as the first movement of Beethoven's C minor Symphony; the danger that the analysis may ignore the flowing paragraph in its fascinated study of the pregnant word. When such one-sided analysis is made a basis for the teaching of composition, the results may be paralysing or destructive; and there are such things as compositions that have no flow and no real coherence, because the composer has been deceived into believing that a composition can be built upwards from single figures, 'logically' connected by a process which has little more logic in it than a series of puns.

The following fifteen quotations are, then, no more than the first words or leading words of the paragraphs and the processes which they initiate. I quote them thus briefly, not because the melodies are short, but because there are so many different long melodies and long processes based on the same figures that it is convenient to quote their common factors. If this work were a Wagnerian opera, nothing would be easier than to label one pair of bars the motive of longing, and another the motive of ambition, and to imagine that the composer and the dramatist were both equally capable of designing a dramatic scene by permutations and combinations of some twenty such motives and titles, each consisting of six or seven such highly significant notes that the initiated listener is miraculously certain of their meaning. Such a doctrine would not be worth refuting, but for the fact that composers themselves have been misled by it. This concerto refutes it triumphantly. I have heard it admired for the shortness of its themes, and I have heard it blamed for its lack of broad melodies. The answer to the equally mistaken admiration and blame is already to be found in the fact that the first paragraph is an entirely straightforward matter containing three distinct and important themes.

Ex. 1.

Ex. 2.

Ex. 3.

Even so it is not quite complete, but closes into the next paragraph, which works out, in broad melodious sequences of urgent character, a new theme announced in a darker key.

Ex. 4.

The next theme is destined, later on, to express a serene calm—

Ex. 5.

but the modulations to which it here gives rise, lead quickly to an excited climax in an extremely remote key, with a new figure closely allied to Ex. 2.

Ex. 6.

This swings round in five bars back to B minor, where we have Ex. 4 in an inner part below new counterpoints, followed by a further development of Exx. 1 and 2. So far we have heard nothing of the solo violin. What we have been listening to is a fine modern example of the classical opening tutti of a concerto. These six themes have been welded together in a continuous flow of melody. The changes of key, though more remote and more frequent than those of any older concerto, have all been changes possible in a flow of melody; they have not been events marked off from each other by dramatic action. The master who is to hold this large orchestra spell-bound, and set all these themes out on their various different planes, has not yet spoken. We have now reached the moment when the orchestra is eagerly awaiting him. The strings speak of him wistfully, as in the two bars represented by Ex. 1. Their sentence is finished for them by the master himself.

This entry of the solo violin realizes in a new way the true relation between the solo and the orchestra in the classical concerto form. After a short but broadly ruminating recitative, the violin, passing through Ex. 2, discusses Ex. 4 with the orchestra. Then Ex. 3 (which, by the way, is obviously closely allied to Ex. 1) is developed through a wide range of keys as a rich transition passage, drifting slowly but surely, with the aid of its ally Ex. 6, to G major. In this key Ex. 5 now blossoms out as a broadly lyric second subject. After this has been given free expression we are surprised for a moment by the appearance of Ex. 1 in its original key, a phenomenon which, however, does not mean a return to the tonic, inasmuch as one of the subtleties of the opening tutti was that its first chords were ambiguous in key. Thus the oracle proves its tragic infallibility, for the key turns out to be F sharp minor, the dominant minor. Ex. 4 is worked up, with various derivatives from Ex. 1, and a new counterpoint from the solo violin, to a great climax in which Ex. 3 also plays its part; until at last the full orchestra crashes in with an impassioned tutti beginning with Ex. 4 and passing through remote keys with a still more impassioned development of what was once the calm lyric strain of Ex. 5. Ex. 1 joins powerfully in the stormy dialogue and soon brings the development round to the original key.

Suddenly the storm subsides, and the solo violin re-enters, completing the half-spoken word of the orchestra as on its first entry, but with a quite new meaning, while muted horns murmur the rhythm of the first bar of Ex. 4. The effect is quite clearly that of a return to a recapitulation; and what now follows has all the manner thereof. In actual fact it is very free. The main theme of the second subject (Ex. 5), for instance, appears almost at once below the meditative florid figures of the solo violin, and executes some beautiful remote modulations before the violin resumes the transition themes, Exx. 4, 3, and their accessories. It then appears again in sequences that recall its tentative appearance in the opening tutti; and when at last it settles down to a real feeling of recapitulation its key is not the tonic, but D major. This establishes the same balance of keys that Schubert has in his Unfinished Symphony; but as the original course of Elgar's second subject swerved from G major to the dominant F sharp minor, it now has to take a different direction to swing round from D major to B minor, the main key. This it effects with more sombre dramatic force than before; the entry of the brass being particularly impressive where the violin resumes the discussion of Ex. 4 in B minor. From this point the coda grafts itself on to the recapitulation, and, with the impetuous intervention of Ex. 2, brings the movement to its impassioned end with the first theme, Ex. 1, and its variant, Ex. 3.

The slow movement is in the extremely remote key of B flat. There is something quaint in the fact that two modern violin concertos which are almost at opposite poles of artistic outlook should both be in B minor, and both have this exceptional key relationship

in their slow movements. Of Saint-Saëns's third Violin Concerto
it may be said without offence that it is all publicity, whereas
Elgar's Violin Concerto is one of the most intimate works of this
century. In most respects the comparison between the two works
sheds little light on either of them, but it is interesting to compare
the most obvious single feature in the slow movement of each.
Everybody who remembers the slow movement of Saint-Saëns's
B minor Violin Concerto instantly thinks of the passage where the
violin plays arpeggios in harmonics two octaves above a clarinet.
Everybody who remembers the slow movement of the Elgar Violin
Concerto thinks of the way in which the orchestra first states eight
bars of naïve melody, whereupon the solo violin enters with an
equally naïve counterpoint *as an inner part.*

Soon the violin leads the orchestra into remote regions; and new
themes appear—

which rise to a climax in D flat.

In this key the first theme (Ex. 7 with its counterpoint) is resumed,
and leads through Ex. 8 to a broad new theme in D natural.

This, though it sets out very firmly in D, does not remain there long
but fetches a compass quickly back to B flat, where, with the

return to the main theme, we also have other themes freely recapitulated in their order. The last words are said by the orchestra with Ex. 10 pianissimo, answered by the violin with Ex. 9.

The finale is very rhapsodical and dramatic. Its outstanding features are an opening in which the solo violin seems to be playing a kind of prelude on a figure of rising turns. This requires no quotation until an inner part of the orchestra interpolates a theme which afterwards becomes important.

Ex. 12.

This appears to be a determining point, inasmuch as it brings the harmony to the crisis of closing in the key of B minor, which all this improvisatorial opening is intended to establish. It is obviously right that after the slow movement in the remote key of B flat, the main key of the work should be specially emphasized. This impression once clearly conveyed, the harmony, after all, swerves boldly aside, and in D major there enters the most prominent theme in the finale.

Ex. 13.

Other themes that are used with a sense of being transitional material are Ex. 12 (soon taken up with majestic passion by the whole orchestra) and a combination of it with new figures—

Ex. 14.

foreshadowing the second subject itself.

Ex. 15.

Out of these materials the scheme of exposition and recapitulation is easy to follow, and soon runs its course. It accordingly lands us in B major; and now, in what is formally speaking the coda of the work, comes the real series of events for which all this is a prelude. The second theme of the slow movement, Ex. 8, enters in B major adapted to the tempo of the finale, and is brought by both the solo violin and the orchestra through a wide range of key to a climax over which the themes proper to the finale (Exx. 13 and 12) return in full vigour.

Suddenly the music dies away into the minor, and the themes of the first movement reappear slowly and mysteriously (Exx. 1, 4, and 5) in the cadenza, which has become famous as one of the most original dialogues between a solo instrument and an orchestra that have ever been imagined. The device of the 'pizzicato tremolo', which Elgar has invented in this passage, ought henceforth to be a matter of common knowledge in orchestral music. There is nothing like it for filmy harmonious transparency and mystery; and it is one of the simplest things in the world. But we wrong this cadenza if we ascribe its aesthetic value to an orchestral effect. The priceless thing is to find such devices invented in the service of music which enshrines a soul. It is not a sensational effect; and those who have heard of it by reputation and expect to be startled by it will be disappointed. It is simply a common-sense solution of the problem of providing an exquisitely faint harmony that will keep entirely in the background on any notes required. After the cadenza, the introduction to the finale is resumed and leads to a brilliant coda in which Exx. 8, 15, and 13 conclude the work in triumph.

ARTHUR SOMERVELL

CXIV. VIOLIN CONCERTO IN G MINOR

1 *Allegro moderato.* 2 *Adagio.* 3 *Allegro giocoso.*

There will never be too many violin concertos in the world. They are immensely difficult to write, even on post-classical or experimental lines; and while violinists clamour for additions to their repertoire, they find more difficulty in learning new concertos than in keeping their classical repertoire up to the demands of their engagements. Accordingly a new concerto will have a better chance if its design is a light post-classical framework for the display of the violin than if it is either on full-sized classical lines or experimental in the latest phases of revolution. Nevertheless, some living composers are so fond of music that the full-sized classical form of concerto still gives them a greater stimulus to musical invention than any other; and so Sir Edward Elgar designed his Violin Concerto with a broad opening tutti and a full exploitation of the consequences thereof. And now Sir Arthur Somervell does likewise. The two works resemble the classics no more than they resemble each other. They agree with the classics and with each other in being individuals, in owing their form to their matter, and (a third way of saying the same thing) in being the work of masters who know their own minds and are not diverted from saying what they mean by any consideration as to whether 'one can do this nowadays'.

The Somervell Violin Concerto is easy to follow, and is in fact so much less complex than the Elgar that the comparison between the two cannot possibly illuminate either of them. Unfortunately the comparison is quite certain to be made by most people who know that both works are violin concertos and both are by contemporary Englishmen. Accordingly, let the possibility of comparison here be mentioned as a subject hereafter under taboo. The Elgar Concerto is obviously the more difficult to understand and to play. The Somervell Concerto will, like most of its author's works, attract the listener at once, and will not present him with anything evidently difficult to understand. The wise listener will, nevertheless, refrain from concluding that what he appreciates on a first hearing comprises the whole work in all its dimensions and implications; nor will he be worried by that most destructive of prejudices, the belief that what pleases immediately must always be wrong somehow. This belief has never been shared by great masters. They know that bad works may be 'best sellers'; but they have no conviction that good works may not; and their own criteria are far too humdrum to impress as profound criticism. The highest praise ever given by one great composer to another was Haydn's oft-quoted assertion to Leopold Mozart; but usually only the unimportant half of it is quoted. 'I assure you', said Haydn, 'that your son is the greatest musician I have ever seen or heard of.' Very generous and superlative, but not so pregnant as the continuation: 'he has taste and the most thorough knowledge of composition'.

And now let us all devote what taste and knowledge of composition we possess to the enjoyment of a violin concerto by a composer who has abundance of melodious and rhythmic invention, and whose technical resources are all devoted to making his music clear. This end he attains so thoroughly that probably few listeners will realize how free his rhythms are, and how impossible it is to predict what turn the end of a phrase will take. I purposely quote the themes only as far as the first square section: the continuations are always inevitable when we have heard them, but never predictable. The harmonic style is in keeping with the themes and rhythms; the treatment of the minor mode is tinged with the Doric and Aeolian of English and kindred folk-song, while the key-system of the whole work is by no means tied down to classical precedent.

The opening tutti begins with the following main theme—

Ex. 1.

The figure (*a*) of the first bar is used in several other themes, as later quotations will show. In the rhythm ♩ ♫ ♪ | ♩ it pervades the next theme (unquoted), which makes a deliberate symphonic transition to the complementary key (B flat) in which the second group of themes is to be cast. The procedure is that of Joachim's Hungarian Concerto, a modification of Beethoven's in his C minor Concerto, but less symphonic than either. Beethoven's C minor tutti was so thoroughly symphonic that when his second group began in its complementary key Beethoven found himself compelled to shift it back to the tonic before the pianoforte could enter at all; and then the pianoforte had no chance of diverging from a strict recapitulation of the tutti up to that shifting point. Joachim found it possible to let his second group die away before the orchestra had gone far into it; and so his solo arose out of it quietly but dramatically, and there was no difficulty in continuing with freedom throughout. Somervell's tutti has contrived, somehow, to keep its processional and preludial aspect throughout in spite of its apparently symphonic form. The orchestra gives out the two main themes of the second group. Of these the first is a fine example of a long and close-knit musical sentence. I am strongly tempted to quote the whole 18 bars (closing into a 19th as first of the next theme), but the listener may learn more by finding out for himself what comes of the simple-seeming first 4-bar clause.

Ex. 2.

As the melody approaches its close it makes use of figure (*a*) in smooth rhythm. That figure then takes an entirely different form in the energetic next theme.

Ex. 3.

The above three quotations show that this opening tutti has at

all events this difference from its classical models, that its material
shows three radically different time-measures instead of only one.
There is, nevertheless, a common denominator implied, however it
may yield here and there to rubato. The half-bar of Ex. 1 is the
same size as that of Ex. 2, and as one-third of the bar of Ex. 3.

The orchestra disposes of Ex. 3 in 18 bars, which die away in
evident anticipation of something dramatic. And the solo violin
enters with a solemn meditation in recitative, alluding to figure (*a*),
and punctuated by pizzicato chords which descend in chromatic
steps from D (the dominant) to the tonic G. The pizzicato chords
settle into a swinging accompaniment to Ex. 1, and the solo violin
proceeds to translate the whole opening tutti into its own language.
But it cannot confine itself to the lines laid down by the orchestra;
it must have a new transition theme, though (*a*) is still latent.

This leads through one or two new incidents to a regular solo
version of the whole second group (Exx. 2 and 3); to which the
violin adds a serene closing-theme made of figure (*a*).

A horn repeats this while the solo adorns it with arpeggios. Then
the orchestra intervenes and starts the development in B flat minor.
There is no trace of the classical procedure which is to reproduce,
with or without some new modulation, a substantial portion of the
opening tutti; the orchestra and violin plunge at once into a
discursive development of figure (*a*) in dialogue and in various
forms new and old, seldom giving more than the first $3\frac{1}{2}$ bars of the
theme as in Ex. 1, but producing several contrasted episodes from
it. Eventually the second group (Ex. 2) intervenes in C major and
moves towards E minor. The solo violin alludes to its opening
cadenza, and the orchestra, apropos of figure (*b*), enters with a
short crescendo that lands unexpectedly in the tonic major, G.

Hereupon the recapitulation begins, with a triumphant translation of Ex. 1 into the major mode. The solo violin diverts the
continuation to its own purposes and leads to Ex. 4 in E minor, from
which point the recapitulation becomes exact. The end of Ex. 5

leads to the cadenza. This, though on different lines from those of the first entry of the solo, somewhat recalls that entry by its ruminative recitative style and its development of figure (*a*). During its course the muted strings of the orchestra enter with an augmentation of Ex. 2, while the solo violin breaks into arpeggios. The cadenza, however, extends beyond this incident and leads eventually to a serene coda devoted to Ex. 1 in the major mode. But at last the tone changes and the theme returns to its original heroic mood, in which the movement ends.

The slow movement (in E flat) begins with a 4-bar phrase for low-pitched wind, anticipating and closing into the main theme. This is given out by the solo violin in a big paragraph with subtle rhythm, involving in two places a two-beat bar of two beats instead of three. I give the first six bars, which overlap with the longer continuation initiated by the entry of the horn.

Ex. 6.

At the end of the theme a transition-passage leads to a middle section in the bright key of G major. Its main theme begins in dominant harmony, thus—

Ex. 7.

and is continued with an allied theme, also hovering on a half-close—

Ex. 8.

which is used separately later on.

The return to the main key and theme is effected in twice two bars of such masterly poetic power that I must quote them. They arise out of the tonic chord on which the solo violin has at last succeeded in resolving the persistent dominant of its themes. And so the main theme returns, as it were, in mid-stride.

Ex. 9.

The recapitulation is terse, and on to it is grafted a peaceful coda beginning with Ex. 7, alluding, in cadence, to Ex. 6, and ending with a tonic pedal below an expanded version of the procedure shown in Ex. 9.

The finale is a joyous rondo on lines differing from classical precedent in certain matters of key-relation which need not worry the listener. The quotation of its main themes is all that is needed.

Rondo theme.

Ex. 10.

The second strain of this theme is on a contrasted figure. There is also a new transition theme arising out of the close, and leading to—

First Episode, or Second Group.

Ex. 11.

Starting in the orthodox dominant, this soon goes to remoter regions, such as F major, a thoroughly unorthodox key, from which, however, the return to G (and to Ex. 11) is effected with insolent ease, the orchestra seeming to stretch itself in a slow yawn while the solo violin blows smoke-rings.

Second Episode.

Ex. 12.

The supertonic, A minor, is a key which, though closely related to the tonic, is never chosen by classical composers for cardinal features of form. The present unorthodoxy is partly a natural result of the previous unorthodoxy of F major, and for the rest it forms the right base of operations for the subsequent adventures that take us through various other keys and surprise us with incidents like the tutti outburst of Ex. 11, in B major. This outburst eventually shortens the normal course of the finale considerably, for when next the main theme (Ex. 10) returns (on a trumpet) there is no need for another explicit recapitulation of the whole first episode (Ex. 11) in the tonic, but it can be dealt with allusively together with all the other themes, including the unquoted transition theme, in a spacious perorative coda.

CXV–CXXXV. VARIATIONS AND CONCERTOS WITHOUT RITORNELLO
JOACHIM
CXV. VARIATIONS FOR VIOLIN WITH ORCHESTRA

Joachim's violin works are full of technical difficulties produced with unconscious ease by the masterly player handling his own instrument. But not a note is there for display. Joachim never wrote a bar that did not aim instinctively for clearness and completeness in the presentation of true musical ideas. It has been well said by Moser that Joachim's playing and teaching inculcated 'the utmost simplicity together with the utmost presence of mind (*Besonnenheit*)'. In his compositions the *Besonnenheit* has an immense field for exercise. All his compositions are early works, and they show a richness of invention which needs all the organizing power that a composer's technique and experience can give. Joachim's early musical ideas and ideals might easily have occupied him as a composer for the rest of his life, had they not found easier and more direct expression in his playing of the classics. I once ventured to ask him how it came that he ceased to compose, and this was substantially the explanation he gave me, adding thereto: 'and then, you see, there was Brahms'. Nothing in the history

of music is more delightful than the early passages in the careers
of Brahms and Joachim in which the two composers kept up a
regular correspondence in the exchange of compositions and mutual
criticism. At the outset of this intercourse Joachim was by far the
more experienced master of the two, especially in the handling
of the orchestra. In spite of one or two obstinately conservative
habits in the treatment of trumpets, Joachim's orchestral scores
are remarkably rich and free; nor does it seem to make much
difference whether the orchestra is acting as an accompaniment to
his solo violin or is independent, as in his Overtures to *Hamlet* and
to a comedy by Gozzi. Popularity his works never sought, and
virtuoso players will not find in them opportunities of display
comparable to their difficulty. This greatest of players will always
be a composers' composer. Thus the interest of his works will
grow with the passage of time; for it depends on ideas that stand
on their own musical merits without regard to fashion.

The Variations for violin and orchestra are a culminative growth
from the following short melody, which is announced by the wood-
wind after a ruminating introduction by the violin.

Ex. 1.

In the 1st variation the violin restates the theme an octave lower.
The 2nd, 3rd, 4th, and 5th variations embroider it with increasingly
rapid rhythms. In the 6th variation the melody is in a lively hunts-
man's rhythm for the horns and bassoons, while the violin has
dashing scales and arpeggios. The 7th variation springs vigorously
along in anapaests.

In the 8th variation the violin throws down the gauntlet to the
orchestra, being left entirely to itself with a uniform series of
chords. The 9th variation repeats this with the full orchestra. It
is a bold plan and completely successful. It is as if the spirit of the
violin had evoked the orchestra. We can appreciate the point if
we consider how fatal it would have been to change the order of
these two variations.

The 10th variation gives a new and melancholy melody on the fourth string of the violin over the harmonies of the theme, and the 11th variation changes to the major, the violin floating seraphically over the high wood-wind in an even flow of crotchets. This is repeated in the 12th variation by the whole orchestra very softly over a rustling accompaniment.

Variation 13 (*poco animato*) is in a syncopated figure in double stops. In variation 14 this is repeated by the wood-wind, while the violin has a peaceful flowing accompaniment.

Variation 15, twice as slow, is a stream of expressive florid melody.

Variation 16, almost twice as fast again, slides smoothly along in a flow of quavers for the orchestra in dialogue between the strings and wind, while the violin weaves gossamer threads over its three upper strings.

In variation 17 the violin sings a lively hunting chorus, in which it rivals the horns of the orchestra.

Again, in variation 18, the full orchestra takes up the challenge. This variation expands into a coda which returns to the minor mode and leads to the finale, a lively movement on the following new theme—

Ex. 2.

Allegro marcato.

which combines, as shown by the lower stave, with a diminution of the original theme. This combination is worked up with several cognate ideas into a brilliant kind of rondo, and the work ends in triumph in the major.

CÉSAR FRANCK

CXVI. VARIATIONS SYMPHONIQUES FOR PIANOFORTE WITH ORCHESTRA

No two art-forms in instrumental music can be much more unlike each other than the two kinds of variation-work represented by Elgar and César Franck. The Elgar Variations are a series of tone-pictures each asserting its own completeness and its contrast with its neighbours, but, with only three exceptions, all very closely confined to their theme. The Franck Variations are a single flowing series forming little more than an episode placed between an introduction about half as long and a finale more than twice as long. The introduction and finale are on a totally different theme from that of the variations, this variation theme being only hinted at in the introduction and being only brought in as a bass counterpoint in two passages in the finale. Of regular variations there are only six, all flowing without change of tempo out of their theme, which is not a long one. In fact the work is a finely and freely organized fantasia with an important episode in variation-form. All the habits of César Franck's style contribute here to the happiest results. He is before all things a master of the extempore manner. This is a very different thing from being a composer who extemporizes on paper. Except in the hands of a master whose experience is so vast that it has become forgotten in the depths of instinct, the process of extemporizing on paper is disastrous, being too slow for spontaneity and too quick for self-criticism. The memory (on which musical form depends) is in a false position, and drugs itself with mechanical copying of recapitulatory passages in the required keys, instead of developing the healthy imagination which vividly realizes the effect a passage will have when it re-appears in the recapitulation.

The improvisatorial manner of Franck is a very different thing; it is a genuine love of portraying the growth of ideas. His introductions and connecting links are vast and ruminating; but Franck does not fall into the error of making them lead only to each other: they lead very surely to the ideas they aim at. The ideas themselves are epigrammatic, like most good things in the French language; and there is no danger of their being lost in the ruminating profundities which surround them. As for the moods and contrasts, with all their subtlety nothing can be clearer. The manner is always openly dramatic without ever descending to theatrical makeshifts. Franck has been compared to Bruckner, the symphonic composer whom the Wagnerian party of the 'seventies hoisted into the position which they loudly denied to Brahms. It seems a pity that Teutonic patriotism forbade them to discover Franck while they were about it. Franck and Bruckner certainly have in common the completest unworldliness, combined with a style which is dramatic in gesture and range, but constitutionally incapable of adapting itself to the theatre. Otherwise, to compare the two composers is unilluminating: it is difficult to exaggerate the clumsiness of Bruckner and the deftness of Franck.

The introduction to these Symphonic Variations states with dramatic roughness a figure (a) which is dimly suggestive of part of the variation theme. The pianoforte, however, answers with something really much more important, figure (b).

Ex. 1.   *Poco allegro.*
                Strings.

These two themes are worked up in dialogue in Franck's delightful ruminating style, together with another idea which I do not
quote. Soon the time changes to 3/4, and the strings (pizzicato,
with staccato wind over a roll of kettledrums) give out two phrases
of the variation theme as it is going to be. The pianoforte, however,
intervenes with a sustained and impassioned speech on the theme
of figure (*b*). Then the orchestra re-enters, and the dialogue is
resumed in ominously dramatic tones. After a fierce climax it
calms down, and at last the pianoforte is free to give out the
variation theme in the shape of the following quiet melody, much
on the lines of that of the middle movement of Franck's Symphony.

Ex. 2.

The first variation is in dialogue (figure by figure) between
pianoforte and orchestra. In the second variation the violoncellos
have the theme. The third is in flowing movement for the pianoforte accompanied by pizzicato chords for strings, the winds
gradually joining in melodically. The fourth variation takes the
theme fortissimo, passing through various keys, in terms of figure
(*a*) in Ex. 1. It expands dramatically and leads to a softer but not
less lively fifth variation in the same rhythm in D major, with an
easily galloping pianoforte accompaniment. This fifth variation
(if it is rightly so counted) dies away into the original key (F sharp
minor) before it is complete; and the sixth variation sails in slowly
in F sharp major. A beautiful meandering counterpoint ripples

throughout the pianoforte part while the theme, in the violoncellos, forms the bass for the first eight bars (you can follow it from Ex. 2). The rest is given by the wind instruments.

Then the mode changes to minor, and slowly, below the flowing arpeggios of the pianoforte, the violoncellos spell out a wonderful dream on the theme of Ex. 1, figure (*b*). There is no more thought now of variations: the rest of the work is concerned with building up a brilliant finale on this other theme. The dreaming passage which leads to this finale is obviously the most poetic part of this very poetic work. The finale itself is quite reckless in its innocent gaiety. It represents the variation theme only by its first two notes (*a*); and the other theme (*b*) is too happy to be shocked at its transformation into a dance-tune.

Ex. 3.

Later on the variation-theme appears to the extent of a clear eight-bar phrase as the bass of one of the episodes in the dance.

Ex. 4.

There is, shortly after this, one hint of dramatic darkness, which gives way to a brief pianoforte passage of peacefully flowing meditation; but soon the lively tempo returns and the work dances cheerfully away to its happy end.

ARTHUR SOMERVELL

CXVII. 'NORMANDY': SYMPHONIC VARIATIONS FOR PIANOFORTE WITH ORCHESTRA

The title of this work refers to its theme, a folk-song sung at the present day by the peasants of Varangeville. The notion of 'symphonic variations' may perhaps also indicate something a little more definite than the mere general importance of the orchestra in their design: certainly it means more than Schumann meant by *Études Symphoniques*. Sir Hubert Parry's Symphonic Variations are strict variations on a short theme, but grouped in four great sections in tempi corresponding suggestively to the first movement, slow movement, scherzo, and finale of a symphony.

Sir Arthur Somervell's variations are, after the first two formal counterstatements of his 'Norman' theme, free fantasias which cannot possibly be numbered off into single variations. The theme, for that matter, is not a closed melody but rather a thing that returns into itself. But these free fantasias have a very obvious resemblance to the four movements of a symphony; though on this view we must regard the three opening statements of the theme, with the following cadenza and allegro, as an introduction; beginning the main movement at the alla breve time, including its important 3/2 section as a middle part, and calling the later group of variations in 4/4 time either a return to the introduction or the first part of the slow movement. All these questions, however, are of less importance than the natural flow and inexhaustible variety of the whole work, which (in times when the motto of musical fashion is *omne absurdum pro magnifico*) are perhaps not so justly appreciated as the opposite qualities would be revered. At present, when a living composer says anything which can readily be understood, there is a real danger that the arbiters of musical fashion will assume first that they have understood all that he has said, and secondly that he has said nothing. Neither progress nor permanence in the fine arts has ever been secured by arbiters of fashion: it is even doubtful whether they have been hindered by them. When a work of art says a great deal, even the most favourable fashions can popularize only a fraction of its meaning. And, as Ruskin pointed out in one of his clearest and most accurate passages, it is really the loose and obscure writer that is least misunderstood: the clear and accurate writer is always taken up in mid-sentence by the careless reader who thinks he agrees with him.

We have here to deal with a clear and spontaneous work of art, so highly organized that its form is free, and so full of point that its clearness does not exhaust its meaning at a single hearing.

After a short and solemnly dramatic introduction, into which the figures of the theme are introduced by the brass instruments intervening softly in a remote key, the pianoforte states the theme in full, each of the two strophes being repeated by the orchestra.

Ex. 1.

The oboe then takes up the theme, which thereafter bursts out in the full orchestra, coming at last to a pause which gives occasion for a cadenza for the pianoforte. Then, in a quick flowing tempo (allegro), the pianoforte begins a free development from figure (*d*) of Ex. 1, and continues, in dialogue with the orchestra, by an impassioned discussion of the three notes comprised in figure (*b*)— the most important and variously treated figure in the work. In spite of the interest of this whole passage it does not advance beyond an introductory manner; the slow tempo returns, with the mood of the original theme; and the figure (*e*), from its close, droops away in dreamy modulations; when suddenly a new movement (molto allegro in 2/2 time) starts with a vigorous awakening.

Ex. 2.

Ex. 2 gives its introductory start, showing figure (*b*). The main new theme, beginning on the tonic, is only harmonically connected with 'Normandy', but when it shifts its key to B flat the orchestra surges up with figure (*d*), and then, in D minor, gets into dialogue with the pianoforte on a new version of (*b*). At the climax there is a pause, and with a change to 3/2 time the pianoforte, imitated by various single instruments, works out a sustained and melodious new development of (*b*).

Ex. 3.

The orchestra interpolates a sentence which puts figure (*d*) into a similar new light. The pianoforte then resumes its sustained treatment of (*b*) with a shifted accent and a more flowing accompaniment. Soon the inner parts of the orchestra get to work on the theme of the molto allegro. The hint is not taken at once; but eventually, after very remote modulations, the pianoforte asks suggestive questions, and the horn gives impressive warnings (figure (*a*), across the 3/2 time). The main theme of the molto allegro then swings back in such a way that the precise moment of the change back to 2/2 time is imperceptible. It continues on the same lines as before, but coming to its climax in the tonic, which gives it a distinct air of allusion to the form of a symphonic first movement. Its final close plunges into a return to a slower tempo, exactly half its pace, and slightly suggestive of the mood of the opening. What follows is in the manner of a sustained variation of 'Normandy', chiefly in terms of figure (*c*). The pianoforte takes it up serenely with a sudden change to the major mode; and this change is followed up with increasingly intense calm and happiness. Here for the first time some development is made of the last figure (*f*) of the theme. Then the note deepens, as the pianoforte recalls the rhythmic figure of (*a*) (which has been absent for some time); and with a change of time a new section begins, which that figure pervades in great solemnity, with masses of deep harmony in the brass.

Ex. 4. *Adagio.*

This is worked up with great breadth and swing twice to a solemn climax and a not less solemn quiet close. When it has died away the drum turns the rhythmic figure of (*a*) into a lively introduction to what may fitly be called a scherzo; of which the main theme is as follows:

Ex. 5.

It alternates with a trio in which still more of the figures of 'Normandy' are neatly embodied, while the drum maintains the rhythm of Ex. 5.

Ex. 6.

Modulating widely, this trio leads back to Ex. 5 in a new key, from which it easily swings back, not to its starting-point, E minor, but to its second key, G major, and thus rushes straight on into the finale. This begins in a very original way, with a series of wide

curling arpeggios ending in violent chords on the fourth beat of
a 4/4 bar. This explosive utterance conceals a ground bass—

Ex. 7.

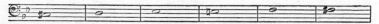

on which the first part of the finale proceeds. The eleven variations
on this ground show great variety in their unity; with the fifth
there is a change to triple time, to say nothing of the happy entrance
of the major mode for this one variation; at the ninth the 4/4 time
returns, and the eleventh is a fierce climax. Meantime the figures
of 'Normandy' have been very happily interwoven at various points
above the ground-bass, so that when the fury of the climax is spent
nothing can be more natural than that the tune itself should,
especially in its second part with figure (c), swing lustily in and
stride from key to key with growing zest until the whole orchestra
brings the work to a triumphant end.

DOHNANYI

CXVIII. VARIATIONS ON A NURSERY SONG, FOR ORCHESTRA
WITH PIANOFORTE, OP. 23

The composer has dedicated this work 'to the enjoyment of lovers
of humour and to the annoyance of others'. And we know that the
man who can write comedies as well as tragedies makes better and
wiser tragedies than the man who is annoyed by comedy. There is
nothing unreal or undignified in the artistic organization and emotional range of this work, which must rank high among the modern
classics in one of the severest of art-forms.

The work begins very tragically, the brass being specially afflicted.

Ex. 1.

Through this 'symphony in Woe minor', a solemn canto fermo of eight notes—

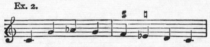

Ex. 2.

(with sharps and flats that come and go) looms large in the horns. The tragic introduction dies away—

Ex. 3.

—with a bang; and then the pianoforte enters with the theme—which explains the solemn canto fermo. (Nothing will induce me to quote it.) The string orchestra accompanies with delight, in harmonies that become increasingly learned as confidence is gained; until at the last clause a bassoon bursts out with the venerable ecstasy of the parent of the Jabberwock-slayer who 'chortled in his joy'.

The first six variations follow the theme closely in combinations and dialogue with different groups; of which we may mention the two-flutes-and-piccolo *versus* two-bassoons-and-contra-fagotto of Var. 4; Var. 5, with its combination of pianoforte, harp, and bells (the bells giving the theme in its form of canto fermo with the sharps and flats that come and go); and the astonishingly ingenious Var. 6, an étude for pianoforte and wind instruments without parallel in classical or modern orchestration.

Ex. 4.
Wood-wind.

Pianoforte.

With Var. 7, the theme blossoms out into a spirited Viennese Waltz, developed at leisure.

Ex. 5.

Var. 8 is a March, glum but dogged. Into the guileless tonality of
the underlying theme, the sharps and flats come and go with such
freedom that the foundations of the key settle and heave with
alarming irregularity.

Ex. 6.

The next variation is a scherzo full of grim surprises—

Ex. 7.

—such as the unison of the piccolo and contrafagotto with the
canto fermo; and it culminates in a desperate recitative of the
pianoforte which leads to Var. 10, a passacaglia, or solemn dance
on a ground-bass—the ground-bass being our canto fermo in the
minor mode. As the first of the eight notes of this canto fermo is
the same as the last, its recurrences overlap the eight-bar rhythm
by one note. Röntgen hit on the same device in the Waltz in
his *Azzopardi Variations*, a *jeu d'esprit* I hope some day to describe.

Ex. 8.

The pace gradually increases until the whole orchestra finds itself
wailing like the brass in the introduction (see Ex. 1), and at last the
theme bursts out in the major (Var. 11) as a chorale. The harmonies, as usual, become more and more chromatic as the tune
proceeds, drifting into the whole-tone scale of Deomnibussy (which
is a more eclectic affair than that of Debussy). It dies down, and,
after a dispute between the pianoforte and the wind as to what
the key shall be, the finale breaks away in a merry fugue.

Ex. 9.

The subject and counter-subject of this fugue are just as happy inverted as right side up, and after a brilliant climax the original theme of childhood returns. It is not surprising that its adventures have taught it a new and elegant phrasing which it had not possessed when it first appeared. There is some little argument over its last notes, but the contrafagotto agrees with the piccolo as to how that should be settled, and the orchestra gathers itself up and hastens to reach the end in time with the pianoforte's final glissando.

SPOHR

CXIX. SCENA CANTANTE FOR VIOLIN WITH ORCHESTRA

1 *Allegro molto, leading to* 2 *Adagio, leading to* 3 *Andante, introductory to* 4 *Allegro moderato.*

Spohr was one of the best of men; and he enjoyed an amiable self-satisfaction which is one of the rarest rewards of virtue. He was never more satisfied than when he had invented a new art-form; a feat which he accomplished with consummate ease, because with him the new form required no change of matter. Once upon a time he gave a concert at Milan. Fearing that the public there would not appreciate a symphonic concerto, he had the brilliant idea of writing a concerto in the style of an operatic scena. His delight at the success of this new art-form resembled that of a hen which should have the intelligence to be pleased rather than frightened when its clutch of supposititious ducklings took to swimming. Of course a concerto in operatic scena form is bound to succeed; for the classical concerto form itself is a glorification of aria form, and has in fact no other origin. For the rest, Spohr's experiment produced in later times the G minor Concerto of Max Bruch, besides a host of kindred phenomena in the concertos of Saint-Saëns and other adroit masters.

The opening Allegro requires no quotation, the orchestral theme being a formal prelude (in A minor and a marching rhythm) to a recitative by the violin. This leads to an aria in F major, of which Ex. 1—

Ex. 1.

is the first subject; Ex. 2—

Ex. 2.

the second subject; while the middle section, in remoter keys, is in
2/4 time—

and is a *locus classicus* for the power of a solo violin's fourth string
to penetrate a high-lying and elaborate accompaniment skilfully
devised for transparency.

Another recitative (andante) leads to the finale, a symphonically
developed movement (Spohr's fear of the Milan public has
vanished) with a theme unusually majestic for a concerto finale.

The second subject, however, shows the aristocratic composer's
most seductive frivolity—

and so does the indolent middle episode.

Schumann very wisely warned the superior person against supposing that Spohr's facility was a thing any one could easily imitate.
One need not at this time of day hear enough of Spohr to find his
mannerisms cloying; but in his best concertos and violin duets
(which are really astonishing *tours de force* in sonorous handling
of small material resources) his mannerisms do not overdo themselves; and his sense of beauty is such as only an unhealthy taste
will despise.

MENDELSSOHN

CXX. VIOLIN CONCERTO IN E MINOR, OF. 64

1 *Allegro molto appassionato, leading to* 2 *Andante, leading to*
3 *Allegretto non troppo, leading to* 4 *Allegro molto vivace.*

How often do we hear the most remarkable stroke of genius in
this most popular of violin concertos? I had not heard it in 1921,
when I wrote this analysis. The manners of British concert-goers
have improved since then; and even then my audience was not
offended at being told that a burst of applause between the first
movement and the andante obliterates a dramatic orchestral effect
and reduces the introductory bars of the andante to one of those
ugly misconstruings which produce the conviction (ascribed by
a Master of Balliol to the British schoolboy) that no nonsense is
too enormous to be a possible translation from a classical author.
I have never been able to make out why, when disaster overtakes
this connecting link, conductors do not adopt the only possible
remedy, which is simply to repeat the short final tutti, and so secure
that Mendelssohn's intention shall somehow be realized.

Mendelssohn is supposed to be the typical classicist in music;
that is to say, he is supposed to be the master of those who after
a classical period imitate the classical forms faithfully and skilfully.
As a matter of fact, the best works of Mendelssohn have all in
their respective ways been the starting-points of some musical
revolution. Mendelssohn may truthfully be said to have destroyed
the classical concerto form, inasmuch as his perennially beautiful
Violin Concerto and his two somewhat faded pianoforte concertos
revealed to all contemporary and later composers an easy way of
evading a problem which only Mozart and Beethoven could either
state or solve in terms of the highest art. In the Violin Concerto
Mendelssohn's inspiration is high and vigorous. He is not so much
evading a classical problem as producing a new if distinctly lighter
art-form. It is not unprofitable to speculate whether the pathetic
and tranquil second subject (Ex. 3) would not have gained in depth
and dramatic power if some hint of its melody had been given
with force and passion in the first energetic orchestral tutti. This
could very well have been managed with no notable increase in
length of that tutti, and would have instantly brought the first
movement into the lines of a genuine development of Beethoven's
concerto style, besides anticipating by some forty years Brahms's
re-discovery of the true function of the orchestra in a concerto.
But the possibility escaped Mendelssohn's notice, and was indeed
very unlikely to occur to a man who had twice before deliberately

suppressed the orchestral tutti, function and all, in his treatment of the concerto form. His Violin Concerto thus became the
original type of the majority of modern concertos; and being, as
it is, an original inspiration, it is far greater than any work that
has ever followed its tradition. Again and again it turns up as a
source of inspiration for later composers, many of whom would
be horrified at the notion of confessing a debt to anything so
old-fashioned. Yet I rather envy the enjoyment of any one who
should hear the Mendelssohn concerto for the first time and find
that, like *Hamlet*, it was full of quotations. This being so, I will
leave the rest of my description to the most necessary of the
quotations, viz. the first theme—

Ex. 1.

&c.

given out in full by the solo violin and worked up to a climax on
which the orchestra breaks in; the transition theme—

Ex. 2.

given out by the orchestra and developed by the solo violin; and
the second subject—

Ex. 3.

&c.

given out by the wood-wind above the famous long holding note
which the violin supplies as bass. The usual procedure in concertos
is for the brilliant passages of the solo player to culminate in a shake
closing into the re-entry of the orchestra. Mendelssohn here makes
his brilliant passages an accompaniment to the first theme. They
do culminate in a shake; but, by one of Mendelssohn's wittiest
inspirations, it is the orchestra that bursts out with the shake,
which the violin answers with impassioned dialogue from the first
theme. The development begins with the transition theme and
comes to its climax in a remote key with one of those intensely
quiet passages of slow return to the tonic which Mendelssohn

always executes with consummate mastery, and sometimes, as here, with the poetic power of a great composer. On to this passage is grafted the cadenza which, both for its unusual position in the movement and its extraordinary skill and effectiveness, constitutes one of Mendelssohn's most famous strokes of genius. Here, as elsewhere in the concerto, Mendelssohn's example has been imitated with disastrous consequences by less adroit composers, notably in a once well-known and well-meaning violoncello sonata by Rubinstein. You must not transplant Mendelssohn's cadenza *totidem notis* into every place where you find it better than anything of your own invention.

Mendelssohn's cadenza is of extreme simplicity, which conceals an almost Greek subtlety of fitness. It is thoroughly dramatic in the way in which it prepares for the return to the opening theme. The orchestra softly brings the first subject into full swing as the arpeggios of the violin settle to a rapid spin; and the recapitulation follows an easy and effective course, omitting much and expanding nothing, until the coda, which moves in faster tempo to a stormy end. But hush!—what is this that emerges from the last chord?

Ex. 4.

Few things in music are more essentially ugly than a vague and meaningless introduction to a lyric melody, designed with the avowed and sole aim of marking time 'till ready'. Of such introductions this opening of Mendelssohn's andante has most unjustly been made the prototype. It is no such thing, except when untimely applause has made it begin with a nonsensical entry of the bassoon on nothing in particular, followed by a few other fumbling notes which can only drift from the unintelligible to the obvious. What Mendelssohn wrote and meant was one of his most romantic changes of key and mood. And it is perfectly naïve: all the spurious imitations in the world will not rob it of its freshness.

The movement has true breadth and dignity. Its middle episode, which I need not quote, achieves a real expression of agitation and anxiety without the fussiness which Mendelssohn was too often apt to express instead; and the serene coda is of that childlike truth and simplicity which it is an insult to call pretty.

The wistful little allegretto that connects the andante with the finale is also quite an unspoilt child. The finale has perhaps been the cause of some unpleasing perkinesses in ill-bred descendants— but there is no doubt about its own good-breeding. Its first theme I quote in its combination with a sedate new theme that first appears in G major in later developments.

Ex. 5.

The second subject—

Ex. 6.

is undeniably 'cheeky'; but we can stand this from Mendelssohn in this work—just as we can stand it from Rossini. I doubt whether Mendelssohn was particularly tolerant of it in Rossini: 'cheekiness' is an aristocratic schoolboy term of reproach, and no two schools can abide each other's 'cheek'. But all schools unite in the detestation of an outsider's imitation of their own 'cheek'; and we can enjoy these indiscretions of Mendelssohn and Rossini because the delinquents are not imitators, but complete if unscrupulous masters of the situation. And so this finale spins along in high spirits, in which no one need be ashamed to share. It is not in Schiller's world of Joy as attained by Beethoven—the world where 'all men are brothers'; but if it cannot ignore the superior person it has every right to poke fun at him.

SCHUMANN

CXXI. PIANOFORTE CONCERTO IN A MINOR, OP. 54

1 *Allegro affetuoso.* 2 *Intermezzo: Andantino grazioso, leading to*
3 *Allegro vivace.*

There is a depth and a breadth in Schumann's lyric vein which
already shows that it was no mistaken ambition that led him to turn
from it to larger designs. His career was shortened and clouded by
illness, but this concerto is one of at least a dozen large works which
utterly refute the Wagnerian judgement of Schumann as a might-
have-been. A work so eminently beautiful from beginning to end,
so free, spacious, and balanced in form, and so rich and various in
ideas, is more than proof that Schumann was justified in attempting
any and every art-problem. It is a worthy monument to the sanity
of art; and while it illuminates the tragic pathos of Schumann's
later years, it is itself untouched.

The first movement, composed in 1841, had an independent
existence for four years as a fantasia for pianoforte and orchestra.
Thus, though it has all the essentials of a very big first movement
in sonata form, it never professed to be the first movement of a
classical concerto. The orchestra makes no attempt to muster its
forces for its own full connected statement of the themes. At the
climaxes it bursts out with a short triumphant passage in the
manner of a ritornello; but for the most part it behaves very much
as the strings behave in Schumann's quintet: though it has far
more colour, and is, for all its reticence, much above Schumann's
normal achievement in its purity and brightness of tone.

My first quotation gives the energetic introductory figure (*a*),
which leads to the first theme, and is used once in the development.

Ex. 1.

After the pianoforte has answered the plaintive cantabile theme,
the violins give a transition theme—

Ex. 2.

of which the figure (*c*) becomes very important later. The second subject is made of a broad stream of impulsive melody derived from (*b*) of the first theme—

Ex. 3.

and using figure (*c*) in the course of its dialogue. Figure (*c*) also forms the text of the triumphant ritornello with which the orchestra bursts in at the climax. Then there is a dramatic change of key to A flat, in which remote region the pianoforte gives out an altogether new version of the first theme (*b*) in slow 6/4 time, in the tenderest of dialogues with the orchestra. When this comes to its natural close, the pianoforte breaks abruptly into the original tempo with figure (*a*), and then proceeds to work up figure (*b*) in an impassioned stream of melody, joined by more and more of the orchestra and driving irresistibly through a wide range of key until at last it resigns itself in a solemn close into the main theme in the home tonic.

From this point the recapitulation follows its normal course, until the point where the orchestra is to break in with its ritornello. But here the pianoforte goes on playing through it, and soon breaks its way into an unaccompanied cadenza. A triumphantly para doxical feature of this very happy outburst of apparently extempore eloquence is that its themes happen to be entirely new until at last figure (*b*) appears below a long trill. Then the threads, new and old, are gathered together, and the orchestra re-enters with figure (*b*) marching at the double, in 2/4 time. Much passion lies suppressed in the gallant spirit of this march, which approaches, makes its climax, and recedes into romantic distance, until at last it flashes out in an abrupt end.

Whatever Schumann may have felt about this fantasia in 1841, his instinct was true when in 1845 he recognized that it was only the first movement of a larger work. The slow movement is of the very centre of Schumann's most intimate and tender vein; childlike in its gently playful opening—

Ex. 4.

while in its sustained, swinging second theme—

Ex. 5.

it attains a beauty and depth quite transcendent of any mere prettiness, though the whole concerto, like all Schumann's deepest music, is recklessly pretty.

Nothing can be more romantic than the coda, in which figure (*b*) of the first movement reappears and leads dramatically into the finale.

From the six or seven important themes of this glorious movement I select the first subject—

Ex. 6.

the second subject with its famous *deux-temps* rhythm—

Ex. 7.

&c.

the new theme which appears in the course of the rich development—

Ex. 8.

and the delightful surprise of another brilliant new theme which cheerfully begins the coda as soon as the recapitulation is over.

Ex. 9.

Never has a long and voluble peroration been more masterly in its proportions and more perfectly in character with the great whole which it crowns with so light a touch. Every note inspires affection, and only an inattentive critic can suspect the existence of weaknesses to condone. Fashion and musical party-politics have tried to play many games with Schumann's reputation, but works like this remain irresistible.

CXXII. VIOLONCELLO CONCERTO IN A MINOR, OP. 129

1 *Nicht zu schnell; leading to* 2 *Langsam; leading to* 3 *Sehr lebhaft.*

Schumann's Violoncello Concerto, long regarded as a thankless task, has been brought to light in the present day by consummate musicianship and sense of beauty on the part of a leader among those violoncellists who refuse to confine the possibilities of their instru-

ment to the obvious. The scoring of this concerto is no obstacle to
its performance, being remarkably free from the dangerous thickness of Schumann's usual orchestral style. In general his orchestral
sense is at its best in his accompanying of solos of all kinds. If
the violoncello seems, on a first hearing, to be at any disadvantage,
this is not because the accompaniment (*Begleitung des Orchesters*
is Schumann's own title) is heavy, but because the form shows
little or no disposition to expand. Terse exposition, short ruminating developments, and interludes all gathered up as quickly as
possible to the business of schematic recapitulation; every feature
indicates Schumann's growing dislike of anything that could be
called display. Still, the work was written before this dislike
merged into the morbid condition which ended in fatal illness. The
qualities of the violoncello are exactly those of the beloved enthusiastic dreamer whom we know as Schumann; and as a flow
of intimate melody the first two movements rank high in his art.
The finale, too, has its point. In the 'eighties Kensington used to
compare Browning with Brahms. The unavowed reason for this
profundity was that both begin with Br: the more conscious reason
was that both were considered obscure, manly, and rugged.
Brahms, who throughout his life spent as much pains in smoothing
his style as Browning took in winning and carrying off his bride,
would probably have not been flattered by the comparison had he
been more conscious of the existence of Kensington or of England.
But there is a real analogy between Schumann and Browning. Both
are the 'essentially manly' poets of people who innocently wallow
in sentiment: and when Schumann is nervous he is apt to develop
exactly Browning's habit of digging you in the ribs and illustrating
grave realities with some crack-jaw quadruple rhyme. And so we
may accept Schumann's finale as Browningesque.

The following list of themes will suffice for all purposes of
analysis.

Ex. 1 is a broad melody, announced, after three opening chords,
by the violoncello, and developed for thirty bars to a climax.

The orchestra enters with an impassioned new theme—

built up into a short tutti, into which the violoncello breaks with ruminating phrases leading into C major. Here they grow into a regular second group. From this one figure requires quotation, with its simplification in the wood-wind, which becomes prominent in many sequels.

The movement runs its course with all Schumann's quiet antithetic rhetoric.

The development begins by introducing an agitated triplet figure, traceable perhaps to a casual ornamental detail in previous violoncello passages.

Later on the violoncello combines with Ex. 4 another figure (which persons who pay super-tax on brains may derive from Ex. 5 by 'augmentation' without making the slightest difference to its intelligibility).

This develops into one of the most thoughtful passages in the work, and leads to the first theme (Ex. 1) in F sharp minor, soon broadly moving to the tonic, A minor, where a full normal recapitulation follows.

A short tutti (compare Ex. 5) leads to a sudden dramatic change of key and tempo, and the slow movement which now follows consists of a single lyrical melody in F major. No quotation is required, but the listener should mark the exquisite moment where the violoncello sings in slow double-stops—a triumph of Schumann's instrumental imagination.

The orchestra alludes to Ex. 1, which the violoncello continues in agitated recitative, combining it with topics from the slow movement and other themes, until it breaks into the finale, with a bluff reaction against sentiment.

Ex. 7.

'Cello.

Ex. 8.

Gentler utterances (especially the main figure of Ex. 1) contrive nevertheless to work their way into the design; and the provocative first theme itself strikes tender notes as a second subject, in spite of gibes from the violas.

Ex. 9.

An ingenious cadenza, remarkable, like most of this concerto, for its predilection for the lower strings of the violoncello, leads to a rapid coda, in which keen listeners will detect an allusion to Ex. 5. Ingenious as Schumann's cadenza is, there is good classical precedent for letting the violoncellist produce something not quite so gruff. Jacobi has written an excellent one, piously in touch with Schumann's *Innigkeit* and efficacious in conciliating us with the finale as a whole. Jacobi having thus broken the ice, I confess to some hankering to try and write a cadenza myself; but Schumann's shyness is very deterrent.

CXXIII. INTRODUCTION AND ALLEGRO APPASSIONATO
FOR PIANOFORTE WITH ORCHESTRA, OP. 92

I cannot account for the neglect of this work, which has always
seemed to me to be one of Schumann's happiest and most inventive
pieces. Even its orchestration is unusually successful, with little
of the thickness and few of the risks of Schumann's orchestral
writing.

The introduction, with its recklessly pretty romantic theme—

Ex. 1.

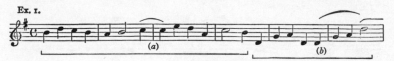

is really beautifully scored; and both the form and matter of the
allegro appassionato are admirably dramatic and in perfect proportion. The Allegro starts in a towering temper in E minor—

Ex. 2.

suddenly yielding to a quieter but energetically rising theme
starting in C.

Ex. 3.

This only establishes E minor more firmly, and a new theme sets
the action of the drama fully in motion.

Ex. 4.

Another figure arises out of this, which I quote as it occurs later,
on the dominant of C.

Ex. 5.

It leads to a second group preceded (as the example shows) by
figure (b) from Ex. 1, which figure now becomes an important
factor in the development.

Ex. 6.

(b)

The second group contains several more themes and is one of Schumann's finest specimens of the art of making flowing paragraphs. The way in which the aforesaid figure (b) insinuates itself into the texture is admirable; and so is the brilliant staccato theme (unquoted) which provokes the trumpets to assert the triplet figure of Ex. 2.

The development begins quietly with Ex. 3 on a chord of F, which promptly leads back to E minor, where Ex. 4 re-enters, soon to modulate further. Ex. 5 is taken up busily, but suddenly the theme of the introduction, Ex. 1, floats in above. With these threads a fine and dramatic development is built up, with none of the stiffness that may be imputed to many of Schumann's longer forms elsewhere. The return comes at the top of a grand climax, and the subtlety of the whole design is revealed by the fact that G major, the key of the introduction, proves to be that chosen for the recapitulation of the second subject, instead of E, the key of Ex. 2. The theme of the introduction again intervenes (in B flat, a soft and dark key in relation to G) at the beginning of the coda, the rest of which is greatly enlivened by a deliciously voluble new theme—

Ex. 7.

such as only the Schumann of the Quintet and the Pianoforte Concerto could invent.

SAINT-SAËNS

CXXIV. FOURTH CONCERTO FOR PIANOFORTE IN C MINOR, OP. 44

1 *Allegro moderato, leading to* 2 *Andante.* 3 *Allegro vivace, leading to* 4 *Andante, leading to* 5 *Allegro.*

Saint-Saëns's Fourth Pianoforte Concerto is, even more than the other adroit and brilliant essays of its composer in this form, on a plan which brings its various movements into a unity of themes without losing their individual character as types of movement.

In many respects it reminds us of his most ambitious orchestral work, the Third Symphony, in which, stimulated by the desire to commemorate Liszt, Saint-Saëns has still more closely followed the general method of transforming themes *en masse* shown in Liszt's *chef-d'œuvre*, the Faust Symphony.

But Saint-Saëns's Fourth Concerto is both more attractive in theme and more terse in form than his Third Symphony. Yet the forms, in spite of the terseness of the whole, are very broad. Saint-Saëns here deals with quite symmetrical and complete melodies, and treats them in a simple but resourceful variation-form. The first movement starts at once with a broad symmetrical melody in two parts, of which Ex. 1 is the opening.

Ex. 1.

Each half of this fine theme is given out by the strings, and repeated by the pianoforte. Then follow two regular variations. In the first variation the 'cellos have the theme as bass to the harmony, and the pianoforte repeats the clauses with florid ornamentation.

In the second variation, the full orchestra gives out the clauses forte; the repetitions give a syncopated version of the melody to the wood-wind, while the pianoforte accompanies with arpeggios. This leads to a climax, in which the pianoforte and the wood-wind break into a new theme, which I quote, for convenience, not in the form in which it occurs here, but in the compressed form in which it later on appears as a scherzo theme.

Ex. 2.

At present it dies away into a cloudy close in the major, and leads to an andante in A flat. After a long passage of dusky arpeggios a chorale-tune emerges. [It is impossible not to be thrilled by Gustav Doré.]

Ex. 3.

It takes shape in four symmetrical phrases, after which the pianoforte gives out a new theme.

Ex. 4.

This is very soon worked up by diminution (quavers instead of crotchets) and, after coming to a dramatic climax, leads to a triumphant re-statement of the chorale. After this, Ex. 4 is worked out again broadly to a quiet conclusion, with a romantic pianissimo cadenza. Thus this first of the two divisions into which Saint-Saëns has grouped the concerto has no resemblance whatever to any other concerto form, but is simply a broad exposition of the material for the whole work.

The second division of the work begins with Ex. 2 in its compressed form as the opening of a brilliant scherzo in C minor. Soon Ex. 1 follows in G minor the dominant, hurrying along in quavers. It soon moves excitedly to E flat major, in which an extremely lively second subject appears. It deserves to break the bank at Monte Carlo, being much stronger than its twin brother the once popular song of that exploit. [Sir Henry Hadow has remarked that the public of that period accepted the illustrator of the *Contes Drolatiques* as a great religious teacher. Compare Ex. 3.]

Ex. 5.

After some development with a few other accessories, the opening of the scherzo returns, and takes a somewhat different course, which, after the climax, dies away dramatically. Then the diminished form of Ex. 4 is worked out in a solemn and mysterious fugue in the original andante tempo, the first phrase of the chorale tune itself being once heard. There is an exciting crescendo; and the pianoforte, breaking into a cadenza, leads to the triumphant finale. This begins by taking the whole chorale tune in a lively triple-time.

Ex. 6.

Here again, as in the first movement, breadth and clearness is attained by quite simple repetitions of this square melody, with varieties of scoring. A diminished derivative—

Ex. 7.

leads to other developments and new accessories. One of these should be quoted (overleaf)—

No. 8.

for the sake of its brilliant combination with a transformation of
Ex. 4, together with an inner part derived from the continuation
of Ex. 6.

Ex. 9.

With these materials, the finale wends its easy way to a triumphant
end.

N.B. The remarks in [ ] are not addressed to concert audiences.

CXXV. VIOLONCELLO CONCERTO IN A MINOR, OP. 33

1 *Allegro non troppo, leading to* 2 *Allegretto con moto, leading to*
3 *Tempo primo, leading to* 4 *Un peu moins vite.*

The worldly wisdom of Saint-Saëns is at its best and kindliest in
this opusculum, which is pure and brilliant without putting on
chastity as a garment, and without calling attention to its jewellery
at a banquet of poor relations.

Here, for once, is a violoncello concerto in which the solo instrument displays every register throughout its compass without the
slightest difficulty in penetrating the orchestral accompaniment.
All the adroitness of Saint-Saëns is shown herein, and also in the
compact form of the work, which, following Mendelssohn in
abolishing all orchestral tuttis, except connecting links, goes
further than Mendelssohn inasmuch as it relegates to the finale
the function of the recapitulation in the first movement, and thus
combines the effect of three movements with that of a single design.

The violoncello opens at full speed with a lively subject in cross-
rhythms that evidently means business.

Ex. 1.

The second subject is a Schumannesque epigram, of which the
tender mood is soon broken into by the business of Ex. 1.

Ex. 2.

An orchestral interlude on new material—

Ex. 3.

leads to a development that, instead of going to remote keys, returns to that of Ex. 2, which it expands, leading peacefully into B flat. (Saint-Saëns has often made effective use of keys a semitone apart, as here, A minor to B flat; the B minor Violin Concerto with its slow movement in B flat; the C-minor-D-flat pair in his Third Symphony; the C minor Violoncello Sonata, &c.)

The middle movement, a slow-movement scherzo, suggests a group of those little dancers supported on a tripod of bristles that move so prettily if you put them on the lid of a pianoforte and play.

Ex. 4.

The violoncello enters ruminatively—

Ex. 5.

and accompanies the dance with sustained melody, taking up its figures only at the end, to subside into Ex. 4 in deep bass: whereupon the orchestra brings back the business of Ex. 1 and leads to the finale.

This begins with a new melancholy tune (compare Ex. 5)—

Ex. 6.

which is followed by a bustling semiquaver theme which I do not quote.

There is a calm middle episode, giving the lower strings of the violoncello a welcome opportunity to sing.

Ex. 7.

III   O

After Ex. 6 returns, the design of the whole work is completed
by further use of Ex. 1, and by the reappearance of Ex. 3 in A
minor. Whereupon the violoncello triumphantly sings quite a new
tune in A major. And so they lived happily ever after.

MAX BRUCH

CXXVI. VIOLIN CONCERTO IN G MINOR, OP. 26

1 PRELUDE: *Allegro moderato, leading to* 2 *Adagio.*
3 FINALE: *Allegro energico.*

When Max Bruch died at the age of 83, the news came to many as
a revelation that he had lived so long. Though he never dominated
the musical world as Spohr did in his own day, yet he was the type
of artist universally accepted as a master, about whose works no
controversy could arise because no doubt was possible as to their
effectiveness and sincerity. Like Spohr, he achieved this mastery
in all art-forms; and, unlike Spohr, he developed no irritating
mannerisms. If it were possible to imagine a large work by Spohr
in which there were no cloying chromatic harmonies, the idea
would closely correspond with that of a masterpiece by Max Bruch.
At present it seems the correct thing to say that his G minor Violin
Concerto is his only surviving work; but the two other violin concertos (both in D minor) and the Scottish Fantasia need nothing
but the attention of violinists to prove quite as grateful to performers as to the public. Moreover, I find myself entirely in
agreement with the writer of the article in Grove's *Dictionary*
who says that Bruch's greatest mastery lies in the treatment of
chorus and orchestra; and I have not the slightest doubt that a
revival of Bruch's *Odysseus* (which the writer regards as his most
successful work), and perhaps still more of his last choral work,
a Kyrie and Sanctus, which I heard in Berlin in 1907, would
make a fresh and stirring impression on any audience that will
listen naïvely to beautiful music for music's sake. Poorer things
have survived from the enormous output of Spohr, simply because players periodically rediscover their effectiveness. Spohr
and Mendelssohn were so completely idolized by a masterful
majority of musicians in their own day that grave injustice was
done to all music in which new and refractory elements were
struggling for expression. The result was that kind of so-called
classical period which should accurately be called pseudo-classical.
The injustice of a pseudo-classical period produces with the swing
of the pendulum another kind of injustice in the next generation.
No art is then allowed to have any merit that does not consist
almost exclusively of new and refractory elements nobly struggling

for expression. This does not repair the older injustice, it merely
transfers it. Clever people tell us that you can train a poodle to
produce pseudo-classical art. If this is true, you have only to shave
your poodle hind part foremost and let its hair grow where formerly
it was shaven, and the very same poodle will produce art in which
refractory new elements are nobly struggling for expression. But
after all, in the long run mastery tells.

The lot of a fastidious artist, conscious of mastery as a gift
entrusted to him during a period of destruction, is not enviable;
nor, perhaps, do the wisest of masters so regard their own personal
mastery or their own period. Brahms's mastery was so great that
it gave rise to furious controversy, but he knew how to extricate
himself from encounters with the shockable; and on the few occasions when he encountered Max Bruch his disposition to tease
appeared at its worst. Lovers of music ought, at this time of day,
to show more gratitude to those who devote themselves to making
beautiful things. It is not easy to write as beautifully as Max Bruch.
'But', you will say, 'that does not go to the root of the matter:
perhaps the very reason why this beauty of yours bores us is that
we see it is a mere matter of mastery over difficulty.' If you can
see that in the case of Max Bruch, I give it up; but I find his case
quite different. It is really easy for Bruch to write beautifully, it
is in fact instinctive for him; and such instinct is a matter which
all modern critics and psychologists will agree to rate very high.
Further, it is impossible to find in Max Bruch any lapses from
the standard of beauty which he thus instinctively sets himself.
I have only to call attention to the second subject of the rondo of
this concerto as a touchstone. There are several popular violin
concertos which now hold the field, and in all of them the second
subject of the rondo is a most regrettable incident, and is also the
most popular feature of the work. I forbear to name the instances
but it is surely significant that this most successful of Max Bruch's
works shows one of its noblest features just where some of its most
formidable rivals become vulgar.

The concerto is in three movements, only two of which are
complete. Instead of the formidable organization of a first movement in classical concerto-form with a great orchestral exposition
of themes afterwards to be fully developed in sonata-form by the
solo player, Bruch contents himself with a prelude in which the solo
violin enters into a solemn dramatic dialogue with the orchestra.
The themes do not require quotation, though soon after the main
key G minor has been established, a contrasted melody, quite
definite enough for a second subject, appears in the key of B flat.
In spite of this, however, the manner of the whole movement is
introductory; it is an introduction so broad that it tends to take a

definite shape; and we need not do it the injustice to imagine that it
was merely an abortive first movement. Thus its design is not cut
short but is completed when, after the violin has returned to G
minor, the orchestra comes storming in with a vigorous tutti, in
which the gentle second theme has become an impassioned outburst in the minor. When this has run its course, it subsides into
the opening phrases, and the declamation of the solo violin returns
in greater elaboration. Suddenly the orchestra bursts out in
pathetic enthusiasm on the dominant of E flat, and leads to the
second movement, a fully developed slow movement in sonata-
form. I quote the three main themes; the first subject—

Ex. 1.

the all-important transition theme—

Ex. 2.

and the second subject as it appears in the bass below florid
counterpoint (unquoted) of the solo violin.

Ex. 3.

The exposition of the second subject ends with Ex. 2, which is
always used to effect cardinal action in the piece. By way of
development we have an expanded version of the first subject in
G flat, followed by the transition theme, Ex. 2, in the same key
with a beautiful new melody above on the solo violin. By degrees
this works round to the tonic, E flat, with a crescendo; and now
occurs with the entry of the orchestra, a masterly and dramatic
stroke of form which I summarize in outline.

Ex. 4.

This shows how the first bar of Ex. 2 is taken up by one orchestral group after the other, until the second subject enters grandly below and so carries us out on the full tide of its recapitulation. The coda is grafted very simply and naturally on to this and brings the movement to a peaceful end.

The finale begins in the key of the slow movement with an excited crescendo anticipating the figure of its main theme and swinging round to G major. It works out a broad and transparent scheme with the aid of its lively first subject—

and its bold and noble second subject.

There is no lack of rich accessory themes, but they can be appreciated without quotation. Max Bruch's First Violin Concerto thoroughly deserves the great success it has always had. Nobody who can appreciate it will believe for a moment that its composer has written nothing else worthy of the like success.

C. V. STANFORD

CXXVII. CLARINET CONCERTO, IN ONE MOVEMENT, OP. 80

This work, composed in 1902, presents a masterly solution of the problem of a modern clarinet concerto. Although it is described as in one movement, it contains, like the Violoncello Concerto of Saint-Säens in the same key, all the essentials of three closely connected movements; a first movement, a slow movement, and a finale. Of these three the slow movement is a complete design. The first movement and the finale complete each other, and surround the slow movement with their own symmetry. The character of the clarinet is revealed in its full range, including that earliest of its functions which the classical treatment of the instrument has relegated to obscurity, its military tones. These are indeed idealized as chivalry, but they provide plenty of contrast to the more feminine accents, to the dramatic ecstasies and sweetnesses of this most resourceful of wind instruments. Most of the themes throughout the work are derived from two figures which I first give in their common formulas.

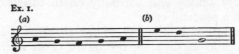

Ex. 1.

The first theme starts at once vigorously in the full orchestra and is promptly challenged by the clarinet.

Ex. 2.

My quotations show by the letters (a) and (b) how far the themes may be referred to the two formulas given in Ex. 1. Before the key changes another theme requires quotation, part of its purport being to combine with figure (a).

Ex. 3.

Soon after this, a highly organized transition is made to another key, and the clarinet gives out a second subject where you see figure (b) brought into daylight.

Ex. 4.

This is broadly developed and brought to a peaceful end. Then the orchestra re-enters as if to develop the first theme, but the idea of a normal development is carried just far enough to assert itself duly, and the clarinet guides the course of events into the slow movement. This begins with what may well pass for a beautiful Irish melody, being, as it is, pure Stanford.

Ex. 5.

Nothing could be more convincing than the naïve way in which the clarinet takes this tune up, expanding it by echoes. (Those who know their way about the orchestra could tell mythologists that the real end of the story of Echo and Narcissus was that Echo's soul passed into the clarinet.) The middle of this slow movement, beginning with an impassioned outburst on the clarinet with its most dashing arpeggios, leads to the following second subject.

Ex. 6.

From this a straightforward return is made to the first theme (Ex. 5), which, after a certain amount of dramatic expansion, is allowed to bring the movement to a peaceful close.

Hereupon the orchestra re-enters with the interrupted middle tutti of the first movement as if to continue its development. The wind instruments, however, turn figure (*b*) into one of the themes of the finale in 2/4 time.

Ex. 7.

Soon the clarinet enters in its fighting mood, with the following derivative of figure (*a*).

Ex. 8.

It works this up with some other figures including Ex. 3 and the following—

Ex. 9.

(a)   &c.

and in a surprisingly short time enough has been said to suggest that we are listening at the same moment to an independent finale and to a recapitulation of the second subject of the first movement. At all events the 2/4 version of that subject sails in happily on the violins, while the clarinet is warbling Ex. 9 in the tonic major; and it is not long before the design is grandly crowned on an altogether broader scale by the reappearance of the theme of the slow movement (Ex. 5); thus revealing the calm depths which underlie the brilliance of the happy end.

ELGAR

CXXVIII. VIOLONCELLO CONCERTO IN E MINOR, OP. 85

1 *Adagio, introductory to Moderato, leading to* 2 *Allegro molto.*
3 *Adagio, leading to* 4 *a recitative, leading to*
5 *Allegro ma non troppo.*

Although the musical language of this work is unaffectedly classical, its forms are unlike those of any other concerto; conspicuously unlike, for instance, the elaborate classical design of Elgar's Violin Concerto. The Violoncello Concerto is a fairy-tale, full, like all Elgar's larger works, of meditative and intimate passages; full also of humour, which, in the second movement and finale, rises nearer to the surface than Elgar usually permits. Though the work is highly organized, an elaborate analysis is not necessary so long as enough themes are quoted. Lucidity is the aim and the achievement of its form and style; not the thin mundane lucidity of a Saint-Saëns concerto, nor yet the arrogant lucidity of the epigrammatist who has not got over his famous discovery of the stupidity of most people.

Mutatis mutandis, this violoncello concerto well represents its composer's Schumannesque mood. This term will seem grotesque to those numerous musicians to whom orchestration is the *sine qua non* of musical thought; but Schumann's helplessness in that category rather reveals than conceals the shyness that goes with such intimate moods. The shyness is, however, just as compatible with consummate mastery of the orchestra; and indeed Elgar's orchestration is as unworldly as it is masterly. In the Violoncello Concerto

the orchestra is throughout concentrated on the special task of
throwing into relief a solo instrument which normally lies below the
surface of the harmony. Brilliant orchestration is thus out of the
question; but there is no lack of subtle and beautiful tone-colour,
inexhaustibly varied within narrow limits and by the simplest
means.

After a short recitative-like introduction by the violoncello—

the first movement begins with an indolent sequential theme,
announced unharmonized by the violas—

and repeated by the violoncello. The movement is not in sonata
form, but is a simple lyric design with a middle section in 12/8 time.
This is introduced by the following theme—

which then blossoms out into the major mode thus—

There is a free recapitulation of the main section (Ex. 2). Then,
after a momentary allusion to the introduction (Ex. 1), the second
movement, a lively scherzo in G major, begins tentatively with the
following figure:

This soon gathers speed and seems about to work itself out, with
a few other themes, as a free sonata-form movement, with a second

subject beginning in the remote key of E flat, which, however, it soon abandons.

Ex. 6.

Having produced just enough effect of development to take us beyond lyric forms, the impish little movement scurries back to its G major and vanishes with the detonation of a burst bubble.

The serene slow movement, in B flat (the Ultima Thule from E minor, the key of the concerto), is a single broad melody. For future reference I number its first two phrases separately.

Ex. 7.

Ex. 8.

The movement ends on the dominant, with its first phrase (as in Ex. 7), and thus leads into the introduction to the finale. This introduction begins in B flat minor, with an adumbration of the future main theme, which is turned by the violoncello into a recitative not unlike that at the beginning of the concerto. The finale then begins, in full swing.

Ex. 9.

It is a free rondo, with a mischievous second subject, slightly suggestive of dignity at the mercy of a banana-skin.

Ex. 10.

The movement is spaciously developed on a large scale, with many and varied episodes. A complete surprise awaits us towards the end in a new slow theme of romantically abstruse harmony and full of pathos.

Ex. 11.

The metre, already new, changes to 3/4, where yet another fresh theme—

Ex. 12.

rises to a climax of passion, thence to subside into the second strain of the slow movement (Ex. 8), and from that to the opening of the concerto (Ex. 1). Then the main theme of the finale works up tersely to a spirited and abrupt end.

DELIUS

CXXIX. VIOLIN CONCERTO

In the art of to-day, there is no more intimate note than that of the later works of Delius. He was never a sensational composer; and the large orchestra and brilliant technique of his early works never displayed any tendency incompatible with the almost oriental depth of meditation which he has attained in recent works such as the Violin Concerto and the Double Concerto.

It would be a mistake to infer, from the shortness and number of the themes here quoted, that the Violin Concerto is either a disjointed or a complicated work. It is, on the contrary, so continuous a stream of ruminating melody that the shortness of the quotable themes is really, as with Wagner's Leitmotivs, a symptom of the length of the paragraphs; while, on the other hand, the course of Delius's work is subtle only (and a very important 'only') in its emotional reactions, and extremely simple in plan. The themes follow in a natural sequence of discourse, with no more complex link than might be supplied by the clause 'and that reminds me': until a point is reached at which it is agreeable to recapitulate some of them from the opening. The classical key-system is only occasionally alluded to, and most of the harmonic phenomena depend on regarding chords of all degrees of artificiality as direct tone-sensations, unanalysable as the taste of a peach, with none of the classical sense of their individual notes as coming from given directions in order to 'resolve' on explanatory notes.

In Delius's art, even more than in Debussy's and Cyril Scott's, the instrumental tone-colour of every chord is quite as important as the actual notes. For the most part the tone-colours are exquisitely soft and mellow; and even when Ex. 3 finds itself forced to the extreme high notes of the trumpet, there is a technical mastery in the scoring which ensures that with first-rate playing the effect is glowing rather than shrill.

The function of the solo violin is to sing and to decorate; chiefly to decorate. The difficulty of its part arises entirely from the almost complete absence of familiar harmonies and intervals, and at no point is the difficulty connected with technical display.

After two introductory bars for the strings, the solo violin pours out the three following themes in a wayward stream of meditation.

To these may be added a majestic outburst of the brass.

The middle section (if one may use the term of such unsectional music) is in a slower time, and comprises two important cantabile themes.

Ex. 6.

A short cadenza leads to a recapitulation of the first four themes with a change in the direction of key. Very unexpectedly a quaint new section, in a naïve dancing rhythm, creates a diversion from the ruminating mood of the whole.

Ex. 7.
Allegretto.

It alternates, however, with a variation of Ex. 5 in the following form.

Ex. 8.

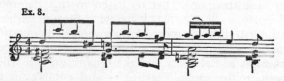

Finally the figures of Ex. 1 conclude the work on a chord once known to theorists as the 'added 6th'—one of the very few names in musical theory that fit the facts.

Ex. 9.

For more reasons than concern theorists we might well regard this music as an example of the Lydian mode, as Milton would describe it—

> And ever against eating cares
> Lap me in soft Lydian airs,
> Such as the melting soul may pierce . . .

RICHARD STRAUSS

CXXX. PARERGON TO THE 'SINFONIA DOMESTICA', FOR PIANOFORTE WITH ORCHESTRA, OP. 73

The relation between this work and the 'Sinfonia Domestica' is, apart from a few allusions to fine details of melodic figure, based on the all-pervading presence of a theme which in the 'Sinfonia' represented the Baby. The 'Sinfonia Domestica' is one of Strauss's largest symphonic poems, and represents a day in the life of himself, his wife, and his infant son. The son is now a doctor in a learned profession and has edited his father's profoundly interesting correspondence with his operatic coadjutor, the dramatist Hofmannsthal. Paul Wittgenstein, for whom the Parergon was composed, probably knows any number of delightful and witty inner meanings in every detail of the work; but great artists, even when they give their works domestic titles, do not really invite us to examine any of their private affairs except those, most private of all, which they reveal by simply expressing universals without speaking in abstractions. Let us listen to this Parergon as to a piece of music, so that we may learn what Strauss wishes to tell us without interrupting his message by impertinent questions.

Eddington has remarked, apropos of some little difficulties in the theories of Relativity and the Quantum, that when phenomena seem to be specially artificial and complex it is because they are reaching us through the refracting medium of our own oblique point of view. Similarly the theme of Dr. Strauss Jr. (C F G E C A) has some difficulty in adjusting itself to our harmonic expectations when, being by birth and breeding in F major, it is trying to reach us through the key of F sharp minor.

A tragic and feverish C sharp (with muted horns and trumpets) starts us with reluctant steps (*langsam und schleppend*) in that key, of which it is the dominant.

Ex. 1.

The pianoforte soon intervenes dramatically, evidently as convinced as its own tuner that the offending note will be the better for reiterated emphasis.

A declamatory figure—

Ex. 2.

becomes important later. The main theme develops itself, refracted through many keys, but always ruthlessly brought back to the inexorable C sharp. Finally the struggle is abandoned, and in triumphant F sharp major a new theme bursts out in full swing, with nothing introductory in its manner. (But cf. Exx. 1 and 9.)

Ex. 3.

Another figure looms large in the bass (cf. Ex. 2)—

Ex. 4.

and soon a new tune is sailing gracefully over it.

Ex. 5.

The enthusiastic climax of this ends in sudden catastrophe with a plunge into F *natural*.

Dr. Strauss Jr.'s theme shows a deep and worried sense of its responsibilities, and so do the other themes in combination (and sometimes in conflict) with it. The agitation grows as the sequences rise and crowd one on another, until at last the pianoforte, finding C natural (the dominant of F) well established, declaims with more confidence and calm. The fatal C sharp has learnt to explain itself away as D flat—Browning's Abt Vogler would say he had 'blunted it into a ninth' (so that mysterious expression means something at last!).

Then the pianoforte states a happy melody in the most innocent F major.

Ex. 6.

The wood-winds restate it, and the pianoforte, imitated by the orchestra, follows with an adaptation of Ex. 3. Immediately the time changes to a quick 2/4, in which Ex. 6 is transformed in a rapid rhythm. Dr. Strauss Jr. joins the game in semiquavers—

Ex. 7.

and new themes, such as—

Ex. 8.

Ex. 9.

swing gaily in and enter into various combinations. In short, all the previous themes join the dance at full speed, Ex. 4 rising to the surface in as high spirits as the rest. The fatal C sharp reasserts itself and refuses to be Voglerized; but the only result is that Ex. 6 dances back in a still faster 2/4 measure. Ex. 5 also swings along over a double-trot version of Ex. 3. Then, while Ex. 8 is roaming in bass sequences under developments of Ex. 4, it becomes evident that there is no great danger in revisiting F sharp again. Thither we drift, and in that key the following combination intervenes—

Ex. 10.

It returns to F natural without trouble and the work concludes brilliantly in the 2/4 time.

The art of left-hand pianoforte solo writing is of great aesthetic interest, and presents the modern instrument in aspects attractive by contrast with the ordinary tendency to exploit the instrument in voluminous harmony which emulates the orchestra without achieving any character of its own. The special restrictions are a stimulus to the composer's invention, and there is a wide field of exploration in this medium where the compass of the instrument is practically unlimited, while the hand carries its own compass with it throughout the whole field.

GLAZOUNOV

CXXXI. PIANOFORTE CONCERTO IN F MINOR, OP. 92

1 *Allegro moderato (with several changes of tempo).* 2 *Andantino Tranquillo.* VARIATIONS *and* FINALE.

In this delightful and compendious work Glazounov amuses himself by combining the rules of two games; one, the game of Liszt in his E flat Concerto; the other, the game of Tchaikovsky in the variation-finale of his Trio. Both these games, as played by their inventors, were meant to be dangerous. Liszt played his with a more than Byronic ostentation of musical wickedness. Tchaikovsky aims at enshrouding in the blackest tragic atmosphere the spectacle of a ruined gambler dancing a trepak on his mother's grave. Glazounov is *jenseits des Guten und Bösen* in all the musical possibilities of these moods. To him the transformation of themes is as easy as his art of orchestration; and is limited only in two ways. He will not make a pedantic transformation, nor will he transform his own themes into other people's. The opening theme of this Concerto begins gravely and goes through many transformations—

Ex. 1.

It sometimes almost merges into the third theme of Liszt's E flat Concerto—

but the Lisztian perkiness does not after all venture into the precincts of this Russian Olympus; and the first movement works

out its design with noble breadth, associating the transformations
of Ex 1 with a tragic pianoforte theme—

Ex. 2.

which lends itself to diminution—

Ex. 3.

and a consolatory second group in the remote key of E major—

Ex. 4.

which is also much developed by diminution.

Ex. 5.

As if by way of slow movement, the orchestra propounds a
beautiful theme for variations, beginning as follows—

Ex. 6.

The variations all retain the outline of the melody. The first three
are simple embroidery, which becomes 'chromatica' in Var. 2,
'eroica' in Var. 3, and 'lyrica' in Var. 4. The 5th variation is a
lively intermezzo in a mixture of tonic minor and E major. Var. 6
is a slow fantasia in the minor. Var. 7 is a mazurka in A major,
which borrows the triangle from the scherzo of Liszt's E flat Concerto; but Var. 8 is a scherzo, also in A major. At last, on moving
to the key of F, the tonic of the concerto, the theme becomes a
march—

Ex. 7.

and is worked up, with mysterious episodes, into a neatly rounded-
off finale in combination with the themes of the first movement.

SIBELIUS

CXXXII. VIOLIN CONCERTO, OP. 47

1 *Allegro moderato.* 2 *Adagio di molto.* 3 *Allegro, ma non tanto.*

Perhaps the Violin Concerto of Sibelius has not yet had time to become popular; but I can see no reason why it should not soon take place with the Violin Concerto of Mendelssohn and the G minor Concerto of Max Bruch as one of the three most attractive concertos ever written. Personally I am impelled to place it above those two famous works, nor do I think that my present enjoyment of it will wear out. Of course the great concerto form of Mozart, Beethoven, and Brahms is another story; instead of being lighter than symphonic form, it is perhaps the most subtle and certainly the most misunderstood art-form in all music. But in the easier and looser concerto forms invented by Mendelssohn and Schumann I have not met with a more original, a more masterly, and a more exhilarating work than the Sibelius Violin Concerto. As with all Sibelius's more important works, its outlines are huge and simple; and if a timely glance at an atlas had not reminded me that Finland is mostly flat and water-logged with lakes, I should doubtless have said that 'his forms are hewn out of the rocks of his native and Nordic mountains'. The composer to whose style the word 'lapidary' (*lapidarisch*) was first applied by the orthodoxy of the 'nineties is Bruckner; and if the best work of Sibelius suggests anything else in music, it suggests a Bruckner gifted with an easy mastery and the spirit of a Polar explorer. Strange to say, the results are of no inordinate length. Sibelius, unlike Bruckner, has an instinct which saves him from misapplying the classical sonata forms to a music that moves at quite a different pace; he does not design motor-cars with a box-seat for the driver, nor does he build reinforced concrete skyscrapers in the style of the Parthenon. There is plenty of sonata form in his works; but it is not a nuisance to him as it was to Bruckner; nor, on the other hand, is he, like Bruckner, at a loss when he diverges from it. The real problems of musical form are always, in the last resort, problems of movement; and Sibelius has his own special sense of movement, which delivers him from the need of Bruckner's desperate and dangerous gesture of 'I pause for a reply'. It gives him complete command of the arts of rousing expectation and of slow gradation to a climax. He does not aim at the time-scale of classical sonata forms, and therefore is not liable to the difficulties of those composers who are not conscious that the time-scale has something to do with the effect of the musical events that are to happen in it. One of Sibelius's most famous and successful devices is that of building up a

symphonic finale out of broken figures that come together, like the
Vision of Dry Bones, into a broad melody only by way of supreme
climax at the end. (Very clever critics have been known to discover that this form lacks the eventful variety of the classical
symphonic finale.) But the acid test comes when the inventor of so
effective a device has to write a finale where it will not work; as, for
instance, in a violin concerto, where it is impossible to ask a solo
violin to live upon scraps for three-quarters of the finale, and then
to dominate the full orchestra by giving its celebrated imitation
(on one string) of the three trombones at the end of the Tannhäuser
Overture. Hence there is nothing of the kind in the finale of this
violin concerto: the characteristic 'lapidary' vastness is achieved
by equally drastic simplicities, accurately to the purpose.

The first theme is a ruminating melody given out by the solo
violin.

Ex. 1.

Clarinet.

Nothing is more characteristic of Sibelius than the austerely dia-
tonic dissonance of the first note, with its rhythmic position just as
far off the main beat as its harmonic position is off the chord. I
mark with (a) and (b) two figures that are used in other combinations; but a detailed analysis, though interesting to a student, is
unnecessary for the enjoyment on a first hearing of a work which is
always lucid, and never more so than in its most original features.

The violin works its melody up to an impassioned climax ending
in a cadenza; and, without any transition passage, the orchestra
announces the second subject, in B flat and 6/4 time.

Ex. 2.

From this arises an allied figure, to which the solo violin adds an
important comment in 4/4 time. We shall find that the style of

Sibelius is nowhere more distinguished than in its novel and yet inevitable cross-rhythms.

The violin brings this meditatively to a close in B flat minor, and then the orchestra breaks out grimly with a new theme.

This yields to a gentler strain—

which, however, is punctuated by fierce accents, and ends in a low-pitched crescendo, which leads to a despairing cadence theme.

When this has died slowly away in utter darkness, the violin re-enters and, while the basses continue to hold B flat, changes the key to G minor. An allusion to the main theme (Ex. 1) turns unexpectedly towards A minor, which key is affirmed in an angry gesture from the orchestra. And now the violin plays a highly developed cadenza, modulating widely and working out the main figures of Ex. 1 in an admirable style of extemporization governed by organic life. It returns to G minor, and in that key a recapitulation begins, with the main theme (Ex. 1) in the bassoon. The

violin resumes it with the second phrase. When, at the climax of
this solo, the orchestra intervenes, it is in order to start a new and
impassioned development with rich modulations, the main theme
being welded to a new figure (*x*) which develops a life of its own.

Ex. 7.

At the climax, in B major, trombones thunder out the despairing
notes marked (*f*) in Ex. 6; and then phrases from the middle of the
second subject (Ex. 3) build themselves up, in combination with
the solo violin, reaching a climax of tenderness in the key of D
major, our tonic, which darkens to the minor. The violin solo has
settled into a long trill, beneath which the theme is mournfully
pulsating away. Suddenly there is an uprush of energy, and the
remaining themes (Ex. 4 and 5) enter *in extenso* with a brilliant
counterpoint for the solo violin. The final theme (Ex. 6) gains its
full meaning by the following bold combination with Ex. 1—

Ex. 8.

and thus brings the first movement to an end for which brilliance
is an inadequate term.

The slow movement, after a wistful introduction—

Ex. 9.

settles down to a noble paragraph of melody for the solo violin—

Ex. 10.

When this has come to its close, a dramatic interlude arises from the wistful introductory figure. The following specimen of Eurythmics—

Ex. 11.

shows what Sibelius can make practicable and natural in the way of cross-rhythms. Both the upper parts are played by the solo violin.

Soon the great main melody returns, this time in the orchestra, the solo violin having fine counterpoint until it resumes the melody in its last phrase; after which a single line of coda suffices.

In less than fifty lines of full score the finale achieves gigantic proportions and brilliant high spirits without banality. The form seems elementary, but the spacing is Handelian; that is to say, there is no means of discovering how it has been achieved.

Only two themes need be quoted; the main or rondo theme— evidently a polonaise for polar bears—

Ex. 12.
Strings.

and the second subject, in a rhythm known to Couperin, Bach, and Handel as that of triple-time with the 'hemiole' as in a French courante, but taken by Sibelius at a pace and with a swing alto- gether shocking to the eighteenth-century dancers of courantes. It quibbles upon the distinction between twice three and thrice two; and Sibelius used it steadily throughout the middle movement of his third symphony.

Ex. 13.

With this we can safely leave the finale to dance the listener into Finland, or whatever Fairyland Sibelius will have us attain.

FRANZ SCHMIDT

CXXXIII. VARIATIONS ON A THEME OF BEETHOVEN FOR PIANOFORTE WITH ORCHESTRA

The high courage which has inspired Paul Wittgenstein's art receives another fitting tribute in this delightful and humorous work. The witty little scherzo of Beethoven's F major Violin Sonata lends itself, with the aid of an orchestra, to the art of left-hand solo 'pianistics' in many ways which reveal the possibilities of that art and shed unexpected new lights on the theme. The most obvious example is furnished by the last note of the whole composition, which avails itself of Beethoven's little joke, sometimes taken by critics of more severity than experience for a defect of ensemble in the performance.

If a set of variations on a humorous theme is to have an introduction, one of the chief functions of the introduction will be to mystify us as to the purport of the theme. The following solemn polyphony might do for a funeral in a certain corner of Kensington Gardens.

Ex. 1.

The horns indicate a later strain of the theme that is to come. Another more hymn-like aspect—

Ex. 2.

leads to florid developments which, falling into A major (or B double-flat, through D flat), lead to a more animated rhythm.

Ex. 3.

echoed below

The solemn introduction is explained away by the theme—which is *not* buried in Kensington Gardens.

Ex. 4.

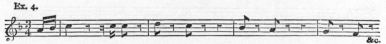

We now learn that Ex. 3 foreshadowed the second part.

Ex. 5.

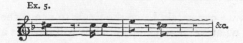

It was a stroke of genius to select this theme. But strokes of genius are tested by the way they are followed up. This is followed by another *genialer Zug*. Franz Schmidt produces a splendid ritornello effect, useful alike to orchestra and pianoforte, by using the trio as well as the scherzo!

Ex. 6.

Then, by way of a first variation, the two themes are combined. This combination of course produces what Pepys or Purcell would have called 'divisions', and Handel, Bach, or the French clavecinistes would have called a 'double'. The next variation is a 'double' in triplets, and the third variation a 'double' in semiquavers.

And now it is time to go farther afield. We have a change to D major 6/8 time, *ruhig fliessend*, and the orchestra waxes erotic, while the pianoforte mocks it in the original tripping measures.

Variation 5 dances a bolero in B minor, which ends in B major, and is followed therein by a slow declamatory variation for pianoforte alone, in common time.

Variation 7, in E major, deals in slow and solemn 3/4 time, primarily with the trio.

Variation 8 (*sehr lebhaft*) in E minor runs away with the scherzo, fugally in 2/4 time.

Variation 9 (*sehr ruhig*, A major 3/4) is a quiet slow waltz with undulating figures.

Variation 10 (*alla-breve* time, *Massig bewegt*) turns the scherzo into a figured chorale in A minor. The pianoforte gradually betrays that *cucullus non facit monachum*, and we are soon rushing along in every conceivable kind of counterpoint to a brilliant and highly developed finale.

Tub-thumping, however, is not its profession. Much butter may have melted in its mouth; but the end is peace, though the hearthrug be in pieces.

RESPIGHI

CXXXIV. CONCERTO GREGORIANO FOR VIOLIN

1 *Andante tranquillo, alternating with Allegro molto moderato and leading to* 2 *Andante espressivo e sostenuto.* 3 FINALE (*Alleluia*).

Ottorino Respighi was born at Bologna on July 9, 1879. He studied at home and at the Liceo Musicale of Bologna until 1899, gaining diplomas as violinist and composer. He then went to Russia to study composition under Rimsky-Korsakov, and afterwards to Berlin to study under Max Bruch.

The Concerto Gregoriano was produced in 1922. It is a subtle and intimate work inspired with the mystic tones of the plain-chants *Victimæ Paschali* and the *Alleluia: Beatus vir qui timet Dominum*, which pervade the second and third movements.

The first movement, though treating the key of A minor in a modal style, is not on Gregorian themes. The orchestra announces a hymn-like Aeolian figure—

Ex. 1.

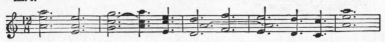

after which an oboe gives out the main theme, a plaintive pastoral melody taken up by cor anglais and bassoon—

Ex. 2.

The strings resume Ex. 1, upon which the solo violin enters with Ex. 2 (substituting F natural for F sharp). It develops this theme meditatively and soon breaks into an allegro moderato beginning in C major with the following pentatonic theme—

Ex. 3.

Arising out of this a new figure—

Ex. 4.

asserts itself, eventually combining with another as follows—

Ex. 5.

This dies away in F major and the solo violin combines Ex. 1 with it. Then Ex. 2 returns and brings the movement gradually to something that would eventually be a close but for an outburst of energy on the solo violin which gathers up Ex. 4 and Ex. 2 in a spacious slow cadenza leading to the second movement.

II. *Andante espressivo e sostenuto*

In pure Dorian (D minor without leading note) the violin sings the *Victimæ Paschali*.

Ex. 6.

&c.

Arising from this an impassioned free continuation—

Ex. 7.

&c.

&c.

leads to a Dorian form of F minor, where the *Victimæ Paschali* looms in the bass with profoundly agitated figures and rhythms above. The plainchant having run its course in the bass, its figures are developed more quietly, but with intense emotion and much beautiful and varied colouring. An ominous figure of wordly trouble appears in the bass—

Ex. 8.

&c.

and dies away in an extremely low drum.

Then the *Victimæ Paschali* appears in the chords; D sharp minor, solo violin accompanied by high muted strings, celesta, and solemn chords for violoncellos and basses.

Once more Ex. 7 appears, but leads now to another calm setting of the chant, given to low clarinets and developed so as gradually to bring the movement to a close in D major. The bass sustains D while the solo violin in dialogue with horn, oboe, and bass clarinet work out the final paragraph.

III. *Finale.* Alleluia.

The Alleluia is set like a rousing march, and Respighi does not scruple to add two most secular bangs on the last beat of the accompaniment—

Ex. 9.

Another plainchant forms a second part—

Ex. 10.

As in the slow movement, Respighi builds up a series of settings of this pair of plainchants in various contrasted keys and colours. Towards the middle (after a quiet variation in B flat) the violin, in ethereal mystic tones, gives out another plainchant—

Ex. 11.

Passing from Dorian-Aeolian D minor to D major, this leads to excited development of Ex. 9 on the dominant of E, and thence through F minor to B minor, where the violin has a big cadenza accompanied by the drums. Horns re-enter in B (as dominant of E) with the Alleluia, and then there is a brilliant climax with figure of Ex. 10 on the home dominant. From this there is a slow and solemn decrescendo dying into extreme darkness. Then the solo violin on its sonorous fourth string sings the Alleluia over a conquered world (Ex. 8, from the darkest part of the slow movement, appearing in the bass). It rises to a climax and leads the orchestra on to a dramatic and brilliant end.

WILLIAM WALTON

CXXXV. VIOLA CONCERTO

1 *Andante comodo.* 2 *Vivo, con moto preciso.* 3 *Allegro moderato.*

The style of this work is modern in so far as it could hardly have achieved its present consistency before 1920 (the actual date is 1929); but it does not consist of negatives. Hence it will arouse the anger of many progressive critics and composers in these days of compulsory liberty. Walton's music has tonality, form, melody, themes, and counterpoint. The counterpoint, and hence the harmony, are not always classical. Classical counterpoint is harmony stated in terms of a combination of melodies: classical harmony, when correctly translated from whatever instrumental conditions may have disguised it, is the result of good classical counterpoint where the inner melodic lines are not meant to attract attention. Modern counterpoint tends actually to avoid classical harmony. It prefers that the simultaneous melodies should collide rather than combine; nor does it try to explain away the collisions.

It wishes the simultaneous melodies to be heard; and if they har-
monize classically the combination will not assert itself as such.
Hence modern counterpoint is no longer a technical matter at all;
its new hypothesis has annihilated it as a discipline. But this very
fact has thrown new responsibilities on the composer's imagination.
A technical discipline becomes a set of habits which, like civilization
itself, saves the artist from treating each everyday matter as a new
and separate fundamental problem. The rule-of-thumb contrapuntist need not trouble to imagine the sound of his combination;
his rules and habits assure him that it cannot sound wrong. The
composer who has discarded those rules and habits must use his
imagination for every passage that he writes without their guidance.
It is by no means true that mere haphazard will suit his purpose.
Nor, on the other hand, is it true that any great classical master
used rules as a substitute for his imagination. One of the first
essentials of creative art is the habit of imagining the most familiar
things as vividly as the most surprising. The most revolutionary
art and the most conservative will, if they are both to live, have this
in common, that the artist's imagination shall have penetrated every
part of his work. To an experienced musician every score, primitive, classical, or futurist, will almost at a glance reveal the general
question whether the composer can or cannot use his imagination.
About details I would not be so sure. To the experienced musician
Berlioz has no more business to exist than the giraffe; 'there ain't
no such animal'.

Walton is no Berlioz; a glance at his score will suffice to show an
art that has been learnt as peacefully as any form of scholarship.
And it is possible to read the first twelve bars of this Viola Concerto
carefully without finding anything irreconcilable to an academic
style in the 'nineties. After the twelfth bar the range of style
expands. But let us note that it thereby differs from the many other
modern styles which contract. Walton's style is not sentimental;
but neither is it anti-romantic.

Similarly, it is neither theatrical nor sensational; and its forms
do not at first seem to have more than a slight external resemblance
to sonata forms. Yet it has essential qualities of sonata style in its
ways of getting from one theme to another and in its capacity to
give dramatic meaning to the establishing of a new key. Walton's
dramatic power has asserted itself in oratorio; but its unobtrusive
presence in this thoughtful piece of purely instrumental music is
more significant than any success in an oratorio on the subject of
Belshazzar's feast. The sceptical critic can always argue that an
oratorio, especially on such a subject, can hardly go wrong unless
the librettist's intellect is subnormal. But when a composer can
write an effective concerto for viola (an instrument with a notorious

inferiority complex) and can move in it at something like the pace of a sonata, it is as obvious that he ought to write an opera as that Bruckner, Wagnerian though he was, ought not, and fortunately did not.

The concerto begins with two bars of orchestral introduction which I do not quote, though I shall have to allude to them later. The viola enters with a broad lyric melody in A minor.

Ex. 1.

The collision between C sharp in the accompaniment and the C natural in the melody is bold, but it is resolved in the classical way. Nevertheless it is destined to become an unresolved thing in itself and, as such, to be the initial and final motto of the whole work. Accordingly I give this motto here in its tonic position—

Ex. 2.

though its first appearance (during the counterstatement of Ex. 1) is at a high pitch in the course of a sequence that sweeps round a whole enharmonic circle of keys. But the figure soon detaches itself as an individual actor in the drama, and claims derivation from the first two notes of Ex. 1.

What may conveniently be called the second subject (though as my readers know, I have reasons for deprecating the term) first appears in D minor.

Ex. 3.

Its essential feature is the coiling of a sequential figure across the rhythm and across the harmony at every sort of angle. Its transformations are shown in every subsequent cantabile that is not derived from Ex. 1. Another new figure—

Ex. 4.

originates most of the rapid passages in the sequel, and from it, if we wish to use classical terminology, the development may be said to begin. Ex. 1 becomes fierce in an entirely new rhythm—

Ex. 5.

which, sometimes reduced to monotone and ragtime—

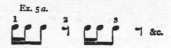

Ex. 5 a.

alternates dramatically with developments of Ex. 3, which steadily grows in beauty and pathos. As the drama unfolds, the motto, Ex. 2, asserts itself. The last phase of the development is introduced when the viola makes its exit with Ex. 4, and the orchestra, entering with Ex. 5 in ominous agitation on the dominant of C sharp minor, rouses itself to tragic passion, and with grand classical breadth works its way round to the home dominant, and so to a pathetic slow decline in which the later figures of the main theme (Ex. 1, the part marked 'N.B.') are heard solemnly augmented.

Over the still reverberating dominant pedal the viola re-enters with a two-part version of the (unquoted) introductory bars, expanded into a short cadenza and leading to the return of Ex. 1. While the viola breaks into a running accompaniment, the melody, softly delivered in a higher octave, makes a single simple statement rounded off with a pathetic cadence, and the viola adds a line of coda alluding to Ex. 3 and ending with the motto, Ex. 2. The whole movement must convince every listener as a masterpiece of form in its freedom and precision, besides showing pathos of a high order.

The middle movement is a lively rondo in E minor with plenty of ragtime rhythms which, unlike those of jazz, are allowed to throw the music out of step, so that the composer has now and then to change the time-signature for one or two bars. The listener need not worry about these changes; an odd bar of 3/4, 3/8, or 5/8 is merely a practical necessity for conductor and players; it happens whenever the composer has found that his groups of 3 or 5 quavers across his 4-quaver bars will land him on a main beat either too soon or too late for his whim. Much has been said in favour of jazz; but jazz, though a composer may be generous in his acknowledgement to it, never kept a movement going like this. A list of themes must suffice by way of analysis; letters and figures in the quotations will show a few significant points in the thematic and rhythmic structure. In general scheme the three movements of this concerto agree in the common-sense device of reserving the display of the full orchestra for a penultimate stage in which it can make a big climax, leaving room for a coda in which the solo instrument can deliver its final summary.

Here is the main theme of the scherzo, delivered by the viola, with wood-wind echoes.

From its scale-figure (C) many things result; especially a habit of making accompaniments out of bits of scale marching up or down in obstinate little groups of 3, 4, 5, alone, or in 3rds, and always inclined to collide with beat and harmony. The continuation—

arises out of figure (b) and shows how the ragtime refuses to explain itself away. Jazz has often lulled me to sleep by its underlying monotony; but Walton's rhythms keep me on the alert.

A transition theme, using a figure akin to (b)—

leads to the main theme of the first episode.

The second episode is the beginning of extensive development, starting in F and modulating widely.

Ex. 10.

As the 5-note underlying scale and the semiquaver figures show, it lends itself easily to 'conflation' (as the palaeographist would say) with the other themes; and the transition-theme, Ex. 8, appears conspicuously in the sequel. As in the other movements of this concerto, the orchestra eventually arises in its might, bringing the development to its climax, and leading, at its own leisure, to the final return of the main theme in the tonic. The viola resumes its control in the ensuing compound of recapitulation and coda. The movement ends, according to its nature, with Haydnesque abruptness and Bach-like punctuality.

The lyric qualities of the first movement, and its moderate tempo, have already supplied whatever need this work may have for a slow movement. Yet it is a bold stroke to follow so typical a scherzo by a finale which also begins in a manifestly grotesque style which the bassoon and contrafagotto can do nothing to bowdlerize.

Ex. 11.

But the grotesque is, as Ruskin has defined it, the sublime refracted by terror; and this finale is no joke. In its total effect it is the majestic and pathetic conclusion of a work that is throughout large in all its aspects. The form will explain itself: here is the main figure of the transition theme—

Ex. 12.

and here is the 'second subject'—

Ex. 13.

from which an important figure arises.

Later in the movement the viola draws a long line of pathetic cantabile over an ostinato development of the first theme.

This cantabile becomes tragically important before the end of the movement.

Another point that may be quoted is the following combination of Ex. 14 with an augmented version of the main figure of Ex. 11.

When the orchestra, as in the previous movements, gathers up the threads Ex. 11 reveals itself as a purely majestic subject for a fugal stretto, and the listener will soon become convinced that the total import of the work is that of high tragedy. This is wonderfully realized in the coda. What happens at the end is this: the main theme, Ex. 11, has settled into an ostinato in 9/4 time, and over this the viola brings back the lyric melody of the first movement, Ex. 1, with which the concerto ends, not in the same way as the first movement, but with similar Bach-like punctuality.

There are so few concertos for viola that (even if I happened to know any others) it would be a poor compliment to say this was the finest. Any concerto for viola must be a *tour de force*; but this seems to me to be one of the most important modern concertos for any instrument, and I can see no limits to what may be expected of the tone-poet who could create it.

PRINTED IN GREAT BRITAIN
AT THE UNIVERSITY PRESS, OXFORD
BY VIVIAN RIDLER
PRINTER TO THE UNIVERSITY